D1475034

The Other Women's Lib

The Other Women's Lib

Gender and Body in Japanese Women's Fiction

JULIA C. BULLOCK

University of Hawai'i Press
HONOLULU

Library of Congress Cataloging-in-Publication Data
Bullock, Julia C.
   The other women's lib : gender and body in Japanese women's fiction /
Julia C. Bullock.
      p. cm.
   Includes bibliographical references and index.
   ISBN 978-0-8248-3387-9 (alk. paper)—ISBN 978-0-8248-3453-1
(pbk. : alk. paper)
   1. Japanese fiction—20th century—History and criticism.   2. Women in
literature.   3. Japanese fiction—Women authors—History and criticism.
4. Feminist literary criticism—Japan.   5. Gender identity in literature.
6. Human body in literature.   7. Women—Identity—Japan.   I. Title.
  PL747.82.W64B85 2009 /o
   895.6'35093522—dc22
                                             2009032034

University of Hawai'i Press books are printed on acid-free
paper and meet the guidelines for permanence and durability
of the Council on Library Resources.

Designed by University of Hawai'i Press production staff
Printed by Sheridan Books, Inc.

Contents

Acknowledgments   vii

Note on Citation Format   ix

INTRODUCTION
Bad Wives and Worse Mothers? Rewriting Femininity
   in Postwar Japan   1

CHAPTER 1
Party Crashers and Poison Pens: Women Writers
   in the Age of High Economic Growth   13

CHAPTER 2
The Masculine Gaze as Disciplinary Mechanism   53

CHAPTER 3
Feminist Misogyny? or How I Learned to Hate My Body   77

CHAPTER 4
Odd Bodies   97

CHAPTER 5
The Body of the Other Woman   127

CONCLUSION
Power, Violence, and Language in the Age of High
   Economic Growth   153

Notes   169

Works Cited   185

Index   193

Acknowledgments

It is impossible to thank all the people who should receive thanks for a project of this length. Personally and professionally, I've benefited from the guidance and support of far too many to acknowledge here. I only hope that they will see their imprint in my work and feel that it does them justice.

I've been fortunate to have three intellectual homes during the course of my work on this project: Stanford University, where I earned my PhD; Jōsai International University, where I did my dissertation fieldwork; and Emory University, which has supported my academic career since. The Department of Asian Languages and the Center for East Asian Studies at Stanford provided numerous sources of funding early on. A generous grant from the Fulbright-Hays Doctoral Dissertation Research Abroad program allowed me to spend a year at Jōsai, in the company of brilliant feminist scholars of literature who helped me to clarify the contours of this project from its earliest stages. I am especially grateful for that opportunity. I've also benefited tremendously from the considerable financial support of Emory University, particularly the University Research Committee (URC), whose grant provided me with a semester of leave to work on this project when I needed it most, and the Emory College of Arts and Sciences and the Graduate School, whose subvention fund underwrote some of the costs of publication of this book. The Institute for Comparative and International Studies (ICIS) also provided funding for two research trips to Japan to collect valuable materials unavailable to me in the United States. Finally, I must thank the Scholarly Inquiry and Research at Emory (SIRE) program for providing me with a wonderful student research assistant, Siobhain Rivera, who patiently combed through databases, made endless photocopies, organized files, and lugged books back and forth to the library more times than I can recall. I owe particular thanks and kudos to her.

I've also had the benefit of so many brilliant and supportive colleagues that I'm almost afraid to list them for fear of leaving someone out, and yet conscience obliges me to give particular thanks to the following: to Jim Reichert, for going above and beyond the call of duty as dissertation adviser by providing a model of scholar, teacher, and advocate that I could only hope to replicate in my own career; to Mizuta Noriko and Kitada Sachie, whose support meant more than they could possibly know or I could ever express; and to Juliette Apkarian, Elena Glazov-Corrigan, Cheryl Crowley, Lynne Huffer, and Mark Ravina for nurturing my development as a junior colleague and for making Emory feel like more than just an academic home. Jeffrey Angles, Jan Bardsley, Rebecca Copeland, Sally Hastings, Vera Mackie, Mark McLelland, Sharalyn Orbaugh, Atsuko Sakaki, Chris Scott, Bob Tierney, James Welker, and many others generously commented, encouraged, and especially challenged me at crucial junctures when this manuscript was finally coming together, and I hope that I have been able to do justice to a fraction of the intelligence that they have brought to the evaluation of my work. I owe a similar debt of gratitude to two anonymous reviewers, whose insightful comments made this project much better than I could have managed on my own. Thanks to all of you for your thoughtful feedback. Any remaining deficiencies are entirely my responsibility.

Personally, I've also been extremely fortunate to feel supported by family and friends, even when (especially when?) they found it difficult to understand what all the fuss was about. To my family—my mother, father, and sister, as well as the newest addition to our family, my niece Riley Marie—I thank you for indulging me through all those times when I was tired, cranky, or otherwise too involved with this project to be a good daughter/sister/aunt. I promise there is a vacation in our future somewhere. And yes, I'll actually join you this time. I am also humbled to recognize more friends than I can list here, for their support through times when this felt harder than it really needed to be. First of all, to Dave, who never let me get away with it when I tried to sell myself short. Jules, Vanessa, Pam, Tavishi, and Emiko led by example, just by being amazing women who inspired me to keep on going, even when I didn't feel like it. As new friends enter my life, I will try to remember to give as much to them as they did to me.

Note on Citation Format

For works originally published in Japanese, both the Japanese-language title and an English translation of the title are provided the first time a work is cited here. For subsequent citations, I employ the English-language title only. Where a published English translation of a work is available, I have used the English version of the title employed by the translator, and when quoting from that work, I have quoted the translated version so that readers wishing to consult the translation can easily locate that quote. Where no published translation exists, all quotations and English glosses for story titles are my translation. In the works cited, both original Japanese texts and English translations are cited where available. Where no translation is available, I have provided English glosses for Japanese titles.

Personal names are referenced according to cultural custom—last name first for Japanese and first name first for Western—except in cases where an author with a Japanese name has Western-style ordering for works published in English.

Introduction

Bad Wives and Worse Mothers?
Rewriting Femininity in Postwar Japan

"Woman-hating." That title just leapt right off the page. I was more puzzled than offended because the essay in question was by a woman writer whose work I admired for her portrayal of bold, independent, and bravely eccentric female protagonists—women who challenged the status quo, bad girls, some so deliciously bad that you couldn't wait to see what they would do next. Aha, I thought, she's going to give those male chauvinists what for. But upon reading the essay, I encountered the following: "I myself have a strange fear of people with whom rational language doesn't communicate. In spite of the fact that I'm a woman, I have a fear of women and children."[1] Women were described as infantile, superficial, materialistic, insipid, and generally inferior to men. And this from an author I had come to think of as "feminist." What was going on here?

I reread the essay, sincerely wanting to understand why a woman might make such statements about other women. I tried to set aside my own assumptions about what "counted" as feminism and began to notice a degree of rhetorical complexity that had escaped my previous, less patient reading. What I found was a text that was profoundly conflicted, with respect to both the various meanings assigned to the term "woman" and the author's position regarding those "feminine" qualities. For such an extraordinarily brief essay, the author oscillated with dizzying speed between identifying herself as a woman and critiquing "women" as if this category had nothing to do with her. The text seemed to recognize "woman" as a cultural construct even as it simultaneously appeared to present that term as an essential and fixed category. In short, I finished the essay with a strong sense that the author herself felt profoundly ambivalent about her own gender and at the very least did not want to be a "woman" if that meant conforming to conventionally "feminine" norms.

The author in question was Takahashi Takako, and the essay, "Onnag-irai" (1974), sparked my desire to understand this thing called "feminin-ity," which could motivate such an angry diatribe against one's own sex. As I read more by Takahashi and her contemporaries, I realized that many other women writers of her generation seemed to share a profound sense of unease regarding what it meant to be a woman in Japanese society. This seemed to have much to do with the fact that during the 1960s, when so many of these women made their debuts on the literary scene, Japanese society was experiencing a resurgence of the prewar "good wife and wise mother" ideology—a stereotype of femininity that many of these women resisted. These writers defied models of normative femininity through their literature, crafting female protagonists who were unapologetically bad wives and even worse mothers: frequently wanton, excessive, or self-ish and brazenly cynical with regard to "traditional" conceptions of love, marriage, and motherhood—when they did not opt out of this system entirely.

Born in the late 1920s to early 1930s and raised in a country mobilized for total war to contribute to the Japanese empire by becoming "good wives and wise mothers," this generation of women faced a brave new world of opportunity after World War II, when sweeping Occupation-era reforms sought to legislate equality between the sexes. And yet prewar models of femininity persisted into the postwar era, as high economic growth from 1955 to 1973 was underwritten by a strictly gendered division of labor that required women to take full responsibility for the domestic sphere so that their husbands could devote themselves to rebuilding the nation's economy through paid labor. In the 1960s, women were still discursively constructed as "good wives and wise mothers" even as more and more of them began also to work outside the home.[2]

The term "femininity," as understood in Japan during the 1960s, thus primarily denoted qualities associated with women's nurturing and supportive functions vis-à-vis men. It was also understood as the comple-ment and logical opposite of "masculinity," so that, for example, women were expected to respond to male activity and self-assertion with passive and self-effacing behavior. In attempting to rewrite femininity, these women writers therefore struggled against binary models of gender that assumed a direct correspondence between the terms "male/masculine" and "female/feminine," such that bodies were expected to exhibit the gendered behaviors considered "natural" to them. Furthermore, because these terms were understood to be mutually exclusive and complementary, it was expected that there would be no overlap between the characteristics that were considered "masculine" and those considered "feminine." Embracing one side of the polarity thus meant denying the other.

In a context where those who inhabited female bodies were required to produce a corresponding range of behaviors coded as "feminine," what possibilities existed to resist these norms? When gender is structured according to a set of binary oppositions that require the subject to choose one of two mutually exclusive positions, how can a woman avoid becoming entrapped in stereotypical notions of the "feminine" without presenting herself as "masculine"? When the terms "female" and "feminine" cannot be thought separately, how is it possible to critique feminine norms without also criticizing the category of "woman" itself, thus opening oneself up to charges of chauvinism or misogyny? And how can the term "woman" retain its structural integrity as an essentialist and totalizing category when, in spite of binary discourses of gender to the contrary, there appear to be as many differences *among* women as there are between women and men?

The authors whose works are analyzed in this study were keenly interested in these theoretical concerns at a time when raising such issues placed one firmly outside the boundaries of culturally ingrained "common sense." In their fictional works, and often in nonfiction essays as well, they persistently grappled with the problem of feminine subjectivity against a discursive backdrop that rendered this "logically" impossible. In their willingness to radically challenge binary models of gender, they share much in common intellectually with the "women's liberation" activists of the following decade, who argued in explicitly political terms what these writers had already envisioned in the realm of fiction. This volume represents the first systematic analysis of the narrative and representational patterns through which normative femininity was contested by women writers of this period, in advance of the flowering of "second-wave" feminism in Japan in the 1970s. In the sense that both fiction writers and activists sought to critique and subvert hegemonic discourses of femininity that confined women to the "traditional" roles of wife and mother toward a broader range of permissible expressions of feminine subjectivity, I argue that both groups should be understood as espousing a feminist position.

Histories of feminism in Japan tend to give prominence to the Seitō (Bluestocking) group of writers in the 1910s and then touch on the "housewife feminism" of the early postwar period before moving on to the more exuberant generation of women's liberation activists in the 1970s. Vera Mackie's landmark study, *Feminism in Modern Japan*, provides a considerably broader spectrum of feminist activity, as Mackie gives equal attention to women's organizations that aided the war effort during the 1930s and other lesser-known or more politically problematic activists like the women of the Red Army. However, much of the existing literature on Japanese feminism seems to concentrate primarily on women's political activism as a crucial marker of their participation in projects to alter normative constructions of gender.

Thus discussions of radical feminism in the 1960s tend to focus primarily on student-movement activists who would go on to create the philosophical base of the women's liberation movement in the 1970s.[3] From the massive anti–Security Treaty demonstrations that paralyzed the Japanese Diet in 1960 to the takeover and occupation of university campuses during the worldwide unrest of 1968–1969, young women organized and struggled alongside men during this turbulent decade, which included inter- and intrasectarian violence and pitched street battles with riot police. However, as in the United States and other countries that experienced such counterculture movements, many Japanese women became disillusioned with the New Left organizations that emerged during the 1960s because of the chauvinistic treatment they received from male comrades—ranging from their relegation to kitchen duty to sexual harassment and even rape. In the 1970s, such frustrations erupted around the world into a flurry of "women's liberation" movements or woman-centered political organizations and theoretical attempts to redefine women's roles in society. In Japan, this came to be known as *ūman ribu* (women's lib).[4]

While explicitly political expressions of radical feminism did not emerge in postwar Japan until the women's liberation movement of the 1970s, women writers of fiction began to challenge normative discourses of gender much earlier. In the 1960s, as some women participated in New Left student movements, others contributed to an extraordinary boom in literary publication by women, whose radical and shocking articulations of feminine subjectivity forced a new dialogue on sexuality and gender roles within the community of intellectuals known as the *bundan,* or Japanese literary world. To date their work has been largely neglected in histories of Japanese feminism, most likely because many of these writers eschewed *explicit* political activism in favor of an *implicitly* political rewriting of femininity through literature.[5] However, I argue that their literature must be seen as part of a larger attempt to negotiate alternative discourses of gender during the 1960s. Like the "women's lib" activists of the following decade, they identified everyday relationships between men and women as a primary source of gendered oppression and critiqued the way the power dynamics that structure such relationships suppress or manipulate women's sexuality in order to harness it toward the goals of a patriarchal order. Like the feminists of the 1970s, these writers challenged "commonsense" assumptions of motherhood as woman's "natural" role and attacked binary models of gender that defined woman as man's eternal complement. Like these explicitly political feminist activists, they identified women's bodies as the site of gender oppression and thus attempted to trouble facile linkages between body and gender, biology and destiny.[6]

The contributions of these writers of fiction to emerging feminist discourse helped to lay the theoretical groundwork for a more explicitly political "women's lib" in the following decade. What they imagined first in the realm of literature—from insightful observations regarding how gender roles are constructed and enforced, to problematizing binary models of gender, to questioning the category of "woman" itself—reemerged in later decades as more explicitly political articulations of feminist theoretical discourse. By demonstrating the contributions of these women as theorists of gender, whose ideas were very much a part of larger debates on gender and sexuality taking place in Japanese society at this time, this study bridges scholarship on Japanese feminist history and modern Japanese literature to fill an important lacuna in our understanding of feminist theoretical development prior to the women's liberation movement of the 1970s.

This study centers around a sustained analysis of the works of three of the most famous women of this generation—Kōno Taeko (1926–), Takahashi Takako (1932–), and Kurahashi Yumiko (1935–2005). Kurahashi, the youngest of the group, was the first to capture the attention of the literary world, and her controversial ascent onto the literary stage in 1960, while still a university student, marked the beginning of that decade's boom in women's writing.[7] Takahashi, a fellow student of French literature, has much in common intellectually with Kurahashi, in spite of being slightly older and married at the time of her debut. Kurahashi, a graduate of Meiji University, and Takahashi, a graduate of Kyoto University, were part of the first generation of young women to attain entrance to the prestigious male-dominated universities that had been closed to women during the prewar period. Being somewhat older, Kōno did not have that opportunity, but her passionate interest in English literature (which began during her student years at Osaka Women's University), as well as her evident fascination for the bizarre and the grotesque, makes her a perfect complement to Kurahashi and Takahashi in terms of her willingness to challenge gender stereotypes from unconventional perspectives.

Another reason that these authors were chosen is that all three of them are readily available in English translation, for the benefit of readers who cannot understand the original Japanese texts. Because I have selected texts for analysis primarily on the basis of their employment of common themes and tropes, not all texts analyzed in this manuscript are available in English, but other texts that address similar themes are, and thus the English-language reader can readily compare translated stories to the ones I have included here.

One final criterion employed in the selection of texts for this project was their year of publication. I have limited the scope of this study to works published between 1960, when Kurahashi's debut inaugurated the boom in women's writing of this decade, and 1973, the year that most scholars cite as the end of the period of high economic growth. As noted above, the discursive constructions of gender against which these women writers struggled to define new models of femininity were intimately interwoven with the ideological and structural fabric of Japanese society in the age of high economic growth. They were difficult to resist precisely because they seemed to "work," in the sense that such binary models of gender drove the engine of economic recovery forward. Challenging these models of normative gender effectively meant challenging the very basis of prosperity itself, something that violated contemporary common sense and rendered the challenger a subversive threat to the integrity of a newly stabilized Japanese society. Under the circumstances, then, it was no wonder that in the 1960s such challenges took the form of avant-garde literary feminism, which then morphed into more explicitly political activism once the recession of the 1970s and resultant environmental and social problems made it easier to question the fruits of economic growth.

In order to understand the theoretical contributions of these women to postwar Japanese feminist discourse, it is also necessary to understand the ways that gendered discourses and behaviors were transmitted and enforced through networks of power at all levels of society, from the most official of government institutions to the most intimate personal relationships. In this sense, Michel Foucault's concept of "biopower" is useful in helping to elucidate the way normative models of gender are produced and deployed. In volume one of his *History of Sexuality*, Foucault traces the process by which the social and sexual behavior of Western populations in the modern era came to be shaped, not so much by repressive government controls, but rather through regimes of "biopower," which required the consent and active participation of the individuals they targeted. Modern nation-states required disciplined and healthy populations capable of contributing willingly and eagerly to national projects, whether those be waging war on another country, combating the spread of famine and disease, or contributing labor toward the development of industrial capitalist economies. In addition to government legal and bureaucratic structures, Foucault cites the pivotal role played by schools, military organizations, and prisons, among various other institutions that served to produce the "docile bodies" necessary for such projects.[8]

As Sheldon Garon notes, although with respect to Western nations it is difficult to describe these disciplinary institutions as part of a deliberate and coordinated effort by governments to shape the development of their societies in a calculated fashion, in Japan this is precisely what happened. As Japan suddenly and abruptly opened up to the West at the beginning of the Meiji period (1868–1912) out of a sense of urgency to beat the imperialist powers at their own game, reigning oligarchs explicitly and deliberately crafted administrative institutions and strategies to remake the Japanese people into a cohesive and nationalistic populace capable of contributing to the project of imperialism.

> The [Japanese] imperial state did not rely on repression alone in its efforts to increase national power, promote economic development, and maintain social order. In more positive terms, the government energetically disseminated an "emperor-system ideology" to the public, inculcating patriotism, loyalty to the emperor, and the virtues of diligence and thrift. The state did so by utilizing a highly centralized set of institutions: the national school system, the military, a network of State Shinto shrines, and numerous hierarchically organized associations. If social control in the West implies society's regulation of its members or one group's domination over another *within* society, its Japanese analogue—the emperor system—refers to the unrelenting drive by a transcendent state to control society as a whole between 1868 and 1945.[9]

Garon further demonstrates, in his book *Molding Japanese Minds*, that the kind of "moral suasion" that the Japanese imperial government used to mobilize its subjects before the end of World War II continued, albeit in modified form, into the postwar period, as economic growth came to replace imperialist expansion as the new national project.

Foucault's notion of "biopower," harnessed toward the national project of postwar economic growth, is a useful rubric through which to understand the disciplinary process of engendering that contributed toward the gendered division of labor that increasingly characterized Japanese society during the 1960s. Men and women were exhorted to take up the complementary roles of salarymen and housewives respectively, not simply through repressive governmental controls, but also through institutional and organizational structures that shaped their behavior in less explicit ways. These gender roles increasingly came to seem not only "natural" but also desirable to much of the mainstream of Japanese society, creating the illusion that individual behaviors were a matter of choice rather than the "administrative guidance" that nurtured not only economic growth during this era but also the human capital that made this project possible.

Under such circumstances, when disciplinary mechanisms of engendering are woven seamlessly into all aspects of social life, how is it possible for the individual subject to resist hegemonic discourses of gender? Judith Butler, in her landmark work of feminist scholarship, *Gender Trouble*, explores one way this is possible in her theory of the performativity of gender. By complying with gender norms yet performing them differently—for example, through excessive or parodic expression, as in drag performance—one may highlight the ways in which gender is a learned and socially constructed set of behaviors rather than a "natural" and individual expression of inherent qualities.[10] For feminist critics, highlighting the artificiality of gender norms is a necessary first step toward changing them, and the authors whose works are explored in this book often follow precisely this strategy, using literature as a vehicle for the excessive or parodic performance of femininity in order to problematize such gender norms. Capitalizing on the rich potential of fictional worlds to highlight ironic disjunctions between feminine stereotypes and feminist realities, they actively participated in creating alternative discourses of femininity during the 1960s and early 1970s—even as this era of high economic growth seemed to render such gendered distinctions not only inevitable but also necessary to the cause of national and individual prosperity.

The primary objects of my analysis—novels and short stories written during the 1960s boom in publication by an elite cadre of women writers—represent the perspectives of a new female intelligentsia that came to question dominant constructions of femininity from *within* the *bundan*, the literary world that had previously been dominated by male graduates of prestigious Japanese universities. It was through literature that many female members of this emerging intellectual elite pushed for recognition of women as more than wives and mothers. Therefore, their fictional work serves as an important clue to the way discourses of gender were discursively negotiated at this moment in time—in advance of the more explicitly political discourses of liberation forwarded by the "women's lib" movement of the 1970s.

This is not to say that they were the first generation of women writers to question normative femininity or that they were in any way typical of their own generation in terms of their willingness to question reigning common sense. Generations of female political activists and literary figures, from the early Meiji-era Popular Rights Movement feminists in the 1870s to the members of the Seitō group in the 1910s, to prominent writers like Enchi Fumiko whose educational background earned the respect of male and female contemporaries alike, had each in her own way contributed to the negotiation of gendered discourses in previous eras of modern Japanese history. What made the 1960s boom in women's writing so significant, though, was that for the first time many of these writers were able to speak from a position *inside* the academy—or at least fight for inclusion in that hallowed space from a position of strength. Post–World War II legal and cultural transformations in Japanese society, due to Occupation-era reforms that had given prominence to the elevation of women's status, had guaranteed women the right to attend school alongside men through a system of coeducation that extended from primary school through university, and many of these women were the first to take advantage of this new system. Armed with new social and educational capital that had been denied to their forebears, they began to participate in the literary world in ways that rendered them not merely cloistered writers of fiction but also public intellectuals with serious academic pedigrees who actively participated in debates that included, but were not limited to, the role of women both in the *bundan* and in society more generally.

In focusing my analysis on works of fiction, I do not mean to imply that these literary creations should be understood as transparent representations of the reality of these women's lives. Rather, I see these stories as imaginative recreations of a process of gender role negotiation that was playing out simultaneously in Japanese society at this time. Understanding these stories as discourse—or more specifically, as philosophies of gender in fictional form—allows us to read them against the nonfictional discourses of gender that were in circulation at this time, toward a better understanding of how women like these writers challenged the center of gendered representation from the margins. I am interested not only in what these stories say, but also in how they say it and in what ways this form of expression can be seen as itself produced through negotiation with discourses in circulation in the real world that always seems to hover on the margins of these texts. Real world and textual world are thus seen as separate but mutually imbricated spaces that operate according to analogous rules and structures and shed light upon one another.

Therefore, this book is organized not according to discrete analyses of individual authors but according to the various tropes they employ to challenge, reformulate, and/or lament the constructions of femininity that structure the lives of their protagonists and, by extension, Japanese women like them who inhabit nontextual spaces. In each chapter I read several authors against one another, as well as against the historical backdrop that forms the context for their work, to understand the similarities and differences in expression of each trope or theme. While each chapter is devoted to a different trope, it is important to note that all of these narrative strategies highlight the female body as both the object and instrument of the process of engendering. Women are subjected to feminization in these texts precisely because they inhabit female bodies, and they live in a society that assumes a direct and logical connection between biology and identity or role type. Severing this discursive connection between bodily sex and gender is thus a primary objective of these narratives and a necessary first step toward envisioning a less restrictive model of subjectivity for women in modern Japan.

Chapter 1 is intended to contextualize the work of these authors against the historical backdrop that framed their literature, with particular attention to the production of hegemonic ideologies of gender and the ways in which these writers' fictional narratives sought to resist such dominant paradigms. The next two chapters explore the way that subjects are engendered through both "hard" (formal or explicit) and "soft" (informal or implicit) disciplinary mechanisms. I begin in chapter 2 with a trope that seems crucial to the process of construction of femininity as these authors understand it: the "masculine" gaze—so gendered because society itself, or more properly the structures of authority that permeated Japanese society at this time, is understood to be masculine. Being fixed by the disciplinary gaze is depicted in these texts as a kind of scopic violation akin to rape, an experience that forces the subject to acknowledge herself as female and therefore to internalize appropriately feminine behaviors.

In addition to this oppressive and violent means of disciplining women as "feminine" subjects, these authors also highlight the function of "soft power" in enforcing feminine norms. Chapter 3 takes as its objects of analysis texts in which women are induced to comply with normative femininity through a self-imposed abjection of their own bodies. The protagonists of the narratives explored in this chapter learn to internalize the binary logic that aligns women with the inferior plane of the corporeal in contrast to men, who are envisioned as spiritually and intellectually superior. This "logic" is mastered in the context of intimate relationships with male lovers or mentors, who reward complicity and punish resistance by withholding the affection or respect that is desired by the woman in question.

Once having exposed the artificiality of such gendered constructions, these authors are then eager to problematize the logic of strict binary distinctions between masculine and feminine subject positions, which serve to rationalize the enforcement of gender norms. Chapter 4 illustrates one trope that often serves this purpose in women's literature of the 1960s—the "odd body," which defies classification as either masculine or feminine, male or female. Curiously, many of these embodiments of alternative corporeality are male bodies that are queered in various ways—for example, they are frequently attributed with typically female bodily processes or feminine behaviors—in an apparent attempt to strike at the heart of the sex/gender system. If male subjectivity forms the ground upon which feminine difference is understood, then using male (rather than female) bodies to disrupt conventional linkages between sex and gender effects a more radical "troubling" of that difference.

Finally, the texts analyzed in chapter 5 all attempt to problematize the coherence of the category of "woman" itself by highlighting the differences among women, even as they acknowledge the potential for similarity or connection. The body of the Other Woman is variously figured in these texts as an object of desire, fear, and identification in ways that incorporate other women textually as privileged sites of self-knowledge. The doppelganger, or second-self, motif frequently appears in these texts as a means of depicting an Other that is simultaneously not other yet always somehow out of reach of the protagonist. While acknowledging a desire for relationships with other women, these texts are unanimous in highlighting the impossibility of true intimacy between women, as the protagonist's desire for the Other Woman is continually frustrated and frequently ends in tragedy.

In the conclusion, I highlight specific points of connection between the literary feminist agenda of these three authors and the goals of the "women's lib" movement of the following decade, with particular attention to the function of power, violence, and language in each type of feminist discourse. These three categories of analysis are significant because they represent problems that continually reassert themselves in all the texts analyzed in this study. Each in some way limits the way these authors are able to express, envision, and theorize new forms of feminine subjectivity, even as it enables the production and expression of subjectivity on other fronts. In other words, feminine subjects in these texts are produced *within* networks of power that simultaneously constrain and form them *through* violence, which alternately shapes their possibilities for expression *in* language. Although this yields a form of feminist discourse that is profoundly conflicted in its articulation of "femininity," this conflict is productive not only because it draws the reader's attention to contradictions in hegemonic discourses of gender that oppress women, but also because it helps to define and clarify many of the theoretical problems that would occupy subsequent generations of feminist activists. The result is an alternate version of "women's lib" that shares much with the explicitly political feminist speech of the following decade while differing from it in important ways.

CHAPTER 1

Party Crashers and Poison Pens

Women Writers in the Age of High Economic Growth

Listening to you talk, all the penises of the world would probably go flaccid.

—*Kurahashi Yumiko, "Yōjo no yō ni"*

The 1960s witnessed the debuts of a succession of women writers of fiction whose subversive heroines and controversial themes posed a profound and disturbing challenge to cherished ideals of femininity and "feminine" writing. The decade began with the publication of Kurahashi Yumiko's "Partei" (Parutai, 1960), a wickedly satirical exposé of student-movement dogmatism that took readers aback for its no-holds-barred poison-pen critique. This was soon followed by Kōno Taeko's "Toddler-Hunting" (Yōjigari, 1961), a provocative blend of themes of sadomasochism, child abuse, and pedophilia. As if to say that no sacred cow was safe from slaughter, Kurahashi and Kōno were soon joined by a cadre of other women, including Takahashi Takako, who wrote about incest, partner swapping, abortion, infanticide, murder, rape, bestiality, masturbation, homoeroticism, and a host of other topics that violated assumptions of feminine passivity, sexual innocence, maternal instinct, and marital bliss.

Needless to say, such women writers were exceptional in their willingness to challenge the conservative social mores and practical, upwardly mobile mindset of the dominant society. As members of the "Shōwa One-Digit Generation," it was their age cohort that was charged with the herculean task of resurrecting Japan from the ashes of defeat, transforming the country into the economic powerhouse that it is today. By the 1960s, most members of their generation had adapted to the roles crafted for them by the high-economic-growth society—producing, consuming, and reproducing more producers and consumers—while enjoying a more comfortable standard of living than any of them, having grown up during the war years of privation and instability, could ever have imagined. By contrast, these women writers resisted the gendered division of labor that underwrote the prosperity of the era, which confined women to roles that were strictly supportive of male labor. Their unconventional protagonists, who rejected stereotypically gendered roles and subverted or mocked institutionalized structures of family and state power, forwarded a trenchant critique of the social and political order that had come to define a newly stabilized and prosperous Japanese society.

In this chapter, I demonstrate how the social and political transformations of Japan in the 1960s produced oppressively narrow ideologies of gender, which in turn motivated these women to write against such trends, producing a counter-hegemonic discourse that I describe as feminist. I begin with a brief historical and cultural overview of this era, describing the process of war recovery and rebuilding that led to rising economic prosperity and increasingly conservative social mores. In the next section, I employ Michel Foucault's notion of "biopower" to explain how a gendered division of labor that rhetorically confined women to the private sphere as housewives and mothers, vis-à-vis their husbands' public role of salarymen, diffused itself through various institutions to become the dominant paradigm of femininity. Finally, I provide a brief introduction to the lives and works of each of these three authors, contextualizing their work within the broader spectrum of postwar Japanese literary production with particular attention to the way they subvert hegemonic gender norms in their literature. Despite the fact that these writers are clearly very different from one another in terms of life experiences and literary style, each of them may be seen as challenging dominant stereotypes of femininity that they felt to be overly reductive and restrictive, thereby promoting a broader conceptualization of what it meant to be a woman in Japan during the 1960s. It is on the basis of this subversive intent that I characterize these three authors as feminist.

Japan in the 1960s

The 1960s was an era of remarkable social and political stability, aided and abetted by high economic growth.[1] The seeds of this stability were sown in the 1950s, as Japan emerged from the ashes of defeat and a seven-year Occupation by Allied forces to become an independent nation under increasingly conservative rule. The Occupation had begun with sweeping social, economic, and legal reforms that empowered socialists and union leaders, but the urgency of Cold War politics led to a dramatic "reverse course" in policy during the second half of the Occupation period that favored stability over reform. While the left wing fragmented into factions that disagreed over the terms of the peace treaty that granted Japan's independence in 1952, conservative parties merged into a single Liberal Democratic Party (LDP) in 1955, which dominated Japanese politics until 1993, inaugurating an era of increased cooperation between government and industry that came to be known in later decades as "Japan, Inc." The Japanese economy finally regained its prewar strength in 1955 and then rapidly exceeded this mark as the gross national product (GNP) continued to grow exponentially throughout the 1960s. As a result of these political and economic transformations, the attention of the Japanese gradually shifted from the foreign policy problems and labor disputes that had contributed to the political strife of the 1950s to an enjoyment of the fruits of their labor as a rising tide of economic growth and individual prosperity swept the nation.

In 1960, two events occurred simultaneously to seal the nation's conservative turn. The first was the rioting and civil unrest that accompanied renewal of the U.S.-Japan Security Treaty. Japan had emerged from the shadow of the Occupation only to reenter the shade of the American nuclear umbrella, in the form of a treaty that bound it to U.S. foreign policy (known in Japanese as the Anzen Hoshō Jōyaku, or ANPO for short). This treaty allowed, among other things, for the United States to maintain its military bases in Japan as a staging point for operations in the Korean War (and later Vietnam). Having just experienced the physical and economic devastation of loss in World War II, concerned about rising Cold War tensions, and caught geopolitically between the two main nuclear powers, many Japanese were wary of becoming ensnarled in further conflict.[2] When the Security Treaty came up for renewal in 1960, left-wing parties and student activists led a fierce campaign against it, resulting in massive demonstrations that mobilized ordinary citizens from all walks of life.[3]

At the same time that riots ravaged Tokyo, ongoing labor-management tensions erupted into violence in the Miike coal mine strike of 1960.[4] The resulting melee, which pitted union members against strikebreakers and gangsters hired by the corporation, forced the government to send fifteen thousand national police to quell the disturbance. "The situation had reached crisis point with television broadcasts sending out images of a nation apparently on the brink of revolution."[5] In the wake of the bitter Miike battle, both industry and unions turned toward more conciliatory means of resolving labor disputes, leading to a more cooperative framework whereby union leadership was more or less incorporated into the bureaucratic structure of industry, effectively making unions part of management.

Having successfully navigated two major challenges to the new postwar order in quick succession, the Japanese people eagerly turned their attention away from contentious political and economic issues to focus on happier pursuits closer to home. With standards of living rising, and consumer products like refrigerators and washing machines finally within reach of the average household budget, in the 1960s they devoted themselves to enjoying the fruits of their labor during the era of rising prosperity and consumerism that came to be known as the "economic miracle."

In 1960, Prime Minister Ikeda Hayato announced a rather ambitious goal—to double the GNP over the next decade. Even more remarkable, the goal was met. Through a comprehensive stimulus package that included tax cuts, lower interest rates, and a generous amount of "administrative guidance" of crucial industries by the Japanese government, the unemployment rate plummeted and the standard of living of the average Japanese citizen soared over the course of the 1960s.[6] In 1960 over 70 percent of the population considered itself to be middle class; by the early 1970s this figure had risen to 90 percent.[7] Dubbed the "economic miracle" as early as 1962, this era of high economic growth resulted in profound transformations in Japanese daily life, from increased consumer activity, to soaring demand for higher education, to profound demographic shifts that dramatically altered the fabric of family life.

One immediate result of these changes was increased purchasing power of the average Japanese household. As the high unemployment of the 1950s gave way to labor shortages in the 1960s, wages increased. Consumers were able to spend a smaller percentage of their total household budget on food and more on durable goods and entertainment. Televisions, washing machines, and other household appliances were popular purchases at the outset of the decade; by 1970 consumers had graduated to cars, homes, and overseas vacations.[8] Regardless of how many people actually lived the lifestyle they were being sold in the mass media, the perception that Japanese people had of themselves as middle-class and upwardly mobile consumers increasingly came to define the national self-image, in turn structuring the conservative social mores and role distinctions that shaped ideologies of gender in the 1960s.[9]

Rising aspirations fueled increasing demands for higher levels of education, and competition for slots at all levels of noncompulsory (post–junior high) education grew intense, fueled by both demographic shifts and altered conceptions of a "good enough" standard of living. In 1962 the children of the postwar baby boom were just beginning to graduate from middle school, but a shortage of high schools to accommodate these unprecedented numbers of students led to phenomenal overcrowding, and classes were frequently packed with as many as sixty to seventy students. These numbers reflected a growing appreciation of the need for a high school education, at minimum, to meet the demands of an increasingly technologically sophisticated workplace.[10]

College and university enrollments were more modest, reflecting bitter competition for slots, especially at the more prestigious schools. In 1960, only 13.7 percent of male students advanced to four-year universities, compared to a mere 2.5 percent of girls. By 1970, the figure for males had doubled to 27.3 percent, versus 6.5 percent for girls. The number of girls attending junior college showed a more rapid increase, to 11.2 percent in 1970 (up from 3 percent in 1960), reflecting a cultural assumption that higher levels of education were unnecessary or even detrimental to a girl's future success in the marriage market—still considered to be the primary purpose of education for girls.[11]

For the parents of this postwar generation of young people—in other words, the members of the Shōwa One-Digit Generation that had been charged with national recovery and rebuilding—the need to provide their children with ever-increasing levels of education placed great pressure on both household budgets and family energies. Getting a child into a college or university, particularly a prestigious one, required an enormous investment of time, energy, and money for both parents and children. Fathers worked longer and longer hours to satisfy the demands of high-growth economic productivity, which meant that mothers were increasingly given sole responsibility for managing their children's educational careers—a task that required extensive involvement in school activities, help with homework, arranging for after-school classes and tutors, emotional encouragement, and physical care. The financial burdens of additional instruction pushed many mothers into the workforce as well—albeit in a part-time and poorly paid capacity. In the 1960s, these pressures produced ideologies of gender defined according to a rigid division of labor that charged women with supportive tasks, such as domestic labor and childrearing, so that men could devote themselves to the increasing burden of overtime work that fueled the high-growth economy.

Ideologies of Gender

In 1960, the authors addressed in this study ranged in age from twenty-five to thirty-four—precisely the age at which young women were expected to marry and begin a family, according to the gendered division of labor described above. As we will see in the biographies below, these authors failed to conform to socially ingrained expectations of a "proper" life trajectory for women their age. Not surprisingly, their fictional heroines also subverted expectations of normalcy by explicitly rejecting the culturally defined common sense of the 1960s. Before we look at these literary strategies of resistance in detail, let us first examine the ways in which society sought to discipline women to conform to hegemonic ideologies of femininity.

Just as salarymen had their place in society as "corporate warriors," their children could contribute to the nation by devoting themselves to academic success, toward becoming future productive workers themselves. Women, as during wartime, were constructed as the support staff in this national cause, making their husbands' and children's labor possible through their roles as "good wives and wise mothers," a prewar ideology of femininity that found renewed relevance in the postwar period.[12] While women before and during World War II were mobilized to turn their "natural" instincts for nurturing others toward service to the empire—by bearing and raising future soldiers and preserving the integrity of the home even as husbands and children were sent off to war—women in the postwar period were urged to perform similar roles in the service of economic growth.

Michel Foucault's notion of "biopower" helps us to understand how such gender roles can come to seem "natural," as they are ingrained in the individual through formal and informal disciplinary mechanisms that permeate all levels and institutions of society.[13] Individual Japanese contributions to this postwar project of national economic growth, through compliance with gendered ideals of behavior designed to distribute the burden of production to all sectors of society as efficiently as possible, were likewise solicited through such regulatory mechanisms. Formally, government policies established the parameters of what was legally permissible, including a range of behaviors with highly gendered consequences, such as laws governing abortion and birth control. Informally, disciplinary regimes were incorporated into the organizations and institutions that came to structure daily life for most Japanese people—workplace, school, family, neighborhood. These disciplinary regimes reinforced gendered norms designed to produce "docile bodies" capable of channeling individual desires toward contributing peacefully and productively to a new and improved Japan and were themselves reinforced by the mass media, which served to both reflect and produce postwar ideologies of gender.

It is important to note that compliance with these gender norms was achieved not merely through initiatives sponsored by government, industry, and media, but was in large part also the result of cooperation by a substantial proportion of the Japanese population itself. As we will see, the authors addressed in this study may be seen as exceptional in their determination to resist such disciplinary regimes. But first let us survey the specific contexts that produced these norms. In the following sections, we will see some examples of how conformity to these ideologies of gender was solicited and rewarded through both formal and informal disciplinary mechanisms.

ABORTION AND BIRTH CONTROL

During World War II, exhorting women to bear more children was part of a larger attempt to encourage women to contribute to the war effort through heightened expressions of domestic femininity. Women were understood discursively not only as producers of future soldiers, but also as protectors of hearth and home. Keeping mothers at home seems to have been perceived as crucial to maintaining some sense of stability during a profoundly unstable time. This rationale explains why Japan, unlike the United States or other nations during World War II, remained reluctant to make use of the labor of married women, even as it conscripted young schoolgirls to factories and other military support industries.[14]

In the postwar period, the tendency to view the full-time housewife as anchor of home and family persisted, yet the prewar pronatalist rhetoric no longer made sense in light of the nation's altered circumstances: "Beginning in 1947, mortality rates started a long, steady decline and birth rates skyrocketed. Official thinking of these years came to be marked by a profound fear that overpopulation would choke off any hope of economic recovery. With the prewar option of promoting emigration to the colonies no longer possible, the government gradually moved toward support of family planning and birth control."[15] Amid a storm of controversy, abortion was effectively legalized in 1948 as a response to the dire postwar situation. However, conservative attitudes toward women's sexual subjectivity persisted, and many pundits feared that easier access to birth control would encourage juvenile delinquency and lax morals.[16] Government policy in the postwar period was still underwritten by an assumption that the only morally acceptable outlet for women's sexuality was motherhood, so its embrace of birth control was tentative and qualified.

As the birth rate declined precipitously throughout the 1950s, first due to easy access to abortion and later the increasing availability of condoms, government willingness to legalize new forms of birth control (particularly oral contraception) evaporated.[17] From the 1960s on, Japanese elites—in the form of interest groups representing obstetricians and gynecologists, religious groups, pharmaceutical companies, and family planning organizations—battled one another to influence government policy on abortion and birth control. Several attempts were made to restrict legal access to abortion, beginning in 1967.[18] Women in the 1960s were barraged by religious groups with messages that "abortion is murder," even as they were given few options to limit their fertility and little to no education on sexual matters other than exhortations to remain "pure" until marriage.[19] For a variety of structural reasons that had little to do with the promotion of women's reproductive freedom and much to do with the convenience of government bureaucracy, industry, and the medical establishment, abortion and condoms became the primary means of birth control in the absence of other options, a situation that was not remedied until oral contraceptives were legalized in 1999.[20]

There are many implications of this state of affairs, all of which left women at a distinct disadvantage. Certainly from the state's perspective of expanding the economy, it was desirable for women to have some access to birth control so as to limit family size. On the one hand, an increasingly sophisticated technological society could be maintained only by a highly educated workforce, and such a society required an intensive investment of money and time in each child. On the other hand, as the nuclear family structured according to a highly gendered division of labor provided the optimal structure within which to raise such children, it was undesirable for women to have too much sexual freedom, as they might decide to enjoy satisfying sexual lives while opting out of this structure altogether.

Given these social and historical exigencies, it is hardly surprising that the two available means of birth control, condoms and abortion, both required the cooperation of a woman's male partner, and one was an invasive and expensive procedure with potentially serious consequences for the woman's health.[21] Under these circumstances, it is not surprising that the majority of women acceded to social pressures to conform to models of femininity that stressed marriage and motherhood as woman's "natural" roles. As we will see below, all three of the authors under study here resisted this notion of marriage and motherhood as woman's destiny, and while all three eventually got married (although one waited until quite late in life), only one of the three had children.

EDUCATION FOR MARRIAGE

While Western-style ideals of romantic love had some currency in Japan as early as the 1920s, love marriages were in fact relatively rare at this time. Furthermore, as Barbara Sato notes, as the national climate of increasing militarism in the 1930s began to hold sway over the private lives of Japanese citizens, individual desires—including those influencing choice of marriage partner—were gradually subordinated to the needs of the state:

> In 1940, in compliance with the state's policy to increase the population, marriage became women's duty carried out for the good of the country. This policy led to a temporary decline in the trend toward love marriages as official doctrine left no room for individualism in marriage. "We can't think anymore about marriage being for our personal happiness," *Shufu no tomo* [a popular women's magazine] told its readers. "A good marriage is one that will help strengthen the state."[22]

On an individual level, marriages in the prewar period were typically arranged by the head of household—often the father or eldest brother—who managed the lives of family members according to a patriarchal logic patterned after the emperor's rule over his subjects. Individual needs were thereby subordinated to those of the *ie* (household), which was in turn subordinated to the needs of the state, so the emperor was seen as a kind of national father figure. In this way the state was able to make use of traditional values of filial piety in the service of national order; just as one's father must be obeyed unconditionally, so must the emperor. It was not until the new postwar constitution formally dismantled the *ie* system that women (and men) were finally granted the legal right to choose their own spouses. The Shōwa One-Digit Generation was therefore the first to benefit from this increased freedom to marry a partner of one's choice.

By the 1960s love marriages had become an attainable ideal for many in Japanese society and quickly came to signify the promise and rewards of Japan's newly democratized and thoroughly middle-class society. However, while the choice of marriage partner was increasingly left up to the individual, the question of whether or not one should marry, or what sort of marriage one should aspire to, remained very much a matter of state concern. In the immediate aftermath of the war, elite fears of "moral corruption," in the form of rising rates of prostitution and abortion, and the specter of girls and boys being taught together in classrooms for the first time under the new system of coeducation, led the Ministry of Education to develop a sex education curriculum that overwhelmingly focused on "purity education"—that is, abstinence. Educating future wives and mothers in the postwar period thus began early, with young female students indoctrinated to preserve their virginity for marriage. After marriage, they were expected to channel their sexual impulses into the production and rearing of children, as well as into creating a warm and comfortable home for their husbands.

There was no recognition that women might legitimately have sexual desires that were independent of motherly "instincts." Such impulses were actively discouraged as harmful and antithetical to women's maternal destiny. As an example of the majority opinion among "experts" on sex education, Sonia Ryang notes the following about one influential manual written in 1949:

> While there is a conspicuous absence of mention of the "comfort" men could receive from prostitutes or other sex workers outside wedlock or prior to marriage, the author goes on warning against *fukenzenna kōi* (unhealthy behavior) on the part of women, including masturbation which, according to [the author] Numanoi, could turn women into homosexuals and would ruin their marital happiness. Similar warnings against female sexual self-gratification, focusing on clitoral orgasm as a possible cause of mental illness and frigidity (that is, inability to sexually satisfy her husband), abound in purity education and sex education guidebooks.... One can clearly see that *junketsukyōiku* [purity education] was really about female virginity and not male sexual purity, about controlling female sexuality (by way of educating men as well as disciplining women), and about dividing sex into marital and extramarital components from the men's point of view.[23]

According to this logic, then, the only "healthy" outlet for women's sexuality was within the context of marriage. But as Ryang notes, even within this limited sphere of possible sexual activity for women, emphasis was placed on the "product" of sex—that is, the conception of children—rather than the activity itself or the relationship between the partners. Ironically, this "asexualization" of marital sex took place simultaneously with an increased emphasis on (heterosexual) romantic love, yielding a curious state of affairs whereby couples everywhere were incited not to repress their sexual desires but to actively channel them into marriage and reproduction while eliding the sexual content of the encounter through a discourse of "pure love."

These messages were reinforced in the mass entertainment media through narratives of "pure love" like the novel *Ai to shi o mitsumete* (Facing Love and Death, 1963), a best-selling tearjerker about a young couple whose relationship remained "pure" until the untimely end of the virginal female protagonist. The story was subsequently made into a highly popular TV drama and a feature film. "The sexuality and sexual desires of wives were suppressed or displaced by watching soap operas in the living room, while those of husbands were redirected outside the home, as in the cases of flirting with bar hostesses or buying prostitutes."[24] It was not until after the women's liberation movement of the 1970s that public opinion began to shift toward acceptance of the notion that women might legitimately possess and act upon sexual impulses of their own, outside of the context of marriage. Yet well in advance of these developments in the second-wave feminist movement, the women authors whose works form the core of this study produced frank and often shocking narratives of feminine sexual agency that challenged the notion of women as passive (a)sexual objects.

Education for marriage and motherhood was also infused, formally and informally, into other aspects of the curriculum, demonstrating remarkable continuity across the prewar-postwar divide, even as postwar women were granted legal guarantees of access to a higher quality and level of education than ever before. In the prewar period, even at relatively prestigious women's institutions of higher learning, girls had been presented with a dumbed-down curriculum that emphasized graceful acquiescence to gendered roles and placed extreme limits on feminine self-expression through rigorous disciplinary mechanisms.

Even within the higher normal schools, which provided the most advanced education available to women in prewar Japan, the curriculum was dull and out of touch with a changing society. Math courses emphasized bookkeeping; chemistry courses featured lectures on the molecular makeup of household goods; English courses assigned recitations from *Pilgrim's Progress* and Florence Nightingale's biography; and ethics courses reviewed the "do's" and "don't's" of feminine etiquette: how to sit gracefully at a tea ceremony, what clothes to wear for a funeral, which flowers to hang near the lavatory on New Year's. In addition, the male administrators of these institutions spared no efforts in sheltering their young ladies. Dress codes, curfews, prohibitions on news-papers, and wrought-iron gates insured that the higher normal school graduate had a minimal understanding of, or interest in, politics, social reform, or even simply self-expression.[25]

It was understood that the purpose of higher education for women was to prepare them for their future roles as wives and mothers, and those who violated this norm by pursuing a career instead—even through the more or less acceptable route of schoolteaching—were viewed askance as "represent[ing] a threat to 'manliness,' marriage, and family."[26] Although all three authors addressed in this study would have been subjected to this type of "feminine" curriculum during the early years of their education, two out of three went on to study at prestigious and previously male-dominated institutions, and the third, slightly too old to benefit from the removal of legal barriers to this path, nevertheless attended a prestigious women's college.

In spite of postwar efforts to restructure the Japanese educational system to guarantee equal educational opportunity to women, conserva-tive attitudes regarding gender roles nevertheless persisted in the minds of government and bureaucratic officials, not to mention the average citizen. As Donald Roden notes, even during the height of the Occupation-era reformist zeal, there was great resistance to the kind of restructuring of the educational infrastructure that would be necessary to fully integrate women into university environments on an equal basis with men. Roden's research indicates, for example, that Japanese bureaucrats during the Occupation actively worked to obstruct the creation of deans of women at historically male-dominated institutions who might have acted as guidance counselors to encourage and support the first cohorts of young women admitted to such prestigious institutions.[27] Under such circumstances, it is hardly surprising that women of this generation, like Takahashi Takako, recall experiences of chauvinism and demoralization in all-male university environments.[28]

After 1952, the gap between the promises of the new Japanese con-stitution and the realities of Japanese women's lives persisted. In the wake of the Allies' departure and the rising tide of political conservatism, key Occupation-era reforms that had been intended to decentralize the edu-cational system were rolled back. Thanks to this second "reverse course," the Ministry of Education was able to exert a great deal of control over everything from the composition of local school boards to the contents of textbooks.[29] This control facilitated the socialization of children according to rigidly defined gender roles, through both formal and informal mechanisms. In spite of constitutional guarantees of equality between the sexes, in 1958 the Ministry of Education introduced vocational training from the middle-school level that was effectively sex-segregated. As Atsuko Kameda notes, "The postwar educational reforms mandated that all students pursue a common, uniform curriculum at all levels of education. As part of this policy, home economics was made a mandatory subject for both girls and boys at the elementary and secondary levels. At the lower secondary schools level, a course called "industrial arts and homemaking" was newly established in 1958, and boys were taught industrial arts and girls homemaking."[30] It seems that this policy was designed to obey the letter of the law while violating its spirit by considering "industrial arts and homemaking" as a single class, even as boys were assigned the former and girls the latter. Educators were thereby able to claim that they required the same "curriculum" of everyone, even though the contents differed according to the sex of the student. In 1969, home economics was made a required course for high school girls (effective 1973), but this "requirement" was not extended to boys until 1989 (effective 1994), a revision that was freely ignored by many schools even after this point.[31] Thus, educational curricula left young people during the 1960s with little doubt as to their destinies, continuing to craft girls into future wives and mothers, while boys were prepared for careers in the workforce.

The persistence of these gendered attitudes toward appropriate vocational aspirations for men and women obviously clashed with the guarantees of equal educational opportunity of the postwar constitution. In spite of these barriers, the number of young women enrolling in four-year universities continued to rise throughout the 1950s and 1960s, prompting a conservative backlash that erupted in the mass media in the form of widely publicized debates over "coeds ruining the nation." This debate was sparked by an article penned by Professor Teruoka Yasutaka of the prestigious Waseda University; the article ran in the March 1962 issue of *Fujin kōron,* a large-circulation magazine targeted toward an educated female readership. Hiroko Hirakawa summarizes the esteemed professor's remarks on the subject as follows:

> According to Professor Teruoka, female university students were lowering the standards of higher education and wasting not only their own time but people's taxes, since they were only going

to become housewives. In magazines and radio programs, his claims were supported by other (male) intellectuals, though some defended coeds on the grounds that higher education would help women become "enlightened mothers." The presence of these mass-mediated debates indicates that, by the time the Ampo turmoil [of 1960] broke out, the construction of a normative model of the nuclear family, however contested, was already under way.[32]

The contemptuous attitude that Professor Teruoka demonstrated toward girls who aspired to something more than marriage and motherhood must not have been lost on young women of the time, in spite of the increased opportunities that were theoretically available to them. This contempt was surely driven home by the fact that even the coeds' supporters justified their pursuit of higher education exclusively within the rather limited discourse of the nurturing of future "enlightened mothers." The specter of the coed contagion was then taken up in other mass-circulation periodicals like *Shūkan Asahi,* a weekly magazine aimed at a general readership, and in radio broadcasts, and it continued for about a year. The length and extensive coverage of this debate indicates how contested the question of "appropriate" roles for women was at this point in Japanese history, a controversy that exposed critical gaps between the promise of postwar reforms and the reality of most women's lives. Women who attempted to deviate from this "appropriate" path encountered profound resistance not merely from official bureaucratic structures, but in the court of public opinion as well. Mass media portrayals of "appropriate" feminine activity further worked to reinforce these normative discourses, either by explicitly critiquing women's aspirations to anything but marriage and motherhood or more subtly by rewriting other types of activity as expressions of women's maternal destiny.

In light of these historical circumstances, the narratives of the women writers addressed in this study stand out for the way they are not only able to forward trenchant critiques of hegemonic ideologies of femininity, but also for the frank and explicit attention they give to various expressions of feminine sexuality. By boldly engaging head on with such taboo subjects, these writers implicitly challenged conventional binary models of gender that constructed women as sexually innocent, passive, and nurturing maternal figures. In the next section, we will see how relationships between the worlds of work and family life were constructed so as to further underscore a gendered division of labor that reinforced such binary models of gender in postwar Japanese society, before we go on to explore some of the ways these women writers resisted such binary distinctions in their literature.

GENDERED DIVISION OF LABOR

The remarkable persistence of this ideology of domestic femininity in the 1960s might seem like something of a paradox, given the fact that substantial numbers of women worked outside the home and that these numbers increased markedly throughout the period of high economic growth from 1955 to 1973. Of course, women whose families made their living in agriculture or small business had always worked alongside their husbands and children. It was also common for young single women to work for a few years before retiring to get married. But as industry faced an increasingly urgent labor shortage after 1960, many corporations turned to hiring married women to fill the gap, typically on a part-time or temporary basis. The number of women employed in this capacity jumped from 4.4 million to 10.7 million between 1955 and 1970.[33]

However, this increased rate of employment among housewives did little to alter the discursive construction of women as primarily wives and mothers, as the structural characteristics of the Japanese labor market still conspired to prevent most women from earning enough to attain financial independence. Young women were pressured to marry and start a family by age twenty-five, and until the practice was declared illegal in 1966, they were typically required to retire from the workforce upon marriage.[34] Furthermore, the seniority system that dominated corporate employment and promotion practices provided benefits and raises only to workers with many years of uninterrupted service. Married women who reentered the labor force after raising children were thus generally limited to part-time, temporary, and poorly paid jobs that amounted to little more than supplementary contributions to most household budgets so that their salarymen husbands continued to fill the role of breadwinner for the family. Government policies also created incentives for women to confine their efforts to the domestic sphere. Tax and pension schemes were structured on the assumption of a male head of household who worked outside the home, with a dependent "nonworking" spouse, so women who earned more than one million yen per year actually increased their household's burden in terms of tax and pension plan contributions.[35]

In the face of these structural barriers to women's ability to earn a living wage, marriage and motherhood came to seem like the only logical choice for long-term financial security. Under such circumstances, it is no wonder that as late as 1983, nearly half of Japanese people of both sexes aged eighteen to twenty-four agreed with the statement that "men should work outside the home and women should stay at home."[36]

Such attitudes should not be seen as "traditional" in the sense of natural and ahistorical, but rather as the product of disciplinary practices that gradually instilled Japanese citizens in the postwar period with commonsense assumptions of binary and complementary roles for men and women.

Andrew Gordon demonstrates one way in which this discipline-for-growth was disseminated and promoted through the corporate-sponsored and government-supported "New Life Movements" of the 1950s and 1960s. These campaigns, which began as discrete and localized initiatives in the countryside and then spread to urban areas thanks to corporate adoption, encompassed an impressive array of activities and programs intended to professionalize the role of the housewife. They included courses in everything from practical skills like cooking, sewing, and knitting to lectures on efficient and modest household management. By offering wives the training necessary to acquit their household responsibilities well, these programs instilled in women a sense of pride in their contributions to family, company, and nation. Both industry and government stood to gain from channeling women's labor toward maintenance of the domestic sphere, through rhetoric that "spoke of rationalizing the role of housewife, the life of the family, and the home as both physical and social space. But its greater impact was in naturalizing a certain model of gender relations—of proper roles for men as well as for women. A society where women of all social strata managed the home, while their men managed the workplace, came to be understood as the natural way things were and ought to be."[37] Ultimately this resulted in a gendered division of labor that created definitive boundaries between the private and public realms and was increasingly articulated as an ideological distinction between feminine and masculine roles.

Gordon emphasizes that women were not forcibly inscribed within these domestic roles, but rather actively cooperated in creating and disseminating the gospel of "good wife and wise mother," as reinvented in the postwar period under the auspices of the New Life Movement. By performing as competent and "professional" household managers through an internalization of the tenets of modern domestic science, women were able to craft for themselves a role within the high-growth economy that was valued as separate but equally important as that played by their salarymen husbands. For this reason, many women readily acceded to the role of full-time housewife, even as it constrained their lifestyle options on other fronts. Gordon further notes that by the 1970s the movement had outlived its usefulness, ironically because the job of training women for their future roles in the domestic sphere had been taken over by the public schools.[38]

Nevertheless, housewives increasingly returned to the labor force from the mid-1950s on, if only on a part-time basis, while continuing to shoulder the entire burden of housework and child care. Women were hardly oblivious to the challenge this outside employment posed to their discursive construction as wives and mothers, and this structural paradox motivated a series of vituperative "housewife debates," which raged off and on from 1955 to 1976 in the pages of *Fujin kōron*. The debates began with an incendiary essay by Ishigaki Ayako, a female critic who chastised Japanese housewives for being content with full-time domestic work that, she claimed, allowed them to pursue lives of indolence and ease. Ishigaki charged that this thereby stunted their intellectual and emotional growth compared to American women, whose work outside the home challenged them to develop into mature and independent adults. Jan Bardsley summarizes Ishigaki's argument as follows: "In the space of the home, gendered as female, Japanese housewives grow predictably soft and simpleminded, their concerns taking on a rather nervous, petty quality. The marketplace and other public places, [which are] gendered as male, are the site of serious adult work, something that makes the leisured appearance of the housewife and her inconsequential speech stand out all the more because they are so aberrant."[39] The strident tone of Ishigaki's critique may sound unreasonable, given the very real barriers to meaningful employment for women circa 1955. Moreover, her characterization of such women as infantile and intellectually stunted seems to echo uncomfortably well the chauvinist discourse that was employed by men at this time to denigrate feminine potential for anything *but* housework, as the comments of Professor Teruoka (above) amply demonstrate.

However, in the biographical background she provides on Ishigaki, Bardsley offers a likely reason that this ostensibly "feminist" critic might so savagely attack other women. As Bardsley recounts, the course of Ishigaki's own youth was marked by her resistance to restrictive stereotypes of femininity that confined women within the domestic sphere:

> Her family criticized her as a young adult because she showed no interest in marriage or in leading the sheltered life of a middle-

class Tokyo woman. Ishigaki describes how she despaired of finding a job in Tokyo in the early 1920s that would have enabled
her to be self-supporting, and how she berated herself for being
no more than a "parasite" on her family. She also writes about
how her decision to move to New York and to marry a man of
her own choosing brought even harsher criticism, causing her
father to sever all ties with her. When Ishigaki attacks the modern Japanese housewife with such force, she is, in effect, fighting
against the ideal her family had always upheld for her—and the
ideal which, in their minds, she utterly failed to achieve.[40]

Viewed from the perspective of her personal history, Ishigaki's frustration with women who conform to gendered roles is perhaps easier to
understand. The more women comply unresistingly with the expectation
that they confine their efforts to the domestic realm, the harder it is for
exceptional women who dare to challenge these stereotypes to justify their
behavior or aspirations. In fact because of the disciplinary mechanisms
outlined above, which permeated all levels of society, creating a sense of
the "naturalness" of women's destiny to become wives and mothers, it
was an exceptional woman indeed who dared to challenge the "common
sense" of mainstream Japanese society at that time. As we will see below,
the authors addressed in this study may likewise be seen as exceptional
women, whose impulse to challenge restrictive gender roles led them into
conflict not just with societal norms, but also with those women who
complied with them.

Texts and Contexts

This section will explore the emergence of the women writers of the 1960s
within the broader context of the *bundan*. After a brief description of this
milieu, we will see how it functioned to determine the success or failure of
literary careers in both explicitly and implicitly gendered ways. We will also
see how gendered discourses worked simultaneously to shape women's
writing as "feminine" and to construct masculine subjectivity as active
and superior to women, who were discursively rendered as correspond-
ingly passive and inferior. Finally, we will survey the lives and works of
the authors analyzed in this study, with particular attention to the points
of connection between their literary attacks on hegemonic discourses of
gender and the ways these forms of self-expression were shaped by their
experiences with the *bundan*.

"Femininity" and the Japanese Literary Establishment

While the term *bundan* is now rather loosely applied to the center of Japanese literary power and prestige, its composition and function have changed over time in response to broader transformations in literature and society. The term was originally used in the Meiji period (late 1800s) to refer to a literary guild structured according to a close-knit set of master-disciple relations, where young writers labored under the tutelage of established authors. In the early 1900s, the term came to be applied to a coterie of writers inspired by European naturalist literature who developed the *shishōsetsu* (I-novel). This quasi-autobiographical form of fiction stressed the pursuit of "truth" through a relentless interrogation and exposure of self and became the dominant form of the modern Japanese novel in the first half of the twentieth century. As the market for literary production and consumption expanded dramatically in the Shōwa period (beginning in 1926), the center of power gradually shifted from this small fraternity of like-minded intellectuals to the publishing industry itself, as mass-circulation newspapers and journals increasingly took the place of coterie magazines as the primary outlet for original works of fiction.[41] By the 1960s, the term *bundan* had come to refer broadly to those public intellectuals with the "power"—in the form of educational capital and status, as members of the academy or the publishing industry—to determine the success or failure of the literary careers of aspiring writers.

From the beginning of the modern period, the power of the *bundan* was exercised in evidently gendered ways to restrict or shape women's literary production. In the 1890s, as women began to contribute to literary circles and coterie magazines under the tutelage of master writers, it took the explicit form of male mentors who directed the work of their female protégés to conform to what they perceived as appropriately "feminine" style.[42] As the publishing industry grew and such interpersonal mechanisms of control were gradually superseded by editorial decisions regarding literary marketability, the *bundan* functioned not so much to silence or exclude women from publishing as to selectively reward those who conformed to expectations of legibly "feminine" writing.

As Joan Ericson demonstrates, these literary expectations were gradually codified in the form of the emergent "genre" of *joryū bungaku* (women's-style literature), a "style" of writing that came to define literary expression for women from the 1920s on. As more women embarked on literary careers, male writers increasingly sought ways to distinguish their own "pure" (artistically superior) literature from what they saw as an influx of "popular" (stylistically inferior) writing by women. As a result, women's literary work came to be categorized as *joryū bungaku,* a classification that collapsed a variety of writing styles and thematic material under a largely constructed and totalizing category of the "feminine":

> Modern Japanese women writers confronted a specific constellation of attitudes toward their gender that shaped not only their prospects for publication and critical reception, but, in some circumstances, even how the women themselves wrote. Attributes presumed to be natural in a woman's voice—sentimental lyricism, and impressionistic, nonintellectual, detailed observations of daily life—were the result of a confluence of social and literary trends that, in the 1920's, crystallized the notion of a distinct "women's style."[43]

It is important to note here that while this "feminine" style was presented as "natural" and inherent to the female sex, in fact it took on a prescriptive and disciplinary function, thereby creating that which it presumed to describe.

Women writers who conformed to the standard of *joryū bungaku* were rewarded with opportunities for publication and literary prizes. Writers like Enchi Fumiko, who wrote lyrically in a style that evoked the beauty of the great Heian (high classical) female authors, or Sono Ayako, whose works extolled "traditional domestic virtues of marriage and the family," fit comfortably within male expectations of "feminine" style, even when in other respects their work might be said to forward a feminist message.[44] As Chieko M. Ariga notes, even those who did not conform could often be reinscribed within more comfortably "feminine" parameters through critical commentaries that interpreted the meaning of their work for readers in more conventionally gendered terms.[45] Those who could not be recuperated as appropriately "feminine" were consigned to the margins of literary history.[46]

Women who made their debuts on the literary scene in the 1960s thus faced a network of "hard" and "soft" disciplinary mechanisms that operated in emphatically gendered ways and were frequently mutually imbricated. By "hard" mechanisms, I refer to explicit or formal methods of restricting access to publication or bestowing recognition upon an author or her works. In postwar Japan, these methods ranged from editorial decisions regarding whether or not to publish a work in a prestigious journal or *zenshū* (collected works), to positive critical reception (including the conferral of literary prizes), to inclusion in the ranks of those anointed to judge the merit of other authors' works (for example, prize selection committees or roundtable discussions devoted to the critique of new works).[47] By "soft" mechanisms, I refer to implicit or informal methods of control, such as interpersonal relationships and gendered discourses (literary and otherwise) that shaped attitudes toward women and their literary works and to some extent were internalized by the women themselves.

In terms of the way these mechanisms operated to exclude or marginalize women in the *bundan*, it is helpful to think of power as functioning not in absolute or strictly hierarchical terms but through a variety of complex and overdetermined ways that ultimately yield gendered outcomes. Women's careers were often made or broken not through the decree of one powerful male who deemed them unworthy but through a multitude of everyday interactions with members of the male-dominated establishment, each of whom possessed a measure of power and wielded it in subtle and perhaps even unintentional ways. These encounters could include everything from having a manuscript rejected for its failure to conform to legible expressions of "femininity" to allowing the career of one's husband or lover to hamper one's own professional advancement.

The sum of these individual power encounters—particularly when power was employed to contain women (deliberately or not) within conventionally "feminine" modes of self-expression and behavior—created a formidable wall to women's advancement in the literary world that was only gradually overcome and left an indelible mark on the writing of women authors of fiction during the 1960s. The authors discussed in this study all had personal experiences of frustration and failure in attempting to overcome these networks of power, experiences that in turn shaped what they were able to say and how they were able to say it. In chapters 2 and 3, we will see that these authors explicitly grappled with these experiences in their literature, depicting in harsh terms those "hard" and "soft" disciplinary mechanisms that sought to contain their protagonists within appropriately gendered forms of subjectivity.

GENDER IN POSTWAR JAPANESE LITERATURE

Thus far we have seen how networks of power, both formal and informal, shaped the success or failure of women's literary careers, as well as the form of their creative self-expression. The authors addressed in this study had the dubious distinction of pushing the boundaries of "feminine" literature at a time when they were malleable enough to allow for some distortion yet rigid enough to leave a mark on both the author and her work. Women writers during the 1960s could not help but be affected by discourses of normative femininity even as they struggled against them, particularly since such discourses profoundly shaped not only their own life experiences, but also the standards of literary excellence according to which their own works were judged.

These stereotypes were further reinforced by images of women as depicted in the literature of those male writers who were anointed with both critical and popular success during this turbulent decade. At the time the authors of this study were writing, the *bundan* was dominated by male writers who depicted women in their literature in chauvinist, if not downright misogynist, terms. These male-stream narratives were products of a profound crisis in male subjectivity resulting from the emasculating experience of defeat and Occupation in the immediate postwar period, aggravated by the perception that women were encroaching upon previously male-dominated spaces (including the *bundan*) as they attempted to capitalize on the new rights extended to them by the postwar constitution.[48] Postwar narratives by male writers thus tried to rhetorically reassert a dominant masculine subjectivity by rendering women as corporeal objects that facilitated the recuperation and transcendence of their embattled and emasculated protagonists. In chapters 3 and 4 of this volume, we will see how women writers in the 1960s protested, and then subverted, this masculine trope of aligning women with the base realm of the corporeal as a ground for masculine transcendence to the "superior" realm of the intellect. But first let us briefly survey the context for postwar literature of the body that underwrote this struggle to define femininity.

While prewar practitioners of the "I-novel" were still actively publishing after World War II, new forms of literature authored by male writers also emerged from the ashes of defeat to reshape the postwar literary landscape. During the late 1940s, one of the first such genres of fiction to offer a new direction for Japanese literature was *nikutai bungaku,* or "literature of the flesh." As a response to and reaction against the total spiritual and moral devotion to the national project of imperialism, which had been required of Japanese citizens during the war, this literature sought release from ideological bondage in the form of physical and carnal experience. With its attention to the body as a crucial site of mediation between self and other—as well as the prominence it placed on sexuality, both as a means of interaction with the Other and as a vehicle for self-knowledge and identity construction—this genre is one obvious genealogical source for the literature of the body produced by women writers of the 1960s.

The work of Michael Molasky and Douglas Slaymaker is particularly useful for understanding the relevance of *nikutai bungaku* to this study, as both scholars are sensitive to the gendered implications of such literature. Molasky describes male writers who wrote during or about the Occupation period as engaged in a project of "national allegory," wherein female characters are portrayed as literally embodying the fate of the nation, particularly through narratives that dramatize the fraternization of Japanese women with American GIs. In such narratives, the sexual use and abuse of Japanese women's bodies provides male writers with a convenient trope for expressing the indignity that *men* felt as a result of defeat and occupation, while it projects anxieties of sexual violation and humiliation onto the body of the Other.[49] Slaymaker concurs, noting that writers of *nikutai bungaku* promoted an ideology of "living by the body," where bodily experience, and particularly sexual release, served as a means of escape both from the enforced subservience to nation and emperor required of them during the war and from the crushing sense of emasculation and inadequacy that plagued men during the Occupation:

> Male characters in postwar fiction [by male authors] affirm their identity via agency and transgression under the gaze of the Other; insisting on their agency in sexual relations, they thus re-assert an inviolate identity (precisely what they are anxious about) through heterosexual agency, an act that violates the boundaries of a woman. The flesh writers display an assumption (which I suggest is male) that founds the identity of the thinking individual on an agency coded as liberation; the agency they image [*sic*] violates the integrity of the woman.[50]

It is striking that in male narratives of the Occupation, for male protagonists, control over their own body *and* the body of the Other (woman) seems requisite for a sense of masculine subjectivity. "Liberation" is therefore figured in these texts in terms that are specifically both masculine and heterosexual.

Yet while male authors during the Occupation made much of "living by the body" as a means of coping with the postwar malaise, it seems clear that the body in question was not their own but that of a woman. In other words, rather than merely expressing a man's own bodily pleasures and experiences, what these narratives seem in fact to wish for their male protagonists is not so much transcendence *through* the body but transcendence *of* the body. By employing the body of the Other (woman) as a vehicle for their own transcendence of the base, corporeal realm, the protagonists are able to project onto Woman all of the negative qualities that are associated with the corporeal—physical vulnerability, violation of one's bodily boundaries through sexual submission, acquiescence to domination by structures of power—qualities that threaten to emasculate an already fragile male sense of agency. Within this context, what possibility existed for Japanese *women* to establish a sense of agency in the postwar period? This is precisely the question that occupied the women writers addressed in this study, as we will see in subsequent chapters.

As the *nikutai bungaku* of the early postwar period gave way to a new generation of young male authors who came to define literary excellence in the *bundan* of the 1960s, these new male writers continued to depict women's bodies as the ground for construction of a postwar masculine subjectivity. As Susan Napier demonstrates, male writers of this time continued to depict the humiliation of defeat through narratives that characterized postwar Japan as a "wasteland" that could be transcended only through violent action, frequently accompanied by the sexual abuse and denigration of women. In her thorough study of two great male writers of the 1960s, Ōe Kenzaburō and Mishima Yukio, she explains the frequency of works depicting the rape, torture, and terrorization of female characters as motivated by a desire for mastery and potency in a world that they perceived to be chaotic and barren.[51]

Even in stories where women are depicted in more or less positive terms, they serve primarily as "vessels through which male characters work out their fears and desires." For example, Napier finds that the wife of the protagonist in Mishima's "Patriotism" (1961), quite possibly the most sympathetically drawn of any of Mishima's heroines, is positively depicted primarily for her utter subordination to her husband's will: "Reiko's beauty, highlighted by her traditional garb, her obedience, and above all her traditionally submissive character, signify a world of lost calm and security where relationships were defined and control was firmly in the hands of a virile male." Napier then compares this to the character of Himiko in Ōe's *A Personal Matter* (1964), who willingly offers her body up for the protagonist's sadistic and violent sexual use so as to cure him of his impotence: "Himiko's care-taking attitude and her womblike little apartment offer refuge for a male adrift in the atomizing sea of modernity."[52]

Ōe's work is particularly telling in this regard, in part because of the pervasive misogyny evident in his narratives and also because of his stature as a darling of the postwar literary establishment. Anointed by Japanese critics from the beginning of his career in the 1950s as a spokesman for the emergent generation of young (male) writers, Ōe went on to establish an international reputation as a dominant voice in postwar Japanese letters, eventually being honored with the Nobel Prize for literature in 1994. With authors like Mishima and Ōe setting the standards for literary excellence in the 1960s, it is no wonder that postwar women writers felt compelled to counter these male discourses by narrating experiences of the female body from their own perspectives. As we will see below, the authors addressed in this study also produced narratives that combined sexuality and violence in frequently shocking ways yet to very different ends than those of the male writers described above.

AUTHOR BIOGRAPHIES

In this section, I give a brief overview of the careers and experiences of Kōno, Takahashi, and Kurahashi, up to and including the 1960s, when the texts analyzed in this study were written. In doing so, I highlight the way that each of these women defied normative constructions of femininity both in their literature and in their own lives. Personal experience may in this sense be seen as motivating their rhetorical challenges to the ideologies of gender elaborated above. My objective is not to posit a direct and transparent correspondence between biography and bibliography, but rather to demonstrate the ways in which literature offered these women a forum to challenge hegemonic ideologies of gender and sexuality. While I do not want to overstate the importance of biography, given the extraordinary times during which these women lived, it would be surprising if they were unaffected by the historical transformations that impacted the range of experiences and opportunities available to them as women.

One thing that immediately becomes evident when these authors' experiences are examined together is the extent to which each woman's life course was affected by the age at which she experienced a common set of social and historical transformations. These authors were born less than ten years apart, and yet even slight differences in age at crucial moments in history seem to have dramatically influenced the way they experienced war, defeat, and the reorganization of Japanese society that occurred as a result of Occupation-era reforms. Kōno, the oldest, was born in 1926, and not surprisingly memories of war trauma and loss figure most prominently in her work. While Takahashi, born in 1932, employs the war as a backdrop for some of her fiction and essays, her recollection of events during this time seems more detached. War and its aftermath—to the extent that these are addressed at all in Takahashi's literature—seem to serve her primarily as a convenient setting for exploration of the spiritual and religious concerns that increasingly informed her writing as she developed as an author.[53] Born in 1935, Kurahashi, the youngest of the three, seems to have been little affected by the events of the war—at least judging by her self-presentation in autobiographical essays—and her literature seems far more inflected by her young adult experiences during the early 1960s than by the period of her childhood.

These three women may also be compared in terms of the educational opportunities presented to them, which were determined in dramatic ways by their age when Occupation-era reforms went into effect. Kōno was nineteen when the war ended in 1945, and by the time the coeducational system was inaugurated, she was past the age where she could benefit from it. She had spent just four months in college before her education was interrupted—first by conscription to factory labor; then by air raids that burned her family home to the ground; and subsequently by defeat, occupation, and the daily struggle to survive that characterized life in immediate postwar Japan. Her college cohort nevertheless graduated on time, albeit without actually having spent much time in class. Her struggles to support herself as a writer during the following years may be attributed in part to the narrower range of opportunities available to her as a result of these chaotic conditions. While Kōno's own literary work has clearly been enriched through her reading of both the Western and Japanese literary traditions, this seems less a product of her formal educational background and more a consequence of her own love of independent reading.

Takahashi, who was sixteen when her school went coed, experienced a number of adjustment problems to this new system but was able to translate these experiences into opportunities by competing successfully for entrance to the prestigious Kyoto University. The expertise in French literature that she acquired there is echoed in her own literary style; she was particularly influenced by the surrealist fiction of André Breton and the spiritual and moral concerns of French Catholic writers like François Mauriac and Julien Green. This educational pedigree conferred upon Takahashi the kind of academic and intellectual capital that had previously been the exclusive province of men. Yet her experience of being surrounded by male classmates, whom she describes as possessed of a confidence and sense of entitlement that she lacked, produced a deep-seated psychological conflict that only intensified with her marriage to another writer.

Kurahashi, who was just nine years old at the time of Japan's defeat, seems to have benefited the most from Occupation-era reforms while experiencing the least degree of trauma in adjusting to the brave new world of opportunity available to her. Like Takahashi, she was able to gain entry to a prestigious school that nurtured her interest in French literature, which left a dramatic imprint on her literary style. In fact, she has often described her own style as a process of imitation or parody of the writers she admires most—beginning with the "trinity" of Jean-Paul Sartre, Franz Kafka, and Albert Camus.[54] Her educational experiences also brought her into contact with powerful literary critics like Hirano Ken—a professor at her alma mater, Meiji University—who helped to forward her career. While her unorthodox literary style offended some members of the literary establishment, the brash confidence that her protagonists exude in gleefully subverting gender norms provides eloquent testimony to the psychological effects of these unprecedented opportunities for achievement. What a difference a decade makes.

Kōno Taeko

Kōno was born in 1926, the second youngest of five children, to an Osaka merchant family.[55] Her love of literature was sparked by her encounter with the works of Tanizaki Jun'ichirō and Izumi Kyōka, two authors whose fascination with the fantastic, grotesque, and erotic seems to have found echoes in her writing. Her own growth and maturity paralleled the escalation of conflict between Japan and its neighbors that came to be known in Japan as the Fifteen-Year (Pacific) War. Kōno was just eleven when hostilities formally broke out on the Chinese mainland in 1937 and fifteen when the United States entered the war in 1941. Much of her high school "education" consisted of air raid drills, crash courses in first aid and disaster response, sewing military uniforms, and cultivation of fallow land to supplement food supplies, as Japanese society rapidly transformed into a culture mobilized for total war.

At the age of eighteen Kōno was admitted to the Economics Department of what is today known as Osaka Women's University (Osaka Joshi Daigaku) in 1944. During the precious few months that she spent in class, she discovered a passion for English literature, until "nationalistic policies forced her to abandon her newfound interest."[56] Then, shortly after the beginning of the school year, the entire school was mobilized for mandatory service in a munitions factory. Factory labor and contributions to other military support services were required even of teenaged girls during the early 1940s, when Japan had sent most of its able men to the front.[57] Such work was dangerous and exhausting, and the young "recruits" were subjected to extreme forms of discipline that included corporal punishment for infractions such as failure to behave in appropriately deferential ways toward military officers. Any personal indulgence in food, clothing, or other adornments was interpreted as flouting austerity regulations, which were intended to discipline subjects to devote themselves physically and spiritually for service to the empire.[58] Not surprisingly, a number of Kōno's early stories read as thinly veiled protests against the violence and hypocrisy of prewar Japanese militarism, communicated through the experiences of young female protagonists whose childhoods are disrupted by the exigencies and trauma of wartime.[59]

Immediately after Japan's defeat in World War II, Kōno recalls feeling a sense of "liberation" from the grim austerity of life under the militaristic wartime regime; the feeling quickly turned to disillusionment as the fresh start she had hoped for failed to materialize. Her search for a sense of purpose led her to try her hand at writing in 1947, the year she graduated from college. However, her family objected strenuously to this choice of profession and pressured her to get married instead. In fact, the "normal" and accepted path for young women at this time would have been to marry soon after graduation from college.[60] Pressure on young women to marry and bear children at the "appropriate" age was strong, and any woman, like Kōno, who resisted social pressure to comply with this model of femininity faced an uphill battle that pitted her not merely against pressure from friends and neighbors, but against loved ones as well.

In spite of her family's opposition, Kōno took an office job in order to save up enough money to move to Tokyo, the location of major publishing houses and home to many members of the Japanese literary world. However, the rampant inflation that swept Japan in the wake of the wartime devastation of its economy and infrastructure quickly made it impossible to save anything, and she was forced to quit this job a year later due to ill health. Kōno's early career was characterized by a series of false starts resulting from poor health and economic struggles, aggravated by the stress of attempting to pursue a career as a writer while simultaneously holding down a full-time job to support herself. Not a strong person to begin with, this balancing act seems to have taken its toll on her physically, and in 1957 she contracted tuberculosis, a disease that would plague many of her fictional heroines as well.

While it is easy to attribute this parallel between literature and life as motivated by mere autobiographical fidelity, in Kōno's work, the strategic deployment of illnesses like tuberculosis, which render her protagonists sterile, serves as an implicit challenge to ideologies of gender that insisted on the "naturalness" of conflating femininity with motherhood. Kōno herself did not marry until the age of thirty-nine and never had children; her career thus resembled anything but the image of "traditional" house-

wife and mother. Perhaps for this reason, she consistently crafts protagonists who resist conventionally feminine roles.[61] As Uema Chizuko notes,
"Most of the protagonists of Kōno's fiction, usually in their late thirties
to early forties, are unable to bear children due to illness. They attempt
to redefine 'womanhood' in a society where a woman's only role is that
of a mother. Accordingly, such women struggle to find alternative ways
to re-establish relationships with their husbands and lovers when having
children is no longer an expected or a 'natural' way to assure the validity of
their relationships."[62] While many of Kōno's protagonists are sterile, they
frequently do not react to this condition as a properly maternal woman
"should"—that is, they do not seem to feel that they have been denied an
experience that is precious and fundamental to woman's happiness. Either
they are profoundly conflicted about their status—secretly relieved that
they have been spared the burden of children, yet vaguely guilty because
they know they are "supposed" to want them—or they simply experience
their childlessness as liberating and fortuitous.

An example of the former type of story would be "The Next Day"
(Akuru hi, 1965), where the protagonist is profoundly conflicted upon
being told by her doctor that she is sterile due to a case of tuberculosis
that has spread to her reproductive organs. Although she had decided
long ago that she did not want children, she is thrown by this sudden
discovery that her childlessness was not a conscious choice. She seems to
have constructed an identity for herself as a woman who has refused to
have children and feels that identity to be profoundly destabilized by the
discovery that her body has made the choice for her. She imagines that the
illness might be a kind of "punishment" for her decision not to procreate
and even expresses feelings of guilt for using national health insurance
funds to visit a gynecologist when she has no desire for children in the
first place.[63] The implication here is that the only "appropriate" reason
for her to visit a gynecologist would be if she were pregnant or trying to
get pregnant; there seems to be no recognition by the protagonist that
non-mothers also deserve access to reproductive health care. This poi-
gnant scene both exposes the way ideologies of maternal femininity had
eclipsed any other form of subjectivity for women in Japan by the 1960s
and further underscores the role of the state in enforcing these ideologies
through regimes of biopower that penetrated to the most intimate corners
of women's lives.

In other stories, Kōno's heroines are gleefully nonreproductive and
frequently abhor children to the point of harboring violent feelings toward
them. "Toddler-Hunting" is a frequently cited example of this type of

story (see chapter 4). Another example is "Ants Swarm" (Ari takaru, 1964), where the female protagonist is vehemently opposed to having children and then begins to change her mind, but only on the condition that she might have a daughter whom she would be able to treat harshly. As the protagonist is depicted as playing the role of masochist vis-à-vis her husband, this fantasy of abusing a daughter seems to replicate the treatment she receives at the hands of her husband, allowing her at last to take up the position of sadist in this cruel family game. Presumably it is easier to envision playing the dominant role vis-à-vis another woman who is younger and dependent on her than it is for the protagonist to imagine turning the tables on her husband, a man in a position of power over her.[64] This highlights the way that power asymmetries between men and women produce misogynist dynamics, which then reassert themselves in relationships between women.

Marriage in many of Kōno's stories is depicted as an artificial yet virulent structure that produces asymmetrical power relationships between men and women, even when both partners try to avoid such an outcome. For example, in "Dream Castle" (Yume no shiro, 1963), the protagonist, Kanako, is a divorcée who has recently taken up with a new boyfriend. This new relationship gives her occasion to reflect back on the reasons why her marriage failed; the protagonist attributes it to her lack of any desire to build a conventional home and family. The previous relationship is associatively linked with the house that she and her former husband had been saving to build; though she seems to have enjoyed the process of working toward this goal with him, once the house was built, she lost all interest in it (and him). At the end of the story, as her boyfriend is helping her locate a new apartment, he mentions the possibility of living together, and she reflects that in spite of their intentions, they have begun to replicate the patterns of a standard (Japanese) domestic partnership. Upon noticing a Western-style mansion that she finds attractive, Kanako notes that perhaps a foreign domicile would allow them to avoid this fate, indicating that the problem is with the way marriage is structured in a specifically *Japanese* context.

"Twin Arches" (Sōkyū, 1966) takes up this same theme and infuses it with the sadomasochistic dynamics for which Kōno is well known. So long as the protagonist, Fusako, and her boyfriend live together as unmarried partners, he is respectful of her independence and cooperative around the house, yet the moment the couple decides to officially register their marriage, he becomes selfish and abusive toward her. By the end of the story, Fusako has completely given herself over to serving her husband, even happily calling herself his "slave." Ironically, her husband grows discontented with this outcome because he had enjoyed her "queen"-like bearing and is disappointed with the ordinary wifely demeanor she has adopted toward him. Here masochism provides Kōno with a theoretical framework for understanding femininity as embedded in relationships of dominance and submission that she sees as integral to the institution of marriage itself. Such narratives underscore the irresistible force of the gendered roles ingrained into both women and men in Japanese society, roles that are not "natural" to her characters but rather have been woven into the fabric of marriage patterns and prove exceedingly difficult to subvert, even when they are distasteful to the characters themselves.

In spite of her early struggles to establish herself as a writer, with the publication of "Toddler-Hunting" in 1961, Kōno made her mark on the literary world as a writer of serious and provocative fiction that challenged conventional notions of femininity. This story earned her the *Shinchō* magazine prize; over the next few years she received several more prestigious literary awards, including the Akutagawa Prize—the highest honor bestowed by the Japanese literary world—for "Crabs" (Kani) in 1963. Other literary prizes included the Joryū Bungaku Shō (Women's Literature Prize) for "Final Moments" (Saigo no toki) in 1967 and the Yomiuri newspaper's literature prize for her novel *A Sudden Voice (Fui no koe)* in 1969. The following decades brought more awards and other indications of success and critical recognition—for example, the inclusion of Kōno's stories in many important literary anthologies and invitations to serve on nomination committees for the Akutagawa, Joryū Bungaku, and Yomiuri literature awards.[65]

While Kōno eventually earned success and recognition for her literary achievements, she struggled a great deal in the early years of her career, not just with poverty and illness, but also to establish herself as a serious writer of provocative and sexually explicit fiction at a time when Japanese society was taking an increasingly conservative turn. Yonaha Keiko reflects that when Kōno's first critically acclaimed story, "Toddler-Hunting," appeared in 1961, readers were thoroughly shocked by its themes of sadomasochism and child abuse. As Yonaha notes, Kōno defied commonsense sexual mores by portraying women who actively pursued their own, often "deviant," sexual desires within the context of marriage or established heterosexual partnerships. The implication that a legally or socially recognized marriage, which appeared "proper" from the outside, might serve as a façade for unimaginable violence and sexual perversity, was profoundly troubling for much of the reading public at this time.[66]

Even critics who evaluated Kōno's literature positively expressed reservations about its style and content. Davinder Bhowmik summarizes the critical reaction to her work as follows:

> Despite having won Japan's top literary prizes for decades, surprisingly, Kōno has taken a battering from the critical community. While impressed with her writing, many critics fail to comprehend Kōno's trademark masochistic trope, calling it "incomprehensible" (*nankai*) and "abstract" (*kannenteki*). Even feminist critics, whom one would expect to endorse Kōno's many determinedly independent heroines, fault her for the extremely negative portrayals of young girls she repeatedly includes in her works.[67]

As we will see below, Kōno's literary work during the 1960s in fact posed a profound challenge to the ideologies of gender that structured Japanese society at this time, including much of the mainstream feminist discourse that continued to articulate feminine subjectivity through the conventional women's roles of housewife and mother. But before exploring the specific ways in which Kōno intervened in normative discourses of femininity, we will see some similarities in personal background and literary agenda with the two other writers addressed in this study.

Takahashi Takako

Takahashi (née Okamoto) was born in Kyoto in 1932, the only child of an architect working for the Kyoto municipal authorities. She began her post-elementary education at a girls' higher school in 1944, as was prescribed by the sex-segregated institutional structure of the day, and like Kōno, she describes being mobilized to labor for the war effort. However, Takahashi was just sixteen years old when the Japanese educational system was made coed by Occupation fiat, and being younger than Kōno, she was able to take advantage of the superior educational opportunities that the postwar reforms offered.

The educational reforms proved to be something of a mixed blessing, though, in terms of her intellectual and emotional development. On one hand, Takahashi was one of the first young women allowed to compete for admission to the prestigious Kyoto University, which she entered in 1950. On the other hand, the transition from the girls' school course—oriented as it was toward giving girls the domestic skills necessary to fulfill their destinies as future wives and mothers—to the boys' prep school course, geared toward molding young men into future leaders and intellectual elites, seems to have been exceedingly rough for Takahashi. According to her recollection of events, merely sitting in the same classroom with boys or passing them in the hallway was something of a shock to girls like herself who had spent their entire lives (inside and outside the classroom) in strictly sex-segregated environments.[68] Along with a burning curiosity toward these alien forms of life, Takahashi seems to have experienced a profound sense of inferiority with respect to her male classmates, which was no doubt aggravated by her lack of academic preparation for the new system.

Under these circumstances, it is hardly surprising that when Takahashi entered the prestigious Kyoto University, she was one of a tiny minority of female students in an overwhelmingly male-dominated environment. Her experiences in this bastion of traditional male power and privilege are testimony to the fact that sometimes systems change faster than attitudes. She recalls being continually subjected to chauvinist treatment by fellow students and professors:

> There were a lot of brilliant people, and any woman mixed in with such male students...would feel stupid by comparison. Someone attending a women's university probably would have gotten by without feeling that way, but the women at Kyōdai [Kyoto University] really lost confidence in themselves. I was continually scorned by the male students in the French department. Even when they didn't criticize you directly, they had this way of saying things that made you lose confidence in yourself.[69]

Not surprisingly, many members of the postwar male elite, at Kyoto University and elsewhere, felt threatened by the incursion of women into what had until recently been male-dominated space. Male resistance to the implementation of Occupation-era reforms that gave women de jure equality with men was hardly exclusive to the sphere of educational opportunities, and dealing with this resistance therefore became a unifying theme in the literature and personal experiences of women of this Shōwa One-Digit Generation. Raised during the prewar period according to restrictive models of feminine comportment—but then required to personally embody much of the burden of national reinvention at an age when they were too old to forget the past yet too young to fully understand the overwhelming expectations placed upon them—members of Takahashi's age cohort were caught between two opposing and incommensurable models of femininity.

Nowhere was this tightrope act more difficult, or more urgent, than in the realm of personal relationships. In Takahashi's case, the conflict between old and new models of femininity was epitomized in her marriage to fellow writer and Kyoto University graduate Takahashi Kazumi.

Although she married Kazumi in 1954, the year she graduated from college, Takahashi never had children, and she worked to support herself and her husband for much of their married life. In fact, she put her own literary career on hold for many years in order to take on the exclusive responsibility of household breadwinner so that Kazumi could concentrate solely on his writing. During the 1950s she worked odd jobs as translator, tour guide, tutor, and secretary, among others, while simultaneously pursuing a master's degree in French literature at Kyoto University (earned in 1958), as well as supporting Kazumi's work by running interference with publishers and handwriting clean copies of his manuscripts.[70] Her experiences during this period serve as profound testimony to the fact that while many women during this period did work outside the home, such work was coded as supportive to men's labor. Yet precisely because of her unique situation as a woman with an elite education, she found it difficult to relate to conventional standards of femininity or to the multitude of women who conformed to such standards.

Perhaps for this reason, Takahashi, like Kōno, frequently takes aim in her literature at stereotypical feminine roles. As if to mock conventional assumptions of feminine passivity, Takahashi's heroines aggressively pursue sexual liaisons, often with much younger men, in narratives that evoke Kōno's blend of eroticism, dominance, and incestuous desire.[71] Her stories likewise attempt to undermine or expose as artificial the notion that women are naturally inclined toward motherhood, either through female protagonists who refuse this role altogether or through a depiction of mothers who seemingly lack "normal" maternal impulses. "Congruent Figures" (Sōjikei, 1971), for example, explores a relationship between an estranged mother and daughter in which the mother resents her daughter as a kind of vampire who sucks away her life essence. In direct opposition to Confucian beliefs that children are crucial to ensure the continuation of the family line, Takahashi portrays the relationship between successive generations as one of parasitism, with the young sapping the strength of the old.

Takahashi returns to this theme of antagonism between parent and child again and again, frequently using it to explore the demonic side of human nature that is typically suppressed by social structures, which channel women's desires and impulses into the acceptably feminine outlets of marriage and motherhood. "Transformation" (Keshin, 1965), "Endless Expanse" (Byōbō, 1970), and "Summer Abyss" (Natsu no fuchi, 1973) feature mothers who contemplate or actually commit infanticide, and the mother in "Honorable Child" (Kodomosama, 1969) gradually begins to see her child as evil. The protagonist of the novel *To the End of the Heavens* (*Sora no hate made*, 1973) abandons her own child in a burning house during an air raid, sends her husband in after the child in the knowledge that he will not survive, and later steals the infant of a woman she dislikes, determined to raise the girl to be "twisted" by warping her personality through cruel treatment. The title of this novel refers to the final scene, in which the protagonist reflects on her sinful acts while gazing out at the endless expanse of sky, as if seeking salvation.

In *To the End of the Heavens* we see the increasing influence of Catholic themes that would dominate the author's work later in her career, as her protagonists turn to religion as a means of exorcising the frustrations they experience as women trapped in restrictive social situations or unsatisfying heterosexual relationships. Takahashi's interest in Christianity was sparked by her love for the literature of French Catholic writers, nurtured during her years of study at Kyoto University.[72] After many years of exploring such questions through her own literature, she converted to Catholicism in 1975, eventually leaving Japan in 1980 to spend almost ten years living and studying in France.

Takahashi's fascination with infanticidal impulses might seem incongruous (or downright heretical) in light of this author's Catholic faith. But as Yonaha Keiko notes, these themes of religious spirituality and resistance to gender norms can be understood as continuous with the author's relentless pursuit of the self from the earliest stage of her literary career.[73] Mark Williams further notes the role that Takahashi's faith has served in reconciling the "splintering" of self suffered by protagonists who struggle against oppressive models of femininity.[74] Takahashi sees motherhood as an ideology that confines women to the realm of the quotidian, forcing them to subsume their own transcendent potential to the roles of ordinary wives and mothers, and she (and her characters) appear to want none of that, thank you very much.

KURAHASHI YUMIKO

Kurahashi was born in Kōchi prefecture, on the island of Shikoku, in 1935, the eldest daughter of a dentist.[75] Perhaps because of this rural yet relatively privileged upbringing, she seems to have been given wide latitude for self-expression as a child, and she recalls flouting conventions of gender early on by bullying the boys in her class. While other members of her generation recall air raids and near starvation, Kurahashi's memories of this time are mostly of fond experiences playing in the river with friends and collecting firewood. In contrast to the psychological devastation that members of older generations recount at hearing the emperor's declaration of surrender, Kurahashi recalls merely feelings of bewilderment and incomprehension at the behavior of the adults around her reeling from the shock of defeat.

Kurahashi's subsequent experiences seem to reflect the same mixture of individualism and independence that characterized her tomboy childhood years and would later infuse her idiosyncratic protagonists. Thanks to the resources available to her by virtue of her upper-class status, she was able to make use of private tutors and after-school prep courses and seems to have done well in school in spite of frequent absences due to illness. However, she failed her entrance exams for medical school, and she provisionally entered the Japanese literature department of Kyoto Women's University (Kyoto Joshi Daigaku) while simultaneously preparing to retake the exams. When she failed them for a second time, she gave up medicine in favor of dentistry, a career path that no doubt was influenced by her father's ambitions for her as eldest daughter of a family of dentists. After a brief stint at a junior college in Tokyo, she earned an associate's degree as a dental hygienist in 1956, while secretly applying for and earning admission to the French literature department of Meiji University in the same year. She graduated in 1960 and immediately continued her study of French literature at the graduate level of that school, against the wishes of her family.

Kurahashi's experiences during her university days figure prominently in her early fiction, albeit rendered hyperbolically in absurd and perverse form. Her portrayals of the seediness of dormitory life, the ridiculous self-importance of university administrators and politicians, and the logical contradictions of absurdly doctrinaire student-movement activists all evoke the factional strife of Japan circa the anti–Security Treaty crisis of 1960. Kurahashi seems to have taken a resolutely apolitical stance during this period, describing herself as "totally unconcerned" about current events, her attention absorbed entirely by preparation for her graduation thesis on Sartre's *Being and Nothingness*. One wonders how she could have remained almost autistically disengaged from events that shook the fledgling Japanese democracy to its core, yet this ability to resist the centripetal pull of the mainstream in favor of a position on the critical margins of society is precisely what gave this author her unique literary style and voice.

Kurahashi began writing her first published story, "Partei," in 1959, a work that launched her uncomfortably into the spotlight when it won the Meiji University literary prize a year later and was subsequently nominated for the Akutagawa Prize. Thanks to this stunning debut, she attracted the attention of noted literary critics and publishers, who began to lobby her incessantly for further manuscripts. The requests for her work increased exponentially throughout the 1960s, exhausting Kurahashi to the point where she left the country in 1966 to study for a year as a Fulbright scholar in the United States, primarily to escape the increasing demands of her publishers.

While she wrote prolifically throughout the period leading up to her American sojourn, Kurahashi relocated from Tokyo to her family home in Kōchi in 1962, after the death of her father cut short her pursuit of a master's degree at Meiji University. Her decision to return home seems also to have been motivated by a desire to distance herself from the bitter disputes occasioned by the harsh critical reception of some of her early works—"Partei," "Snake" (Hebi), and *Blue Journey (Kurai tabi)*. There she met Kumaya Tomihiro, a photojournalist for the Kōchi branch of Nihon Hōsō Kyōkai (NHK), whom she married in 1964.[76] The couple eventually had two daughters, the first born in 1968, less than a year after their return from the United States. The only one of the three authors examined in this study to bear children, Kurahashi's decision to become a wife and mother is ironic in light of the way she savagely parodies these roles in her early fiction. While some critics suggest that Kurahashi's post-Fulbright life and works demonstrate a conservative "return" to Japanese tradition, Atsuko Sakaki argues against this interpretation, characterizing the change in her literary style as more "neoclassical" for its fascination with Greek tragedy as well as classical Japanese literature.[77] Furthermore, her determination to parody or subvert "traditional" values in her literature seems consistent across this personal divide.

Kurahashi is perhaps best known for her absurdist, Kafka-esque plots, as well as for abstractly drawn characters denoted by an alphabet soup of letters (K, S, L, and M) rather than proper names. There is no denying Kurahashi's intellectual debt particularly to Sartre, Camus, and other cerebral European authors, yet the themes of her stories have much in common with other women writers of the 1960s who used their fiction to explore the changing roles and opportunities available to women in the postwar period, not to mention their own sometimes troubled engagement with the more conventionally "feminine" topics of marriage and motherhood. Kurahashi's concern with such themes is reflected even in the titles of many of her early stories—for example, "Engagement" (Kon'yaku, 1960) and "Marriage" (Kekkon, 1965). Her parodic treatment of normative bourgeois values in such texts belies a not-so-subtle anxiety about her own difficulty in combining the role of professional novelist with her identity as a woman, and specifically with the demands placed on any young Japanese woman to marry and bear and raise children.[78]

Kurahashi's literature inscribes with remarkable consistency a rather cynical and subversive attitude toward the relationship—or what she sees as a lack of relationship—among sex, love, marriage, and motherhood.[79] Reading Kurahashi's early works in particular, one gets the impression that sex is a rather ridiculous business, from which one would do best to abstain. In the short story "Symbiosis" (Kyōsei, 1966), for example, we are informed that sex is an activity that most people perform out of a sense of "duty" to enjoy themselves in this way, and thus they are usually disappointed with the results.[80] Kurahashi heroines (frequently also writers and uniformly denoted as L) typically meet their husbands' sexual advances with the challenge, "What would be the point?" or else with a firm reminder that sexual service was not part of the contract they signed. In fact, marriage in such early Kurahashi stories is more often than not governed by the existence of an actual contract that provides for the writer-wife, L, to be "kept" by her husband while absolving her of most of the typical "duties" of a housewife. One such heroine claims that the terms of her contract with her husband in no way obligate her to cook, clean house, eat or sleep with her husband, or have his children; she is merely required to "support" him. Although what this "support" entails remains unspecified in the text, we are assured by L that it involves "a lot of work."[81]

While such texts contain moments of playful parody, they most often end on a dark note of tragedy. For example, at the conclusion of "Marriage," the contract that should have protected L from the drudgery of conventional matrimony has now apparently been rewritten in conformity with the gendered division of labor commonly associated with middle-class households of the 1960s. L, now pregnant, is confined to the home and devotes herself to the daily production of elaborate meals that her working husband will never be home long enough to eat. While the story begins with a subversion of the structure of marriage from within, it concludes with a return to "normalcy" that is explicitly coded within the text as a most unhappy ending. The emptiness and futility of her new arrangement seem to have driven L mad, and she even begs K, the masculine half of herself that she has had to abandon in order to fulfill her domestic destiny, to kill her. The tendency of such stories to end with L's failure to subvert the structure of conventional marriage underscores two primary themes that link the author's early works: a subtle message of protest at the deadly mediocrity of so many Japanese women's lives and a lament that the centripetal force of bourgeois marriage ideology is so difficult to resist.

Critical assessments of Kurahashi's works seem to focus primarily on her avant-garde stylistic techniques, treating the substance of her literature as little more than a vehicle for technical experimentation. Male critics during the 1960s seem to have been thoroughly oblivious to the challenge her fiction posed to normative ideologies of gender, preferring to debate the merits of her parodic appropriation of great works of both Western and Japanese literature. Many of these critics, including prominent scholars Etō Jun and Nakamura Mitsuo, savagely attacked her for "plagiarizing" these works, denying the legitimacy of her technique. Atsuko Sakaki interprets these attacks as motivated by perception that Kurahashi was attempting to encroach upon male intellectual territory while defying the dominant (masculine) genre of the "I-novel," which was based in a more realistic and autobiographical mode. Writers like Haniya Yutaka, who supported Kurahashi's technical experimentation, nevertheless criticized her for other reasons, such as her lack of commitment to the New Left political causes that increasingly dominated the *bundan* during this time.[82] While Kurahashi maintained her popularity with readers throughout the 1960s, she maintained a tense relationship to the *bundan,* as the bitter disputes surrounding the value of her work continued into the subsequent decade.

Kōno, Takahashi, and Kurahashi are all known for their depiction of independent heroines who shun or mock conventional marriage, as well as for frank, occasionally grotesque, portrayals of sexuality and other bodily experiences from a female point of view. All three were eventually rewarded not only with literary prizes and popular recognition, but also with a seat at the table in the boardroom of the literary establishment. In addition to successfully publishing their own work, they were actively sought for participation in roundtable discussions and other formats that placed them in the position of judging the merits of other writers—both male and female.

Yet these accolades were not easily won—they came at great cost, both personally and professionally. Kōno's award of the Akutagawa Prize in 1963, after years of struggling for recognition for her efforts in spite of poverty and poor health, is a perfect example of such delayed gratification.

She was only the fourth woman in history to accomplish this feat, yet soon afterward, the deluge of women writers awarded this and other prestigious awards prompted one resentful male critic to wonder if they ought not to establish prizes specifically for men since the women seemed to be enjoying such success.[83] Kurahashi's initial critical success sparked such a vitriolic series of debates that from 1963 to 1987 she won no prizes at all, in spite of maintaining a phenomenal popularity with readers as an icon of the 1960s and 1970s counterculture.[84] Takahashi began writing in the late 1950s, but it took more than ten years for her to gain recognition for her efforts, in part because she willingly subordinated her own career to her husband's, and in part because his reputation so overshadowed her own that editors refused to take her seriously. One critic thus describes her as suffering from a kind of "textual harassment"—the assumption that the wife of a famous writer must owe her accomplishments to his support (or ghostwriting abilities), while the considerable contribution of the wife to her husband's literary success is overlooked.[85]

Given the intensity of the struggle these women faced along the road to professional success, it would be surprising if their experiences did *not* influence their literary expression. As we will see in subsequent chapters, that is precisely what happened, as these writers' struggles with the normative discourses of femininity that pervaded the *bundan* and Japanese society generally emerge in their fiction in imaginative form as power dynamics that enmesh their protagonists. The fictional narratives analyzed in this study may therefore be understood, à la Foucault, as nodes of resistance that troubled such normative ideological networks from within, rendering them strange and illogical even as they posed as transparent and natural representations of the way the world should be.

Those disciplinary mechanisms—sexual, textual, and contextual—that sought to contain these authors within appropriately "feminine" parameters of self-expression are rendered in their literature as repressive, violent, and destructive regimes of power that inscribe themselves onto women's bodies and behaviors in frequently horrifying and shocking ways. In such narratives, the female body is consistently foregrounded as the site of inscription of gendered norms, through an engendering process that is experienced as corporeal violation. In the following chapter, we will see how their determined exposure of such networks of power functioned as a potent critique of the masculine gaze—a regime of biopower that rendered female subjects "feminine" through an invasive and sometimes violent process of engendering.

CHAPTER 2

The Masculine Gaze as Disciplinary Mechanism

Sadism demands a story.

—*Laura Mulvey, "Visual Pleasure and
Narrative Cinema"*

It is striking how many Japanese expressions related to interpersonal communication employ the word "eye." In a culture that so prizes wordless communication, apparently the "eyes" have it. Children are admonished to behave lest others look at them with the whites of their eyes. An unpardonable offense can be described as too much for one's eyes. One's superiors in a hierarchical system are said to be above the eyes. Not surprisingly, many of these expressions also imply the power of the bearer of the gaze to discipline or dominate the one who is seen.

Western theorists have likewise been fascinated with the interconnectedness of power, knowledge, and visuality. In his landmark study on the subject, *Discipline and Punish,* Michel Foucault devotes an entire chapter to the topic of "panopticism," or the ways in which power may be exercised most effectively by causing subjects to discipline themselves, through mere anticipation of the gaze of the authorities. Here Foucault draws on the logic underlying the "Panopticon," Jeremy Bentham's ingenious architectural design for a prison in which inmates are arranged in cells monitored by a central tower. The inhabitants of these cells are at all times visible to those manning the tower, but they cannot see the authorities who observe them.

> He is seen, but he does not see; he is the object of information, never a subject in communication....And this invisibility is a guarantee of order. If the inmates are convicts, there is no danger of a plot, an attempt at collective escape....If they are

schoolchildren, there is no copying, no noise, no chatter, no waste of time.... Hence the major effect of the Panopticon: to induce in the inmate a state of conscious and permanent visibility that assures the automatic functioning of power.... The inmates should be caught up in a power situation of which they are themselves the bearers.[1]

Under this arrangement, it becomes unnecessary to discipline or punish the inmates of such a facility—they are induced to discipline themselves merely by virtue of the anticipation of punishment, precisely because they know that any infraction will immediately be seen by the authorities. Foucault goes on to demonstrate that such disciplinary mechanisms characterize not only prisons but also all institutions of modern society, ending his chapter with the wry comment that in terms of the way power functions in and through those who are subjected to it, "prisons resemble factories, schools, barracks, hospitals, which all resemble prisons."[2]

Feminist film theorists have also made use of scopic dynamics to understand the relationship among power, gender, and film spectatorship. Laura Mulvey's pathbreaking article, "Visual Pleasure and Narrative Cinema" (1975), first brought critical attention to the way classical Hollywood cinema constructs the body of woman as object of the masculine gaze. She contends in this essay that the spectator derives pleasure from voyeuristic control and mastery of the onscreen female object, possessing her by proxy through identification with the hero of the tale. As in Foucault's theory of panopticism, there is an implied power differential here between subject and object of the gaze, and in Mulvey's theory this is coded in explicitly gendered terms. Men wield the gaze; women are subjected to it. In a subsequent elaboration of her theory, Mulvey even contends that filmic techniques work to so thoroughly construct the gaze of the viewer as masculine that in order for female viewers to derive visual pleasure from such forms of spectatorship, they must subconsciously adopt a masculine subject position vis-à-vis the women onscreen.[3]

Reading these two theories together tells us much about the complex web of relationships among power, knowledge, and visuality; moreover, it is interesting to note that Mulvey and Foucault each seem to highlight the theoretical blind spots of the other. Foucault has frequently been criticized by feminist theorists, even those who find his work useful, for neglecting to deal explicitly with the gendered aspects of the exercise of power.[4] Foucault's understanding of the functioning of "panopticism" is a perfect example of this blindness to sexual politics. Nowhere in his elaboration of the workings of this disciplinary mechanism does he deal with the question of how sexual difference might alter or nuance the power dynamics that obtain between observer and observed. On the other hand, Mulvey, perhaps because she is concerned with questions of spectatorship rather than human relationships unmediated by a film screen, appears not to recognize the disciplinary potential inherent in the exercise of visual power by a male subject vis-à-vis a female object. In other words, while she explores in great detail the potential for pleasure experienced by the subject who wields the gaze, her theory cannot account for the experience of the female object who is visually subordinated to that gaze.

The experience of women in modern Japan speaks eloquently to the role of visual surveillance in policing behavior, as well as to the gendered effects of such scopic disciplinary mechanisms. For example, during the Pacific War, when Japanese citizens were exhorted to display nationalistic fervor in all aspects of their lives, particular attention was paid to sartorial cues as evidence of one's level of dedication to the imperialist cause. Women, who unlike men could not demonstrate their patriotism by participating directly in combat, were expected to show their solidarity with Japanese soldiers in various ways, most especially by eschewing "Western" adornments like permanent waves and high heels. Instead they were expected to wear traditional Japanese clothing like kimono, and later *monpe*, or work trousers, which announced their total dedication to empire building on the domestic front. Andrew Gordon, in his survey history of modern Japan, provides photographic evidence of the way these sartorial restrictions were enforced by military inspectors, who patrolled the streets looking for women who failed to conform and harangued those whose physical appearance flouted this policy of austerity.[5]

The state continued to actively intervene in the daily lives of women in the postwar period, as economic recovery and growth replaced military imperialism as the national goal. Such intervention frequently occurred with the support and participation of women themselves, who helped to police the behavior of other women. As Sheldon Garon illustrates, women were mobilized to participate in the process of postwar rebuilding through "moral suasion" campaigns that encouraged them to carefully manage every aspect of their lives, from household savings and expenditures to the care of the elderly to their own reproductive potential. Compliance with such initiatives frequently emphasized visual surveillance of women's lives and activities.[6] Scopic dynamics were thus central to enforcement of gender norms, and this state of affairs remained remarkably continuous across the prewar-postwar divide, even as the specific types of desired behavior may have changed.

As this chapter will illustrate, the authors analyzed in this study, whose lives traversed this prewar-postwar divide, were very familiar with the power of such scopic dynamics to regulate the behavior of Japanese women. In their literature, these three writers portray such visual disciplinary mechanisms as an insidious means of enforcing restrictive models of femininity. I will introduce three works of fiction—"Broken Oath" (Haisei, 1966), a short story by Kōno Taeko; "Getting on the Wrong Train" (Jōsha sakugo, 1972), a short story by Takahashi Takako; and *Blue Journey* (*Kurai tabi*, 1961), a novel by Kurahashi Yumiko—that illustrate the relevance of Foucault's and Mulvey's theories to women in postwar Japan. All three of these stories can be said to operate at the nexus of these two theoretical models.

Each narrative features a female protagonist who finds herself subjected to a disciplinary gaze that is invasive and even violent. As per Foucault's theory, the protagonist learns to internalize and reproduce the gaze, resulting in a kind of "voluntary" compliance with societal expectations, but this process of self-discipline is experienced as traumatic from the perspective of the engendered object. Thus, while poignantly illustrating Foucault's model of "panopticism," these stories underscore the fact that the authorities who wield the gaze are anything but gender-neutral observers. Society is explicitly or implicitly figured as masculine in each of these texts, and the effect of the gaze is to induce its objects not merely to behave, but also to behave as *gendered* objects.

Each of these narratives features a climactic moment when the female protagonist, who initially perceives herself to be gender-neutral, is confronted with her own femininity, in the form of a gender identity that is forcibly assigned to her by virtue of the fact that she inhabits a female body. In each case, attempts to resist this process of engendering are overcome by the overwhelming power of the masculine gaze, which recognizes the protagonist only through the lens of conventional markers of femininity such as menstruation, pregnancy, and sexuality that is confined within a framework of monogamous marriage. Failure to identify with these stereotypes of femininity precipitates a crisis in subjectivity as the protagonist turns the gaze upon herself, resulting in a loss of identity and relationship to language. These fictional stories thus provide valuable insights into the way bodies are engendered as feminine, through a complex and detailed elaboration of the relationships between power, knowledge, and visuality.

"Broken Oath"

In "Broken Oath," the protagonist, Momoko, is summoned to court to testify as a character witness for her ex-boyfriend, who has been charged with assaulting a female employee. Through suggestive lines of questioning, the prosecution and the defense attempt to portray Momoko according to opposing stereotypes of femininity. The prosecution would like her to play the role of the scorned woman, whose live-in lover Otaka refused to marry her and then abandoned her as a pathetic old maid, with no chance of a "normal" life as proper wife and mother. In spite of the fact that Momoko never sought marriage to Otaka, her credibility, within the context of these court proceedings, is predicated on an understanding of her as an innocent who was seduced and discarded by an inveterate ladies' man. The defense, on the other hand, is determined to destroy Momoko's reputation by insinuating that she carried on affairs with colleagues behind Otaka's back. Both of these narratives subscribe to a view of femininity as properly confined within a heterosexual framework that assumes fidelity to one man; the "good," and therefore credible, woman is then defined by her adherence to this role type, while the "bad" woman, one who is lacking in credibility, defies this stereotype.

Momoko recognizes these strategies for what they are and attempts to resist them through the creation of an objective persona that transcends such gendered typecasting. Throughout her testimony, she scrupulously monitors her own responses for their truth value, determined to present her story in a disinterested fashion that would render her a neutral participant, rather than a scorned or unfaithful woman. The reaction of the all-male audience becomes crucial to Momoko in determining how well she manages to live up to this ideal—when she is able to respond to a question dispassionately, she feels supported by the gaze directed at her and actively seeks eye contact with individual members of the courtroom to confirm this. Furthermore, her constant attempts to reassure herself that "there is nothing in her testimony to betray her vow" of truthfulness vies with the interrogation of the lawyers in the intensity of its scrutiny of her character, indicating that she has on some level turned the masculine gaze in upon herself. [7]

Momoko's shield of neutral objectivity serves as only a temporary protection, however, as the moment the possibility of other lovers is raised, the crowd begins to turn on her. "The gaze of the people [in the courtroom] all at once stopped being supportive and turned to curiosity" (294). Her body begins to fail her as the stutter she thought she had conquered years ago returns under the pressure of cross-examination. "Momoko wanted to tell the truth. She hurried to tell them that she didn't begin to stutter because of confusion or perjury. It was because the moment the subject [of infidelity] was broached in questioning, people already began to doubt her" (295). The more Momoko tries to defend herself, the worse her stutter gets, and the guiltier she appears before the gaze of the all-male audience. The story concludes with Momoko unable to voice a single comprehensible utterance, paralyzed by a role that she has not chosen for herself and deprived even of her capacity for speech.

From the very beginning of the story, tropes of concealment and revelation are intimately connected with the exercise of power, such that being "discovered" or "known" in a visual sense is effectively equated with being fixed by the gaze of authoritarian structures. As the story opens, Momoko is just arriving at the courthouse, but the narrative quickly shifts to a flashback sequence in which she recalls first receiving the subpoena that has summoned her there. She is thoroughly shocked by the appearance of the officer on her doorstep and shudders at the efficiency with which the authorities have managed to track her down:

> Of course, it was common sense that the police could find out anything that they wanted to. If they investigated Otaka's past, naturally they would find out about the existence of a woman he lived with even for a short time. And it wasn't like she was hiding out or using a fake name or anything, so it must have been a simple job for them to find the whereabouts of a person like herself who was living openly. But to think that the police had been going around and searching for her when she was unaware of it made her feel that the past that she had neatly tucked away had been arbitrarily scattered about again. Though she had not attempted to conceal anything, she couldn't help but feel that it was humiliating and vaguely creepy. Gradually she began to feel like a suspect herself. (272–273)

Since the breakup with Otaka five years ago, Momoko has not seen or talked to him and has no idea of his whereabouts, and thus the officer's discovery of her comes as something of a shock as she is confronted with a chapter of her personal history that she had believed to be over. In fact the relationship is described as something that she has worked hard to put out of her mind and would prefer to leave safely concealed in her past. The fact that the authorities have so effectively revealed what she implicitly seems determined to conceal—from herself, if not also from the outside world—makes her feel violated, as if they have willfully thrown into disarray a part of her life that she has struggled to bring to order. This disturbs her sense of composure, unsettling her before she even enters the courtroom, so she is already in a vulnerable state when she is challenged on the stand—the experience that leads directly to the breakdown in her capacity for language by the end of the story.

As the theoretical frameworks of both Foucault and Mulvey would suggest, there is a clear power imbalance between the parties in this episode. While the authorities appear to know much already about Momoko's relationship with Otaka, she is thoroughly unaware of the crime in which she has indirectly been implicated. The officer who arrives at her doorstep hands her a summons that tells her nothing about the nature of the case in which she is ordered to provide testimony or the nature of the information that they will solicit from her. All she knows is that it has something to do with Otaka and that she cannot refuse to reveal herself to the court. She is required to give information about herself, but they are not required to tell her anything unless it pleases them. Momoko is thus rendered utterly subordinate to a system of authority that knows much and can impel her to reveal even more, yet she cannot even know the circumstances of her subordination. To borrow Foucault's phrasing once more: "He [*sic*] is seen, but he does not see; he is the object of information, never a subject in communication."[8] The days leading up to Momoko's initial interview with the prosecutor are fraught with anxiety; she is unable to sleep and cannot help pulling out the subpoena and staring at it, as if searching for clues to the nature of the crime in which she has been implicated by association. But all the mute document reveals to her is a display of its own authority, in the form of the Kasumigaseki address to which she must report.[9]

Momoko is thus thoroughly intimidated before she even takes the stand, and the persistence with which she admonishes herself to tell the truth reveals how much she perceives herself to be on trial, as if she is taking on the role of both witness and prosecution in her own mind. Based on her previous interview with the prosecutor, she knows before taking the stand that he wishes her to play the role of the abandoned woman in order to destroy Otaka's character, and she arrives ready to refuse this role by giving testimony that neither slanders nor supports her ex-boyfriend. As she prepares herself mentally to testify while waiting outside the courtroom, she reflects:

In the more than twenty days that had passed [since her meeting with the prosecutor], she repeated to herself over and over what she had said to him: "You're terribly mistaken if you think that I still hold a grudge against him for abandoning me. I've hated him to the point that my feelings for him have totally disintegrated. At this late date, there's no way that you can give me satisfaction [by seeing him convicted]. If a fossil from his past will do, then please use me." Regardless of whether or not there was a penalty for perjury, she was determined to be completely faithful to her own feelings in her testimony to the prosecutor.

At the same time, Momoko also decided to give absolutely correct testimony to Otaka's lawyer as well. They were veterans at this. They assumed that because he had abandoned her, she must still be hung up on him, and probably they would try to use that cleverly to elicit testimony from her that would be beneficial to their cases.... I did live with him, but I'm not that sentimental a woman, she thought. However I may appear, I'm tough. (276)

Momoko is thus clearly aware of the intentions of the men who will question her and actively takes steps to prepare herself for this ordeal through a form of self-discipline, "repeated over and over," that is designed to produce an objective and truthful persona.

Momoko's vow to tell the truth seems motivated by two related desires. First, she seems determined not to allow either side to manipulate her into tailoring her story to fit their agendas. Knowing that each man intends to characterize her according to opposite but similarly unacceptable tropes of femininity—as a "good" (scorned) or a "bad" (unfaithful) woman—she strives to refuse either role by aiming for a position somewhere in the middle. She therefore enters the courtroom having crafted an objective persona that is capable of presenting the facts without succumbing to emotional responses to the lawyers' lines of questioning. Second, she seems determined to demonstrate to herself, and to everyone else, that she has dealt with the pain of her breakup with Otaka and has moved on and therefore feels no need to either defend or attack Otaka's character. Having "tucked away" their relationship neatly into the closet of her past life, she is mindful of the potential of the trial to "scatter about" the remnants of her past that she has worked so hard to bring to order. She envisions herself as a "fossil" from Otaka's past as if to will him to stay buried within her own—a desiccated, emotionless relic that no longer poses any threat to her equilibrium. The objective persona that she crafts for herself thus becomes her best defense against the psychological violation that the experience of cross-examination represents for her.

Ironically, while Momoko sees her vow to tell the truth as a kind of defensive strategy to protect herself from the scrutiny of the court, it also requires her to adopt a posture of self-scrutiny that replicates and internalizes the invasive gaze of the men who question her. Poised between two opposing camps both determined to plunder her personal history and warp it into a hackneyed stereotype of femininity with which she cannot identify, Momoko senses that the only way she can forestall this invasion of her memory closet is to maintain a defensive position midway between them. They are seeking not merely factual information but also knowledge of her that can be willfully interpreted to characterize her as a scorned or unfaithful woman, and Momoko's strategy is to provide only those bits of information that will fail to be useful to each case since if she takes the side of one man, she will be rapidly attacked by the other. She is able to deflect the invasive gaze of the Other, then, only by preemptively turning it upon herself, carefully monitoring her own testimony to ensure that she does not provide anything that can be used to make a case for either side. Momoko's objective persona is revealed to the reader to be anything but—her constant reminder to herself to tell only the "truth" is rather a mask for the discipline she has imposed upon herself to edit her testimony so as to remove all emotional content, thus presenting herself defensively as a "neutral" party to the debate.

Momoko is able to maintain this smooth wall of defensive objectivity only as long as she is able to remain deliberately unaware of the gaze of the court upon her. Upon first taking the stand, she manages to protect herself from the eyes of the observers by maintaining a downcast gaze, but she is then admonished by the judge to face forward and speak up. She complies with the judge's order by fixing her gaze upon a safely vacant corner of the opposite wall, so that her line of vision does not intersect with that of anyone else in the room. Her testimony proceeds smoothly after this, and she is able to continue to feel comfortable in her objective persona until, apropos of establishing a precedent for Otaka's violent treatment of women, the prosecutor presses her on the question of whether or not her first experience of sexual relations with him was entirely consensual.

At this point Momoko's confidence in her objectivity begins to falter, as she has remembered the night in question in different ways over the years since the breakup, and the scene has appeared in her memory as alternately violent or romantic (281). She selects a relatively neutral account for the purpose of the courtroom testimony, but her steadiness on the stand begins to waver soon after, when the prosecutor presses her on the reasons for the breakup. She then begins to feel acutely aware of the gaze of the members of the courtroom upon her:

> The reason she had not felt anyone's gaze for some time seemed not to be because she was calm after all. The initial nervousness she had felt when she was sworn in seemed to have simply frozen that way. Now perhaps that had begun to thaw, for the moment she began to search her feelings, she once again was forced to realize that she was all alone on the witness stand in front of the court.
>
> Until just a moment ago, whenever the prosecutor's words emerged from the upper-right-hand corner of her atmosphere, she had been able to produce a correct answer, just like a machine operated by a remote-control device. Even when she had to search her memory about the time in question, she had quickly felt with a palpable certainty that her answer was true beyond any doubt and was able to put into words what she had felt. But suddenly that changed....
>
> Since the judge had told her to face the court, she had kept her gaze fixed straight ahead on the far corner of the room, and within that hazy field of vision the whole court had appeared strangely bright. The gaze of the people in the courtroom that she had only felt up to now with her body now entered her unexpectedly wide field of vision. On the far right, Otaka sat bolt upright and occasionally turned only his eyes in her direction. On the left side, the judge had turned his chair sideways to look at her. Below her the tape recorder behind the court reporter's desk was revolving. After each question was asked, Momoko felt that the whole courtroom became quiet, the gaze of everyone in the room hardened upon her, and even the revolution of the tape recorder reel became more deliberate. Then the memories and words that had seemed to come together instantly fell apart, and she had to search for them again. As this was happening, the prosecutor would change the angle of questioning, and her mind would become even more confused. (282–283)

It is at precisely at this point in the text that Momoko's composure is shattered, and she begins to lose confidence in her ability to respond objectively to the prosecutor's questioning. During the remainder of the interrogation, there are several moments when she seems to doubt her responses or feel unsure as to what might constitute a truthful response. During the cross-examination, as the defense attorney begins to capitalize on her uncertainty and use her previous testimony against her, her stutter returns, and by the final lines of the story she is mute and defenseless on the stand.

This pivotal moment in the narrative, when Momoko begins to lose control of the situation and succumbs to the masculine gaze, reveals much about the role of scopic power as a disciplinary mechanism. While she seems to have been aware of the gaze of the court on some level throughout the proceedings, having "felt it with her body," she is able to maintain her composure until she makes eye contact with those who are watching her. It is as though the Achilles' heel of her psychological armor is the part that is turned inward—her own gaze—and her willingness to discipline herself through a strict monitoring of her testimony, however preemptive and self-protective a gesture that may be, is precisely what leaves her so vulnerable to the opportunistic questioning of the prosecutor. Her need to produce absolutely truthful testimony is what causes her to hesitate on the stand, and the more her confidence in her ability to tell the truth falters, the more the gaze of the audience "stop[s] being supportive, and turn[s] to curiosity" (294).

It is significant that the part of the interrogation that flusters her so relates directly to the problem of her own tenuous sense of sexual subjectivity because it is on this point that both men attempt to make their case about Momoko's credibility as a witness. As noted, while the prosecutor's line of questioning is designed to portray Momoko as a good woman who was an unfortunate victim of the "ladykiller" Otaka, the defense attorney wishes to present her as a loose woman who is undeserving of the sympathy of the court. Both men therefore are invasive in their queries about Momoko's sexual history and relationship with the accused. Was she raped by Otaka on that first night? Did he use force or coercion? What words and tactics did he use to persuade her? Although the prosecutor justifies this line of questioning on the pretext that it is relevant to Otaka's treatment of other women, there is a prurient subtext to his desire to know and expose Momoko's sexual history for the edification of the members of the courtroom, whose curious gaze leaves her feeling even further exposed. Even though the prosecutor is pushing the "good woman" theory of Momoko's character, his questioning at this point gives the impression that she is the one on trial.

When this story was published (1966), it was still very much the norm in Japan for feminine sexuality to be subordinated to the twin projects of marriage and motherhood. Not only does Momoko's experience of having lived with a man outside of marriage mark her as a marginal figure of some disrepute, but she further offends normative models of femininity by expressing little interest in the prospect of marriage. In fact the prosecutor seems somewhat taken aback by her testimony that she never pressed Otaka to marry her (280). As if attempting to reinscribe Momoko within a framework analogous to conventional marriage, so as to make the case for his characterization of her as a "good" woman who was unfortunately used and discarded by a "bad" man, he describes her initially as Otaka's "common-law wife," a characterization that she refuses (279). She likewise declines to support the prosecutor's portrayal of herself as a victim of Otaka's "ladykiller" ways when asked to describe their first night together, opting instead to emphasize her own role in choosing to sleep with him (281).

Unfortunately Momoko's insistence on her own sexual agency provides the defense attorney precisely the information he needs to make the case for her as a "bad" woman. He first capitalizes on her insistence that she chose, rather than was coerced, to sleep with Otaka. He then turns the conversation to an inquiry into her sexual history, wanting to know how many previous lovers she has had, how many "male acquaintances" she had during the time she was living with Otaka, and how many of these she "associated with" during their relationship (293–294). He deliberately uses language that can be interpreted as variously innocent or suggestive, making it difficult for Momoko to answer truthfully without implicating herself in a romantic relationship that she never had with any of these men. Momoko's vow of truth, then, becomes her undoing as she is led down a line of questioning that makes it impossible to protest that she is innocent of what the attorney is implying without making herself seem even more guilty. It is at this point that she begins to stutter, which confirms for the curious members of the courtroom the verdict that she is in fact a "bad" woman after all.

Momoko is unable to resist this outcome precisely because the terms of debate are decided for her in advance. Given that the gaze of the authorities recognizes only two valid types of women—good ones and bad ones—she cannot resist one stereotype without being tarred with the brush of the other. Her attempt to maintain a neutral position between these two options is ultimately shown to be untenable; the members of the court scrutinize her with the explicit purpose of determining whether she is good or bad and literally refuse to *see* her according to any other model of femininity.

Kōno's story thus offers an ironic twist on Foucault's theory of visually imposed disciplinary mechanisms, as her protagonist is twice disciplined within the space of this short story to very different ends. Momoko first adopts a posture of absolute truthfulness, in an almost hyperbolically faithful acquittal of her legal responsibility to give accurate testimony before the court. In a sense she is attempting to protect herself through a parodic performance of her sworn duty to tell the truth, as she is instructed by the court. Yet what the court says it requires of her and what it actually requires of her appear to be two different things. She learns during the course of the proceedings that she is in fact expected not to tell the truth about her relationship with Otaka as per her own understanding of what transpired between them, but rather to play a role that is designed to aid the prosecution in making its case against him.

Momoko's attempt to resist this role backfires, as the more she refutes the "good" woman stereotype, the more the audience sees her as its logical opposite. She is even disciplined to perform in accordance with the bad woman role type, contrary to her own intentions, first by providing information on the stand to support these assumptions, and then by failing to defend herself against them through her loss of speech. It is important to note that Momoko's own perception of herself has nothing whatsoever to do with how she is seen and understood by the members of the courtroom—in fact the more she resists their attempts to fix her in the role of unfaithful woman, the more guilty she seems in the eyes of the spectators. Her silence in the final lines of the story thereby renders her, against her own will, as compliant with the mold of femininity to which she has inevitably been assigned, according to the perception of the male observers who are empowered to so define her by virtue of being possessors of the gaze.

"Getting on the Wrong Train"

In contrast to Kōno's realistic courtroom narrative, Takahashi Takako's "Getting on the Wrong Train" is a surreal and abstract tale of scopic violation and loss of identity. The protagonist's misadventures begin as she leaves home for a class reunion and encounters a mysteriously adult-looking boy on the train whose penetrating gaze intimidates her. During her train journey the main character, known to the reader only as "Watashi" ("I"), becomes hungry and decides to purchase a boxed lunch from a platform vendor. She begins eating the meal, but to her dismay this action draws the gaze of the boy even more persistently in her direction, which unnerves her: "Because of those eyes, I was made to see the horror of the fact that I was eating. No, the boy seemed to be looking at something more than that. Perhaps he was looking at the horror of the fact that I was sustaining my life through eating. . . . Because I had committed the single mistake of eating, the boy began to exist beside me as the very incarnation of misfortune."[10] He continues staring at her, and she experiences the gaze as oppressively coming at her from all sides, as his stare is also reflected in the window beside her.

As a result of this encounter, Watashi begins to experience a bizarre form of physical transformation that is explicitly linked to the "penetration" of the boy's gaze: "The feeling of oppression threatened to flow out of my mouth, so I forced myself to swallow it down. It swelled larger inside me, and along with that mass I was assaulted by an unsteady feeling of being scooped up into the air. This engorged thing reached saturation point and exploded into shards that whirled about with a roar. Inside me, something fundamentally abnormal had formed" (223). Confused by the intensity of his observation of her, she first gets off the train too soon and then mistakenly boards another train going in the wrong direction. She finally disembarks in an unknown town, and as she wanders aimlessly through the streets, she reflects on her situation: "Points of departure and destination had both dissolved into something vague and elusive. A bare self surrounded by darkness and buffeted by strong winds—what was I? Neither male nor female. Ageless. Cut off from past or future, brought to the point of nakedness—it was the fault of this station, but it was that boy's fault that I was forced to get off here. That's right; it seems that my fate was sealed on that train platform when I first got on the train" (226).

But although she momentarily sees herself as a form of disembodied existence that has come untethered from the gendered structures of everyday life, she is soon redirected by a series of arrows that point her toward a house where five men are sprawled on the floor in philosophical discussion of suicide. They first ignore her and then turn on her, demanding to know "what" she is. When she falters and is unable to speak, they punish her for her silence by threatening to "take" her thoughts in what can only be described as a scopic gang-rape. Each pulls out a camera and begins snapping photos of her against her will. While she consoles herself with the reassurance that they won't be able to discover anything about her this way, she is aghast when they return triumphantly with developed photos of the "fetus" that she supposedly harbors within her. She associates the object in the photographs with the gaze of the strange boy on the train that unnerved her so: "The thing in the photograph wasn't a fetus. It was that evil boy who was encased in that womb-like space. He's living inside me with those terrifying eyes that see through everything.

When I stare off into space, the boy's eyes follow my gaze. Even if I close my eyes, that boy's eyes stay wide open in place of mine. Those eyes are guiding me in an unknown direction. A dreadful yet sweet abstract pregnancy" (237).

Watashi seems to lose consciousness from the shock of this exposure, and the story concludes with the protagonist's total loss of identity and capacity for speech. In the final lines of the story, Watashi is aimlessly wandering the streets of this unfamiliar town with nothing but an endless night before her, having literally internalized the masculine gaze. She "hears" the voice of the boy as if it emanates from the strange mass inside her, and her own will has apparently been completely overridden by the demands of the voice within.

As in Kōno's courtroom narrative, Takahashi's story likewise illustrates the futility of women's attempts to remain gender-neutral in a society that insists they conform to feminine norms. The protagonist is first marked as "feminine" when she is fixed by the gaze of the boy on the train, whose eyes seem to rebuke her for eating. The consumption of food is implicitly associated with female corporeality in a scene just prior to this, when Watashi notices a middle-aged woman buying a large quantity of boxed lunches on the platform outside the train:

> From the front of the train emerged a middle-aged woman who went running at a frenzied pace toward the vendor. She called out to him in a voice that resembled a bird of prey descending from the sky to pounce on a corpse....I could see her return carrying an armload of ten boxed lunches or so. She was probably buying for a large group of travelers, but I imagined her devouring them all herself. She didn't buy any tea, I realized. It seemed like she intended to choke down all ten lunches without any tea. Imagining such vast quantities of rice passing through her mouth, mixing with a copious amount of saliva, and making their way to her stomach, I felt my appetite diminish. (220)

The middle-aged woman in this scene seems almost a hyperbolic representation of that icon of normative Japanese femininity, the "good wife and wise mother," whose primary role is to nurture life, especially through her preparation and provision of food. Yet here the stereotype is mischievously turned on its head through a grotesque parody of another aspect of domestic womanhood circa the age of high economic growth—her function as consumer, by virtue of her designated role of household manager.

The unsavory images evoked by the sight of this woman as Watashi imagines her consuming excessive amounts of food cause the protagonist to recoil from her own physiological needs, as if wishing to erase any traces of biological femininity through a kind of extreme self-denial akin to anorexia. However, this strategy proves to be unsuccessful, as she is nevertheless fixed by the boy's gaze and defined as feminine, through a negative association of femininity with bodily desire and need. Revealingly, even the gaze of an immature man-boy seems to have the power to scopically engender the protagonist. The boy's authority as bearer of the gaze is visually underscored by his physical appearance—clad in a business suit and carrying a briefcase, he is the very image of a miniature salaryman, the logical complement to the housewife whose excessive consumption threatens to implicate Watashi as feminine.

Watashi experiences a second kind of forcible engendering at the hands of the male philosophers, whose infliction of the rape-by-camera results in her breakdown at the end of the story. Prior to her encounter with the men, Watashi clearly had fancied herself to be a genderless creature, as is evident by her thoughts just prior to arriving at their house: "What was I? Neither male nor female. Ageless. Cut off from past or future, brought to the point of nakedness." Even after entering the room where the men are sprawled on the floor talking, so long as they take no notice of her, she is able to think, "Well, it seems like I'm really not a woman after all" (230). In fact, envisioning herself as an anonymous and sexless entity seems to provide her a kind of protective camouflage, for she senses that, as on the train, drawing attention to herself as a feminine subject could have dire repercussions: "The men drained their cups and poured more water from the kettle. I was thirsty too. But there were only five cups, for the men. Yes, I can't go on drinking carelessly like that, I reminded myself. Because of that mistake of eating on the train, that boy became aware of me and brought misfortune upon me, didn't he? In this place devoted to talk of suicide, I mustn't wish for life-sustaining food or even water" (234). As with the boxed-lunch incident on the train, Watashi assumes a posture of self-denial designed to conceal her gendered identity through refusal of even the most basic biological necessities, food and water.

Underlying this logic of refusal is an implicit binary distinction between men and women that posits men (in the guise of the philosophers) as rational, logical, and intellectual. In contrast, women are defined as embodied creatures who consume, and if this marks them as "feminine" in a distinctly negative sense, then Watashi's instinct is to conceal her physical presence through an anorexic effacement of her own embodiment. However, as with Momoko's attempt to hide behind a shield of neutral objectivity in "Broken Oath," Watashi's efforts to deny her gender through the suppression of bodily desire fail to protect her from the overwhelming power of the masculine gaze, as the men eventually notice her and succeed in proving her femininity through photographic evidence of her reproductive potential. At the end of the story, she is forced to yield to the dictates of the "abstract pregnancy" that now apparently controls her destiny, as she is literally inhabited by the gaze of the boy.

This story thus posits a femininity that is defined by society, in the person of a male observer, as consumptive and reproductive excess. The protagonist is keenly aware that these "offenses" mark her as feminine in a negative and derogatory sense, and she actively attempts to evade such characterizations by denying these aspects of her own subjectivity. She first reveals herself as "feminine" on the train when she acknowledges her hunger and begins to eat, drawing the penetrative gaze of the boy toward her. Though this unwanted attention prompts her to deny her appetite, she has already been fixed by his gaze, and the result is a curious sort of transformation that suggests impregnation by force-feeding: "I forced myself to swallow it down. It swelled larger inside me." Having been visually violated and impregnated once by the boy, she experiences the same treatment again at the hands of the philosophers, who assail her with visual "proof" of her capacity to produce life—that is, the photograph of the "fetus" within—highlighting another bodily function associated with femininity. In spite of Watashi's sense of herself as "neither male nor female," the men she encounters seem determined to remind her of her feminine (and by implication inferior) subject position.

At the same time, this story also highlights the hypocrisy of such binary distinctions, as the disembodied intellectualism of the philosophers is implicitly called into question. Though the consumption of food or water is necessary to sustain life for any human being, male or female, only women are taken to task for expressing such bodily necessities. When Watashi eats, she is subjected to the accusatory stare of the boy, whose visual penetration of her further feminizes her in an implicitly sexual way. The male philosophers, on the other hand, freely help themselves to the kettle of water that is explicitly marked for their exclusive use. Clearly the men in this story may drink, and presumably eat, without gendered consequences, even as they posture rhetorically about casting off their own lives. Furthermore, their "philosophical" discussion of suicide is permeated with crude sexual references that border on misogyny. For example, one man jokes about "shooting" a woman with a pistol/phallus, underscoring what he perceives as the real source of masculine authority, while unwittingly highlighting his own embodiment (231). Thus, while on one level Takahashi's protagonist is inextricably bound to the negative polarity of a binary opposition that renders her inferior, on another level the author highlights the illogical nature of the fantasies of gender that underpin this structure.

Blue Journey

Unlike the previous two narratives, both of which are short stories that climax with the protagonist's encounter with the masculine gaze, the novel *Blue Journey* offers a more sustained exploration of the consequences of this process of engendering on its protagonist. *Blue Journey*, narrated entirely in the second person by a female protagonist, reads like a series of diary entries written by and addressed to the same person. The story alternates between present and past, with the primary narrative continuously interrupted by a series of flashback sequences. The primary narrative chronicles the protagonist's search for her fiancé, who has disappeared after a long and vexed "platonic" courtship, marked by both parties' open acknowledgment of their sexual affairs with other people. The flashback sequences trace the development of their relationship, from their first meeting in high school to the present, when both are university students nominally "engaged" to one another but with no intention of actually marrying.

The portion of the story of interest for us—an episode that is strikingly similar to the visual rape in "Getting on the Wrong Train"—is presented in a flashback sequence that provides crucial information about the main character's development from girlhood into the woman she is in the present. It is particularly important to the novel as a whole because it helps us to understand the protagonist's highly conflicted feelings about her own femininity, her consequent rejection of normative ideologies of romantic love, and her resistance to marriage as the natural and inevitable denouement of the feminine life course.

In this particular episode the protagonist recalls a painful event from her adolescence, when she was accosted near her parents' seaside villa by a gang of young boys who compelled her to remove her bathing suit and submit to their curious and derisive gaze:

> It was the squeaky voice of that pubescent youth that ordered you
> to open your legs and assume the shape of the letter Y—the most
> vulnerable position, leaving you stripped of any action that might

allow you to cover yourself. They raped you with their eyes, the eyes of those boys assembled in the space between your open legs. The pain of shame pierced you like a hot skewer.... After a long silence, the boys raised their voices in a persistent round of insane laughter, stamping their feet and hooting obscenely at your faint growth of hair.[11]

Rendered speechless and unable to defend herself from the assault, the protagonist collapses onto the sand and loses consciousness. The following day she menstruates for the first time, an episode that is explicitly linked to the scopic violation of the day before in its capacity to inflict trauma on her. Rather than an auspicious transformation from girlhood to womanhood, the main character of *Blue Journey* experiences her first period as an "execution" of her subjectivity, rendering her feminine in ways that force her to assume roles and character traits that are alien to her sense of self.

Though prior to this event she had no perception of herself as feminine, the protagonist describes this experience as having "forced her to know" the fact of her own gender in an emphatically unpleasant way. The text is explicit here in disavowing any "natural" basis for gender roles, emphasizing instead the social construction of feminine identity:

You are adamant about the fact that it's not that you *are* a woman; you are *sentenced* to be a woman, so in accepting this sentence you merely perform as a woman.... Until you accepted this sentence, you were nothing but a cute kid, a flexible existence that was neither female nor male, and as a child bundled in silken flesh, you drank the blessed milk of the breast of society. But everything changed after that, you became a different person as a result of this sudden change, and your harmony with society was severed.... From that time on society became Other to you, an evil executioner.... It was your twelfth summer when your blood first arrived, and that symbol of shame that flowed from the wound raped by society sentenced you to womanhood. (97)

While menstruation is clearly a biological process that occurs regardless of the intervention (or indifference) of society, the text is insistent here on the linkage between the trauma of scopic violation and the resultant flow of blood—both are encoded as a kind of rape that forcibly engenders a girl as feminine. In other words, the biological nature of this corporeal experience is subordinated to the meaning placed upon it by society as a rite of passage and the corresponding societal need to confine female bodies within specific tropes of womanhood.

As in the previous two stories under discussion here, *Blue Journey* likewise highlights the overwhelming power of the engendering gaze, illustrating how it is internalized even by women who attempt to resist it. As a consequence of this experience, the protagonist of Kurahashi's novel begins to scrutinize her own anatomy in an exact replication—or perhaps parody—of the way she was violated by the gang of young boys:

> Glittering with the teeth of a witch and the eyes of a martyr, you made a sacrifice of yourself and offered it to yourself.... You devised a way to gaze at that secret part of yourself in the mirror.... It was a hole, a hideous but seductive brand in the shape of a flower, an open wound torn by the teeth of society.... You can't really say that you felt hatred toward this hole of yours, but it was something that you just couldn't get used to. That hole with rose-colored walls, that concave existence that revealed your eerie interior—that was woman. You squatted in a horrifying posture above your own image, eyes glittering like those of a crazy woman as you wrung out all the knowledge you could [from this experience]. You figured it would be cleverest to make a virtue out of necessity and intoned like a curse, I am a woman, I shall become a woman.... That is, you thought you would have to perform as a woman; that would be fine; there was no other way for you to attain liberation and revenge. (100–101)

The trauma of enforced feminization here yields a protagonist who is literally rent in two, divided against herself into observer and observed, and in replicating the masculine gaze, she effectively takes the explicitly unnatural role of policing gender norms upon herself.

Feminine complicity in enforcing gender norms is further underscored in the protagonist's relationship with her mother, which is irreparably damaged once the daughter realizes the futility of explaining her anguish at this "felicitous" transformation into adulthood: "Shouldn't you have confessed the situation to someone—for example, your mother—and had her deal with it on your behalf? But that way of thinking was alien to you. If you had done so, mother would probably have behaved like a knowledgeable guardian, a co-conspirator, in front of this daughter who had felicitously become a proper <woman>" (100). Thereafter the protagonist begins to conceal her true self behind a "mask" in order to take on the appropriately feminine persona expected of her by society. This performance is so effective that not only does she convince her mother and others of her transformation, but she even loses sight of herself as the distinction between the masquerade and the actress collapses: "From then on you ceased being yourself and became increasingly proficient at donning the mask and playing the role of yourself. Even the word "self" came to mean to you nothing more than the crevice, the vacant passageway, between you and the mask, because from that time on you lost substance" (99).

The "solution" to this victimization by womanhood is to embrace and aestheticize the infliction through a parodic performance of femininity. While on the one hand this amounts to a kind of perpetual self-victimization, on the other, the protagonist is able to control and thus distance herself from the damage to her ego; this is evident in the way the strategy is described as a means of both "revenge" and "liberation."

Of the three narratives under consideration here, *Blue Journey* ironically seems to offer both the most explicitly violent example of forcible engendering and the only strategy for overcoming such trauma. Although the protagonists of the first two stories actively try to preserve their sense of agency, their attempts at resistance are ultimately unsuccessful, and they are left defeated and silenced by their experience as objects of the masculine gaze. Momoko is left catatonic on the stand in the final lines of "Broken Oath," and Watashi of "Getting on the Wrong Train" has evidently gone insane.

In contrast, Kurahashi's protagonist is able to narrate her way out of total psychic dissolution. By complying with yet parodying the role that is forced upon her, but more important by retaining her relationship to language, the main character of *Blue Journey* is able to stand on her own by the end of the story. As Atsuko Sakaki has demonstrated in her study of this novel, *Blue Journey* may be read as a narrative about narration, foregrounding the process of writing in ways that allow the protagonist to reinvent herself by the end of the story as the author of her own tale.[12] In this sense, while she has accepted the self-fragmentation attendant upon "performing" the feminine role assigned to her, she is able to retain a measure of control over the process of performance (or narration) itself, thus preserving some degree of subjectivity.

Though very different in narrative style and structure, these three texts demonstrate striking similarities in their portrayal of the impact of the masculine gaze on a female object. In each case, a female protagonist who aspires to gender-neutral status is abruptly reminded of her femininity through the disciplinary gaze of society, which is figured in the text implicitly or explicitly as masculine and personified within the texts through groups of men who collectively outnumber and overpower her. Although the disciplinary gaze in these stories is figured as masculine, this does not mean that the one who wields the gaze must necessarily be male.

In fact, each of these narratives demonstrates in its own way that feminine complicity is requisite in order for the process of engendering to be successful—whether this gaze is wielded by one woman against another (as in the mother of *Blue Journey*) or is self-inflicted. In each case, the protagonist is isolated, either because there are no other women around with whom she can seek solidarity or because other women ally themselves with the disciplinary mechanisms that seek to engender her as feminine. Alone in her subjection to the masculine gaze, the protagonist's defenses crumble and she loses the ability to speak out on her own behalf. The masculine gaze in each story, therefore, can be understood in Foucault's terms as a disciplinary mechanism that functions to enforce norms of femininity, through the reluctant complicity of the protagonist, as she internalizes the gaze and turns it upon herself. [13]

By highlighting the catastrophic effects of these disciplinary mechanisms on their protagonists—not to mention the hypocritical and self-contradictory nature of the binary structures that contain them—each of these authors effects a powerful critique of normative femininity. Kōno's character may be frozen on the stand at the end of "Broken Oath," but her struggles to remain outside of gendered stereotypes elicit the reader's sympathy. Momoko's experiences further underscore the failure of justice in a legal system that operates not according to standards of objective truth, but on the basis of stereotypically gendered expectations of human behavior that have no basis in reality. Likewise, the experiences of Takahashi's protagonist eloquently attest to the pretensions of male intellectual elites who scorn women as base corporeal objects, even as they prove themselves to be equally embodied creatures of the flesh. Finally, through her explicit characterization of femininity as a "mask" worn by an actress forced to deny any sense of a "true" self within, Kurahashi savagely parodies the lack of substance of gendered conventions that confine women to playing a role that is scripted for them by society.

While my analysis thus far has focused on the role of plot and characterization in forwarding a feminist critique of gender norms, it is also important to note the way narrative style contributes to the effectiveness of this critique. "Broken Oath" is told in the third person and is largely plot-driven, which allows the reader to observe Momoko's victimization from a position of some psychological remove—the reader is able to witness her tribulations on the stand and feel sympathy for her but nevertheless is not directly interpellated by the story itself. On the other hand, "Getting on the Wrong Train," with a first-person narrative that is almost claustrophobically contained within the psyche of the female protagonist, forces the reader to align him- or herself more closely with Watashi, which makes the experience of the rape-by-camera scene markedly more uncomfortable.

Yet both of these techniques pale in comparison to Kurahashi's second-person stratagem in *Blue Journey*, where the reader is constantly interpellated (or even verbally assaulted) by an accusatory "you" that places him or her in the position of the protagonist, as object of the gaze. So when the main character of the novel is forced to strip and submit to the derisive gaze of the gang of boys, the reader likewise experiences this scene as if she—and I use this pronoun advisedly since the experience of this scene implicitly feminizes the reader regardless of his or her biological sex—is violated simultaneously with the protagonist. Kurahashi's avant-garde technique in this scene thus effects a powerfully political gesture, forcing the reader to acknowledge the horrific violence of the engendering gaze and turning the tables on her readers by subjecting them to the same disciplinary mechanism. In this sense, Kurahashi's strategy of feminizing her audience seems to enact, on the level of narrative structure, the very "revenge" against society that her protagonist fantasizes about within the story. Although readers may approach this story with the expectation of a spectator desiring to witness, from a safely distanced perspective, the trials and tribulations of a character that is Other to them, they are quickly and violently repositioned as the objects of the gaze through interpellation as the "you" that is defined as the protagonist of this story.

These stories, therefore, yield very different readings, depending on whether one is concerned primarily with character dynamics within the story itself or the impact of each narrative on the reader. A reading of each story based solely on the fate of the main character would suggest a fairly bleak assessment of the possibility for resistance against disciplinary regimes of engendering, given that two of these narratives end with their protagonists in a state of total incapacitation and the third at best leaves its female character radically alienated from (and divided against) herself. Yet these three narratives performatively effect a critique of such disciplinary mechanisms by placing the reader in the awkward position of witnessing, and even identifying with, a protagonist who is victimized by society's intrusive gaze.

Having explored how gender norms are enforced and internalized through the oppressive and invasive masculine gaze as a disciplinary mechanism, we will turn in the next chapter to a discussion of the incentives offered to women to comply "voluntarily" with such constructions of femininity. Chapter 3, on "feminist misogyny," analyzes fiction that depicts the process of feminine self-abjection, whereby women learn to accept the notion that they occupy an inferior position vis-à-vis men. This sense of inferiority is based on a binary logic that relegates women to the realm of the corporeal so that men may transcend this abject state as spiritual or intellectual beings. This lesson is imparted in the context of intimate relationships with men who serve as lovers or mentors of the protagonists and who discipline these women through a system of rewards and punishments based on the women's willingness to comply. Women are rewarded for embracing a position of corporeal immanence through affective ties with men whom they love and respect, or else they are punished for their failure to do so through the withholding of such affections. In tracing these microchannels of power, the authors of these texts wish to expose the hypocrisy of such power dynamics by demonstrating that they cause women to internalize misogynist attitudes, replicating them not only toward other women but toward themselves as well.

CHAPTER 3

Feminist Misogyny? or How I Learned to Hate My Body

It takes a feminist to know a misogynist, and vice versa.

—*Susan Gubar, "Feminist Misogyny"*

In chapter 2, we saw the importance of the masculine gaze in disciplining women to behave as "appropriately" feminine subjects. While such discipline implies a negative form of reinforcement of gender norms, it is nevertheless clear that in other stories, the desire for positive validation by the men in one's life is equally important in rendering women complicit with social constructions of femininity. In this chapter, we will examine three stories that detail the bond between a female protagonist and her male lover or mentor, underscoring the ways male chauvinism or misogyny is internalized and reproduced by the women themselves in the context of intimate relationships. In each case the hierarchical nature of such relationships, whereby the male occupies a dominant position vis-à-vis the female, encourages the protagonist to compensate for her relative lack of power through compliance with and/or manipulation of the standards used to judge her as "inferior." In the process of trying to outwit the male at his own game, she unwittingly winds up internalizing and replicating negative attitudes toward women, a phenomenon that Susan Gubar has ironically termed "feminist misogyny."

In chapter 1 we saw that in postwar Japanese literature by male authors, women's bodies formed the ground for construction of a masculine subjectivity that rendered women inferior by aligning them with the realm of the corporeal. By disavowing those qualities that threatened them with emasculation in the face of a superior occupying army—physical fragility, sexual vulnerability, submission to authority—and then projecting them onto women, Japanese men were able to posit themselves as superior to women by virtue of their own theoretical invulnerability. Misogynist rhetoric thus served as a palliative strategy for coping with the crisis to postwar Japanese masculinity posed by the Occupation. Julia Kristeva has described this strategy of disavowal and projection of undesirable qualities as a process of "abjection," whereby the abject or "unclean" entity is expelled from the economy of power but is at the same time a crucial structuring element of it. As such, the strategy serves to define the boundary between "clean" and "unclean," "normal" and "abnormal"—or in this case, "masculine" and "feminine."[1]

As we will see in this chapter, Kōno, Takahashi, and Kurahashi challenge this misogynist "logic" head on by crafting narratives that demonstrate the psychological cost to women who are thus rendered "inferior." As in fiction by contemporary male authors, women here are aligned with the realm of bodily specificity so that men may identify themselves with the realm of the spiritual, the intellectual, or some otherwise exalted sphere of existence. But narratives by women differ in their attention to the adverse effects of this logic on women. The male characters in these stories so convince the female protagonists of the validity of this hierarchically gendered value system that the women either accept it at face value and succumb to self-destructive behavior or identify themselves as provisionally masculine in order to prove that they are an exception to the rule of feminine inferiority.

"Bone Meat" (Hone no niku, 1969), by Kōno Taeko, is an example of the first type of narrative, wherein the female protagonist's abandonment by her lover sends her into a state of hysterical self-abjection that may in fact result in her death at the end of the story. "Like a Witch" (Yōjo no yō ni, 1964), by Kurahashi Yumiko, and "Castle of Bones" (Hone no shiro, 1969), by Takahashi Takako, are examples of the latter type of story, in which women's internalization of the "superiority" of men results in a contempt for their own sex and a desire to transcend feminine immanence in favor of a valorized state of existence that is explicitly coded as masculine. Rather than affirming this negative valuation of femininity, these stories expose and critique the way such misogynist "logic" works to trap women in an emphatically illogical and unjust double bind, whereby neither resistance nor compliance serves as an effective strategy for building a tenable feminine subjectivity.

"Bone Meat"

The protagonist of "Bone Meat" is an unmarried woman whose live-in lover abandons her about six months before the time when the story begins. Much of the tale is told in flashback, as she remembers the time they spent together leading up to their breakup. She remembers with particular fondness times when they ate food "with bones or shells" because these meals were accompanied by a specific form of role-playing in which the man took the meaty parts for himself and left the woman with the merest scraps of leftover food. This literal performance of the hierarchical structure of their relationship—wherein the male demonstrates his dominance and the woman gracefully submits—is cited by the protagonist as the very reason that these meals were pleasurable to her above all others.

The woman's pleasure is evident in a remembered scene in which the two eat raw oysters on the half-shell together. As if in deliberate parody of the stereotype of the cheerfully submissive wife, the woman carefully prepares the meal and serves it to the man, taking pleasure not only in watching him eat, but also in denying herself food even when he offers it to her. After watching him eat a few of the oysters, she takes up one of his discarded shells and begins to scrape at the tiny bits of flesh left stuck to the shell, from which she derives immense pleasure. Evidently the ritual nature of their role-playing, during which she repeatedly asks him for a whole oyster and he refuses her, is an important part of the enjoyment for her because when he unexpectedly offers her one, she is disappointed at this "departure from the usual order of things."[2] It turns out that the man simply finds that night's product to be inferior in quality to the oysters they usually buy, and since the meal lacks flavor, he seems to grow tired of the usual game:

> "How is it?" the man asked.
> "Well, I can't really tell," she replied. What she could tell was that it was not nearly so good as the taste of the hinge muscle scraped from the empty shell or the other bit of meat that had given her such ecstasy. And it seemed distinctly inferior to the flavor, the smell, the freshness of the seashore called up in her mind by the voluptuous sound the man made when he raised the shell to his lips and sucked out the oyster. Even the flavor evoked by that sound amounted to little more than imagining a long-past and much-faded sensation. (259–260)

With this rather unexpected turn of events, the meal ends, along with the role-playing that is supposed to accompany it, and the scene concludes as follows:

She felt dissatisfied that the scene they always played when they ate oysters on the half-shell had not been followed. The man took her hand and stroked it. She wished she might feel that on another part of her body....

That evening, however, which ended without the usual fulfillment of the scene she associated with the taste, was the last time they ate oysters together. Before too many more days passed, spring was upon them and the raw-oyster season was over. The summer passed and autumn came, and by the time the air again began to turn cold, the man had already left. (261)

It is clear in this scene that eating oysters together is a pleasurable and even erotic experience for the woman and that her own pleasure is predicated on a posture of self-denial that privileges the desires of the man. It is the sound of him eating and enjoying his meal, not the food itself, that evokes "the flavor, the smell, the freshness of the seashore" and makes the meal of oysters special to her. It is also clear that this scene represents the beginning of the end of their relationship—already "long-past and much-faded" by the time the story itself begins. In fact, enjoyment of the oysters, linked as it is with the sexual play that accompanies the meal, can be read as a kind of metaphor for the relationship itself—neither of which, it is implied in this passage, gives him pleasure any longer.

The linkages between physical and emotional nourishment are further evident in the fact that when he leaves her, the protagonist's appetite disappears and she becomes extremely thin. The passion that she felt for the man, which is intimately bound up with the performance of self-denial that structures their relationship, is apparently inextricable from her desire for food so that she literally begins to starve herself after he leaves her:

Since girlhood, the woman had hardly been what could be described as plump. However, from about the time the man began gradually bringing in his personal belongings, she had started to gain a little weight.

Their tastes concurred, and they both liked dishes with bones or with shells. The woman was poor, and the man's prospects, up until about the time he abandoned her, had not looked good, so in order to serve such dishes often, they had to economize on their other meals. Even so, it was mostly the bones or shells which went to the woman. But although she seldom ate richly, she began to gain weight.

The woman recalled this odd phenomenon as not odd in the least....All those varied bone and shell dishes began to give her the feeling that a sense of taste had been awakened throughout her body; that all her senses had become so concentrated in her sense of taste that it was difficult for her even to move. And when she awoke the next morning, she felt her body brimming with a new vitality. It would have been odd had she *not* gained weight. (262–263)

The woman had never been critical of him when they had dishes with bones or shells, because at those times he never made her anxious or brought her troubles to mind. He coveted meat even more fiercely than before, and she even more wholeheartedly savored the tiny bits of bone meat. They were a single organism, a union of objectively different parts, immersed in a dream. (263–264)

The description of their relationship as like "a single organism" underscores the extent to which the woman's physical well-being becomes dependent on the presence and participation of the man. She is able to thrive even though she eats little because their relationship provides her with an identity and proves that she is necessary to him; what use is a sadist without a masochist, and vice versa? Her feminine identity becomes so structured around this performance of a masochistic subject position that when the integrity of their bond is threatened—that is, when the game ceases to provide the usual pleasure—she begins to pick fights with him in order to provoke the kind of passionate exchange they used to share with food. Her constant refrain, "I'd be better off without you!" seems intended to elicit reassurance that this is not the case, and indeed the fact that he continues to stay with her for some time after she begins to criticize him so vehemently appears to offer her some solace—until the day when he takes her at her word and leaves.

It is not surprising that the story begins with a long description of the woman's attempts to deal with the personal belongings he has left behind, given that throughout the story these discarded material objects are likened to her feelings of abandonment:

The first hints that the man was beginning to think of a life in which she had no part appeared even before his work took a turn for the better. His decision to abandon her had been reflected in

> both his private and public aspects; even the clothing he wore
> was all newly made. She felt the sympathy of a fellow-sufferer
> for the old clothes that he took no more notice of, and yet
> felt scorned by the very things she tried to pity. And thus the
> woman found even more unbearable these troublesome leftover
> belongings. (253)

Not only does she equate herself with these material objects, but it is
also clear that she perceives the man to have left her behind in exchange
for something better. Effectively, he has cast off both her and his own
worn-out things as he moves up the ladder of success. Elsewhere in the
text the woman's poverty is stressed, and it is explicitly contrasted with
the man's more advantageous situation: "She had decided that the best
method of dealing with the perplexing problem of the man's belongings
was herself to abandon them entirely, along with her own, and move to
a new place. But she didn't have the money to move to a new place or to
buy all the necessary things for it. Although the woman would have liked
to abandon it all, she could not, and even her own belongings and the
place itself became repugnant to her" (253). It is as though the man has
managed to transcend the realm of base materiality only by relegating her
to a position of immanence, and her feelings of being discarded along with
his old things are transformed into a level of self-loathing that renders her
indifferent even to her own well-being.

The protagonist's frustration with feeling stuck in her current situation, literally weighed down by the baggage of a failed relationship that
she is too poor to abandon and too distraught to discard, prompts self-
destructive fantasies of escape that may in fact culminate in her death. She
becomes haunted by obsessive thoughts of fire that seem to imply both a
fear of and a desire for this outcome:

> She felt she would like to burn it all—the man's things, and her
> own, and the place. If she too were to burn up with them, she
> thought, so much the better. But she merely hoped for it, and
> made no plans. Strangely, for a woman who wanted even herself
> to be destroyed in the conflagration, she was inclined to be wary
> of fire.... She was tortured by the fear that if she were to start a
> fire accidentally it would seem like arson. (254)

All that the woman had disposed of among the things the man had
left behind was the discarded toothbrush, the old razor blades,

and the cigarettes. A moment before, when she had held the ash-tray in her hands, she had the dreamlike feeling that everything would, happily, burn to ashes like the cigarettes. (254–255)

In the final lines of the story, it is suggested that she has (perhaps unconsciously) chosen self-immolation over continued misery, as a dream of burning the physical remains of their relationship morphs into an image of an actual house fire:

> The siren of a fire engine wailed somewhere continuously. But what caused her dream to recede was less the siren than the words she had just heard in her dream.
>
> From the ashes of the man's belongings, that there should be so many bones and shells! "Is that so? Is that so?" she said nodding, and the siren, to which was added a furiously ringing bell, filled her ears. Was what she had been told in the dream perhaps prophetic? The bell stopped, and just then the siren arrived blaring under her window. But the woman, her eyes closed, nodding "Is that so? Is that so?" simply snuggled deeper into the quilt as it seemed to begin to smolder. (266)

"Bone Meat" thus offers a fairly literal illustration of the process whereby a woman's desire for validation by a male authority figure—in this case a former lover—ultimately results in a self-destructive internalization of the very discourses that render her inferior. The protagonist's complicity with hierarchical power dynamics that encourage and reward her for her submission to their vaguely sadomasochistic role-play is crucial in the success of this process of self-abjection. She even learns to take pleasure in subordinating her own desires to his, and her feminine gender identity becomes inseparable from the masochistic role she plays vis-à-vis her lover. Therefore, when he abandons her, she is unable to extricate herself from the position of identification with his discarded material possessions. The only escape she can envision from this intolerable situation is apparently to destroy herself, along with the rest of the "garbage."

"Like a Witch"

The central character of "Like a Witch" is a writer who returns home to her family in Kōchi prefecture, a rural area in southern Japan where the pace of life and cultural patterns of the inhabitants are far more traditional than the metropolitan lifestyle to which she has accustomed herself as an adult. On the pretext of helping her younger brother reopen their late father's dental practice, she has left her husband "without permission" in the hope of gaining some respite from their married life together, which she finds dull and an impediment to her writing career.

The gap in educational level, attitudes, and expectations between the protagonist and the residents of her former hometown is evident from the very first pages of the story, as she describes the mundane routine of housework and gossip that structures the daily life of the women of the village with a mixture of dismissal and contempt. For example, she likens the voice of the woman next door, a former classmate of hers, to the clamoring of stray dogs and wonders how someone so poor could produce so many children.[3] Though the protagonist is married, she has deliberately kept this information from the villagers because she dreads being held accountable to the expectations they have of a properly wed young woman. She therefore sees her marriage as thoroughly different in content and quality than the norm, as defined by this small town, and is determined to keep it that way (219).

The basic conflict of this story, between the normative feminine role of housewife and the protagonist's status as writer and intellectual, is dramatically illustrated through her relationships with two men—her current husband, whom she views dispassionately and is able to defy seemingly at will, and her former lover, a much older man and mentor whose approval she desperately sought yet who never treated her as an intellectual equal. We know of her relationship with the husband through several phone calls, interspersed throughout the story, during which he repeatedly and unsuccessfully entreats her to come home and fulfill her duties as his wife. She responds by referring to married life as a "prison" and dismisses his suggestion that sexual "service" is an important part of marriage (216). She refuses to express jealousy at the possibility that he might become unfaithful and blithely replies, "If you feel you're being inconvenienced, please go ahead and sleep with another woman. Don't hold back on my account." Even when his language becomes explicitly violent, she is seemingly unfazed:

> "Why do you want to do it with me? Shall I put it in more strident terms? What makes it inevitable that you would do so? It's ridiculous."
> "Listening to you talk, all the penises of the world would probably go flaccid from the poison."

"That's the idea."

"With a woman like you, there's nothing I can do but beat you, tie you up, whip you until you lose consciousness and then rape you."

"Ah, you want to give me the role of masochist. But it would be hard for me to be any more masochistic than I am by being bound by the rope of married life." (215)

Perhaps their banter is intended to be tongue-in-cheek, but the sheer misogyny of the husband's discourse suggests how desperately he is attempting to reassert his authority. As we will see below, even as the wife appears rather cavalierly to dismiss this rhetorical power play, she unwittingly echoes the same sentiments vis-à-vis other women elsewhere in the text.

The protagonist's casual disregard of her husband's demands would make it seem that she is immune to the pressures to yield to masculine authority, but this initial impression is increasingly undermined the more we learn of her relationship with her former lover. Structurally, the story begins with the conversations between husband and wife, and it is almost halfway through the narrative that we first learn of the older man, but at this point her relationship with him, and the impact it has had on her current self, begins to dominate the story. It concludes with her feelings of abandonment by her mentor, which have created a sense of "deepening night" within her, profoundly affecting her personality and the quality of her relationships with others in the present. The story therefore moves gradually from a description of the protagonist's exterior persona, through her ties to her husband, family, and neighbors, to the very core of her psyche, which has been dramatically shaped by the bond she shared with "him," the much older man with whom she fell in love at the age of seventeen. It is this man who represents the essence of masculine authority for her and to whom she has submitted herself emotionally, physically, and intellectually in an attempt to win his approval.

Her feelings about this older man are conveyed through two sequences that interrupt the flow of the narrative and provide psychological depth at crucial junctures. The first is a long flashback sequence to the time when she met him, and it occupies nearly a third of the entire text. Then after a brief return to "reality," in which a subplot concerning the brother is wrapped up, her former lover reappears in a fantasy sequence that intrudes upon the diegetic present and concludes the story with her abandonment by the older man. While the first part of the story revolves around relatively mundane aspects of life in the village—her relationships with husband, family, and neighbors and her feelings of being a fish out of water in her own home town—the introduction of the older man takes the narrative to a more philosophical and abstract level that reveals much about the psychology of the protagonist and how she has come to feel so alienated from her roots. The importance of her relationship with the lover is evident from the way his character, once introduced, completely overshadows the daily life dramas of the first section of the story and the fact that his departure concludes the story itself.

The tension between feminine corporeality and intellectual or spiritual pursuits dominates the lovers' first meeting and is explored explicitly and at length in the dialogue that establishes the basis for their relationship. They first meet when he helps her up after she collapses due to anemia brought on by menstruation. She is horrified that he has seen her predicament—apparently she has dripped blood on his floor—and her discomfort with her own bodily functions then becomes their first topic of conversation. In fact, she seems to believe that having been "seen" as feminine in such a decisively corporeal fashion is much more invasive than being sexually violated, and she concludes that now that he has "known" her in this sense, they might as well become lovers: "OK, look at me as much as you want. I've been seen by you, and it seems that your eyes have taken up residence inside my body" (231).[4] It is interesting that although she claims later to be infertile, here and elsewhere the image of being "inhabited" or impregnated by his gaze is used as a metaphor for the profound effect he would have on her later intellectual and psychological development.

While the older man clearly seems to appreciate women's bodies, and her body in particular, he reveals himself to be less impressed with their spiritual and intellectual potential. In the context of a conversation between the lovers that is part argumentative and part flirtatious, she attempts to earn his respect by appealing to his obvious penchant for intellectualism. His response to her banter is more than a little patronizing:

> "You're a troublesome girl, aren't you? Good girls don't argue like that. It just makes you look pouty and stern."
>
> "You don't respect me for my mind, do you? You underestimate me. Even in this little body I harbor a soul and spirit and intelligence about a meter long."
>
> "That's adorable. Your intellectualism is part of your charm, like the whiskers on a kitten."
>
> "Because cats have whiskers, they can catch mice even at night."

"Catching mice is a trivial game so never mind that. But men are stupid animals who will chase rats with such abandon that they forfeit their lives. Men are made exclusively of spirit so they can become as ugly as they want. Women don't have that. Or even if they do it's one with their body. It burns inside their bones and shines out beautifully from inside their flesh. It's hard to say whether it's flesh or illusion or a ray of light." (235)

While his reference to men as "stupid animals" would seem to suggest some derision, thereby mitigating the double standard that underlines his assessment of women's potential, in fact the effect of this phrasing is to posit men as rather heroic in their steadfast pursuit of a goal. Women, on the other hand, are bound by their corporeal immanence, and to the extent that they can be said to have a "spirit"—here a kind of code word for a selfhood that transcends the mortal coil—it is inevitably trapped within a physical package that although pleasing to the eye, is obviously understood as inferior. This much is clear from the assertion that men can "become as ugly as they want" in a corporeal sense, precisely because they possess spirituality, something that is implicitly more valuable than physical beauty.

The protagonist has evidently internalized these prejudices to some extent because she continually attempts to distance herself from the kind of corporeal experience that would bind her to the stereotype of femininity that her lover describes. She balks at his claim that she is "just a woman" and insists on referring to herself as barren in an effort to disavow distinctively feminine experiences like pregnancy and childbirth (233). Likewise, as noted above, she also clearly harbors feelings of abhorrence for her menstrual periods—understood not as a natural cycle of feminine experience but as a corrosive force of decay that destroys from within: "Menstruation. Yuck. I don't use words like that. My 'monthly guest.' More like an angel of death that comes to pick the vines clean, who spits out the dregs and then leaves. It makes the *him* inside of me particularly testy" (233). Her reference to a male self that resides within the outer feminine shell seems calculated to establish a kind of intellectual authority defined along precisely the lines that he has laid out for her. If only men can be said to possess "spirit" and if he insists on focusing on the feminine exterior, then she must present herself as masculine on the inside, forcing him to recognize her as an intellectual equal.

Furthermore, she is careful to distinguish her own implicitly masculine persona from that of other girls, who only pretend at the sort of philosophical inquiry that marks serious writing:

"You said once that you wrote poetry and fiction, right? You don't anymore?"

"I don't. No way. I'm not the kind of girl that pretends to be a writer. Girls can't become beautiful even if they write fiction. I have some friends who are still writing, but it makes me sick to see them writing out of such feelings of self-love. I can't stand to be near someone like that. I've given up looking in the mirror, and at night, so I won't touch myself, I keep my hands above the covers. I don't use makeup either. But the worst is women who make themselves up using words." (233–234)

It is interesting that her contempt for women's self-expression, or "writing with makeup," is so intimately imbricated with both the beauty myth that she is attempting to resist and with feminine sexuality. This is explicitly in response to his repeated attempts to conflate "femininity" with physical beauty. In a determined effort to distance herself from such stereotypes, she disavows both concern for her own appearance, which would mark her as a conventionally and exclusively feminine creature, and the kind of "self-love," whether explicitly sexual or expressed obliquely through writing, that would validate a feminine perspective.

In fact, the protagonist tries so hard to distance herself from normative femininity that she, perhaps unwittingly, seems to internalize the very misogynist discourse and attitudes that she is attempting to resist. She does so by drawing a clear line of demarcation between herself and other women, presenting herself as the exception to the rules that determine gender normativity for him:

[Man:] "But aren't women creatures who live on beauty? Every woman lives thinking of herself as beautiful. If a woman were to become unable to believe that, she couldn't go on living another day. They live praying to themselves to become more and more beautiful. Even old hags."

"That's stupid."

"You should think of it as tragic instead."

"You should have said comic. It's so amusing I can't stand it. . . . If the kind of woman that fits your definition of 'woman' is the most feminine type, then I can't stand to be a woman. Women who are the ugliest things in the world and yet pretend not to see that and try to find something beautiful about themselves, try to make themselves even 1 percent more beautiful, thinking that if beautiful people are good and proper, then they'll try to be good and proper—women who live lying to themselves like that should be raped and killed. Don't you think you'd like to exterminate all those lady teachers and PTA moms, female critics, and Diet members when you see them?"

"Well, you just have to put up with them, don't you? Anyway, they're incapable of doing anything important. Women don't have the power to destroy the world or anything."

"Bear and raise children and build a family. The happiness of domesticity. Peaceful daily life. It's dull. Makes me yawn." (234–235)

The protagonist's language here is shockingly misogynist and reminiscent of her husband's rhetorical attempts to discipline her during a telephone conversation earlier in the story. Yet it is important to distinguish that what she objects to here is the "good and proper" woman, one who aligns herself with the status quo and/or conforms to normative expectations of feminine roles.[5] Clearly the protagonist sees herself as altogether outside this paradigm and justifies her position by her own adoption of masculinist contempt for such women.

"Castle of Bones"

As in "Like a Witch," the female protagonist of Takahashi Takako's "Castle of Bones" is primarily influenced in her hatred of her own sex by a male mentor, in this case a quasi-religious guru who initiates her into a set of devotional practices designed to transcend the body by literally crushing it underneath a giant roller. Women's bodies are found to be particularly unresponsive to this "training," as they are intimately associated with the realm of bodily existence, and the man is particularly keen on forcing those women most clearly identified with the corporeal to submit to his rather sadistic form of "training." The protagonist, Watashi ("I"), admires this man very much for his pursuit of pure spirituality, but she is seemingly frustrated in her attempts to get him to take her as a serious candidate for transcendence on account of the fact that she inhabits a female body. She therefore sets out to prove to him that she is an exception to the rule of feminine spiritual inferiority by voluntarily submitting herself to the training. Her desire for validation by this man she admires thus leads her to take a misogynist attitude toward other women and to abject her own femininity in order to impress him.

"Castle of Bones" opens with Watashi wandering through the back streets of a large city, where she encounters a mysterious, mummy-like old man in the process of "training." Watashi expresses interest in the training, so the old man takes her to a windowless room eight stories high that he calls the "beauty parlor." Here she witnesses armor-clad men who, on the orders of the old man, force unwilling, naked female victims to submit to the roller. According to the old man, the exercise results in failure because the women refuse to accept the fact that their bodies are ugly.

Strangely enough, though Watashi is also female, the old man does not attempt to train her, and it is this fact that brings Watashi to the realization that she is not like other women. In order to trick the old man into abducting her for training as well, she sets out on a quest to learn to behave like a regular woman, and after much trial and error, she discovers that the thing that most sets her apart from other women is her total lack of concern with her appearance. After ducking into a beauty shop and submitting to a lengthy makeover, which she describes as a "sacrifice" willingly undertaken to qualify her for training, she is finally abducted and taken to the old man's "beauty parlor."[6]

Here Watashi is stripped naked and submitted to the roller, but unlike the other women, she resolves not to scream or betray pain or fear, in an effort to prove her worthiness to the old man. Sure enough, the old man notes with satisfaction that the shadow produced by Watashi's flattened body is black like his own, rather than oozing red like that of the other women. Pleased with this measure of success, the old man favors Watashi by leading her to the "Castle of Bones" denoted by the title of the story. He explains that the castle is constructed of the whitened bones and crystalline eyes of those who have successfully completed the training. In attaining this inorganic state, the trainees do not die; they have merely concentrated their life in their eyes in order to attain the power to see the invisible—in effect achieving a god-like status. Unfortunately, the old man continues, even though Watashi seems like a promising candidate, because she is female it would be unsuitable for her to aspire to the Castle of Bones. Upon hearing this, Watashi realizes that her vision of the Castle of Bones was just an illusion and that she still has a long road to travel before reaching it. Despite the old man's efforts to dissuade her, in the end she cannot bring herself to give up the quest.

In this story, Takahashi portrays an environment that is strictly demarcated into male space, from which women are excluded as unworthy, and female space, in which women's bodies are treated as abject and controlled by men. Yet her portrayal of the protagonist undermines this structure, as men are found to be less "pure" than they pretend to be, and women are more "worthy" than they are purported to be. The result is a text that subverts from within the very structure on which it is built. In the indoor, female space of the beauty parlor, great attention is paid to women's bodies in an effort either to beautify them through the application of cosmetics and hair care products or to emphasize their ugliness by mutilating them through training. While the old man also undergoes training in an effort to transcend the corporeal, it is important to note that for him, this process is not only voluntary and meaningful, but also takes place outdoors in free, open space. Similarly, the path to the Castle of Bones is of course also traversed in open space, and it is taken for granted that the men who travel it have the possibility of reaching their destination. By contrast, for the women who suffer inside the old man's beauty parlor, the training is nothing but senseless torture and their failure to overcome it a foregone conclusion. Furthermore, whereas the Castle of Bones is demarcated as male space into which females must not trespass, within the supposedly female space of the beauty parlor, women are clearly subjected to the control and abuse of men who have absolute power over them. This power differential is underscored by the hyper-masculine signifier of armor-clad men, versus the total vulnerability of women stripped naked and subjected to the male gaze.

In fact, this economy of the visual proves to be an integral part of the geography of power articulated in "Castle of Bones." The ultimate form of power sought by the old man and his followers is the power to "see the invisible," which is defined in the text as a kind of cosmic truth at the "center of the universe" available only to those who have successfully completed the training (29). This power of vision is symbolized by the crystalline eyeballs that cover the surface of the Castle of Bones. As if to underscore his position as arbiter of power in this visual economy, the old man has forbidden his armor-clad underlings from visually observing the women's training—they are allowed to participate but must wear helmets that prevent them from seeing the women's agony.

Thus, Watashi occupies an extremely problematic and disruptive position with respect to the network of power relationships that structure the world depicted in the story. Since she is allowed to witness the training on her first visit to the old man's beauty parlor, not only does she occupy a masculine position with respect to the female victims, but according to the logic of this world that denies the right of vision to all but the most worthy, her status is actually superior in this scene to that of the old man's followers. Watashi initially is favored with the right to the gaze because the old man approves of her utter lack of concern with the feminine objective of self-beautification (17). Yet precisely because of her cosmetophobia, she fails to attract the attention of the old man as a potential target for training. In effect, she is *invisible* to him because though he knows that she is not male, he cannot seem to see her as female either because she does not fit his conception of femininity.

In order to attract the old man's attention, Watashi is forced to "perform" femininity in a way that is experienced by her as exceedingly unnatural. On looking in the mirror, she describes the effect of her transformation after the application of a "sticky film of gaudy makeup" (31) as a moment of nonrecognition of a self that "did and did not look like her" (21). But thanks to this makeover she is finally able to qualify for training. In other words, in order to gain the old man's recognition as an appropriate candidate, she has to learn to perform the role of a woman obsessed with her appearance—the type of woman that the old man himself identifies as simultaneously most feminine and, consequently least likely to complete the training successfully.

Thus, Watashi's gender acrobatics serve to cast suspicion on the old man's motives for attempting to train these women in the first place. He claims to want to train them "just as he does himself," in order to help them to transcend the "ugliness" of the corporeal body in favor of an inorganic and spiritual existence (11). Yet by deliberately choosing only those women who he believes will fail to embrace this transcendence, he preserves his position as sole possessor of the gaze while simultaneously justifying his role as arbiter of power on the grounds that he is closer to spiritual purity than anyone else. Furthermore, despite the old man's self-proclaimed holier-than-thou status, he seems to enjoy witnessing the women's torture, as is evident from Watashi's description of her own experience during training: "Then I saw the old man's eyes lose their gleam of purity and burn with a strange greediness, just as they had done here the other day. Because today I was in the opposite position of being punished, I was able to see clearly what was in the old man's eyes. Those eyes seemed to express a cold pleasure at the women's agonies" (24–25). So although the old man suggests that he is able to renounce corporeal pleasure in favor of a supposedly higher realm of knowledge, his *eyes* betray him—the eyes, of course, being the vehicle by which such knowledge is attained, according to the man's own logic. It is Watashi's renunciation of the masculine role of possessor of the gaze, in favor of a feminine vantage point as object of the gaze, that makes this fact clear to her.

To pursue the visual motif one step further, although the old man bases his theory of knowledge acquisition on the power of vision, this power is accompanied by a corresponding blindness to his own limitations (and those of his world view). In contrast, Watashi's deferral of the masculine gaze in favor of a feminized visual position gives her access to a different sort of knowledge, in effect making the hypocrisy of the prevailing power structure fully visible for the first time. Furthermore, this role reversal subverts the binary of male as subject of the gaze versus female as viewed object by giving the "object" the power to see (and judge) the "subject."

In the end, however, Watashi is unable to renounce once and for all her desire for the very sort of visual power that the old man describes, in spite of her apparent understanding that the economy of the gaze is based on a fallacious distinction between supposedly masculine and feminine attributes. It seems clear that Watashi's primary motivation here is not a hatred of the corporeal or the feminine per se but a desire to earn the respect of the old man, and her various sacrifices are undertaken precisely for this purpose, as she states clearly during her own experience of training: "The screams and groans of the other women increased in proportion to my own pain. But I made no sound. Yes, wasn't that precisely why I had come here? In order to show the old man that I could bear the pain, for that reason only, I had spent days and days wandering around in places I had not chosen at times I had not chosen, and finally through the great sacrifice of that disguise, I had created the opportunity to be abducted by the old man" (24). It would perhaps not be going too far to characterize the old man as a kind of father figure from whom Watashi is seeking validation—so desperately, in fact, that she is willing to resort to self-abuse to get it.

Sadly, in spite of Watashi's attempts to prove her worthiness, the old man seems unable to get past the fact that she is female. Though in their first encounter Watashi and the old man seem to share a kind of intimacy—both demonstrate an uncanny understanding of each other's motives[7]—the disguise she dons to recapture this intimacy actually makes it impossible for the old man to see her as anything but a female body. When she appears again at the old man's beauty salon after her transformation into a visually recognizable female, he is unable to connect this image of her with the person he met before.

Even after Watashi submits to his torture to prove that her shadow is just as black as his, the old man at first offers her a vision of the Castle of Bones only to retract it, accusing her of "arrogantly trying to invade male territory" (30). At this accusation Watashi puts her hand up to touch her made-over hair and face and reflects, "Oh, am I nothing but a woman, then?" (31) Given this Catch-22 situation, it is hardly surprising that Watashi is tempted by the old man's notion of transcending the body in favor of a purely spiritual existence. Regardless of her own image of self, her female flesh marks her in the eyes of the fathers as "nothing but a woman." The "feeling of liberation" she experiences as her body is transformed into a lifeless mass by the roller can be read not necessarily as a hatred of women or corporeality per se but as a desire to be free of the cage of binary male/female existence (25).

It is significant that while embracing this desire for transcendence of the corporeal and the binary logic it invites, Takahashi's text deconstructs its own message by simultaneously suggesting the impossibility of such a feat. Bodies subjected to the roller resume their original form when it is removed. Visions of reaching the Castle of Bones prove to be nothing but an illusion. For those, like Watashi, seeking a way out of the binary gender trap, Takahashi's text offers no solutions, only an invitation to rethink that structure from *within*, by portraying a protagonist who is literally not "visible" through the lens of conventional binary distinctions. In doing so, Takahashi emphasizes the artificial and constructed nature of this difference between binary opposites, ultimately demonstrating the hypocritical and self-contradictory logic whereby women are excluded from dominant power structures.

We have seen that all three narratives discussed in this chapter trace a process wherein women are seduced into complicity with the very structures that render them inferior, in the context of affective relationships that reward properly feminine behavior. Such complicity requires women to accept relegation to the realm of corporeal immanence so that men may pose as spiritually transcendent or intellectually superior beings. The female protagonists depicted in these texts all learn to replicate this misogynist philosophy in order to win the regard of male mentors or lovers whose opinions they respect, with varying consequences. The main character of "Bone Meat" seems to accept her inferiority at face value and even learns to take a kind of masochistic pleasure in it, but this likely results in self-destruction by the end of the tale. The protagonists of "Like a Witch" and "Castle of Bones," by contrast, provisionally accept this chauvinist logic in an unsuccessful attempt to free themselves from the hierarchical structure by proving that they are exceptions to the rule of feminine inferiority.

While their female characters are unable to overturn the ideological structures that bind them, all three authors effect a powerful critique of this misogynist attitude toward femininity by replicating and then parodying it within their texts. The ritual nature of the sadomasochistic role-playing depicted in Kōno's story highlights the performative, and therefore artificial, nature of constructions of feminine inferiority. Kurahashi encodes chauvinist dialogue into her story in order to allow her heroine to explicitly refute it in arguments with her husband. Even as she reproduces these attitudes in an attempt to distance herself from other women who ostensibly resemble the stereotypes, the shockingly misogynist tenor of her claims hyperbolically underscores their lack of truth value, mocking while drawing attention to their artificiality and the self-serving motivations of the men who attempt to enforce them. Finally, Takahashi exposes the hypocrisy of the standards used to judge women as inferior by demonstrating that women can display mastery of the standards used to measure "masculine" excellence yet still be denied recognition for their accomplishments.

Given that all three of these authors had to fight for inclusion in the male intellectual space that the Japanese literary world represented, it is perhaps no surprise that such themes reemerged in imaginative form in their literature. Each story depicts a world ruled by networks of power that structure human relationships according to positions of superiority/inferiority, dominance/submission, intellect/body, transcendence/immanence, and spiritual/material along strictly gendered lines. Each protagonist finds that as a woman, she is automatically relegated to the negative side of each binary opposition, whether she identifies with this position or not.

Each protagonist then faces a choice between complying with the terms of her subordination, or attempting resistance. Kōno's heroine chooses compliance, only to discover that even playing by the rules does not guarantee the security of the fragile identity that she has crafted for herself, as this leaves her dependent on the cooperation of a male partner who can capriciously withdraw his participation at will. Kurahashi's main character chooses resistance and attempts to justify a position for herself on the opposite end of the binary. However, she discovers that only those already in a position of authority have the power to grant inclusion and that merely inhabiting a female body is enough to disqualify her. Takahashi's protagonist faces a similar situation, with the added indignity of successfully passing the test for inclusion, only to be turned away at the gates of the establishment.

The rhetorical power of each text, from a feminist perspective, thus lies in its exposure of the hypocrisy of the "rules" whereby women are rendered abject and subordinated to authorities who pretend to be superior, only to reveal their own lack of credibility. These narratives demonstrate that under such a rigidly illogical system of value, neither compliance nor resistance offers a tenable position for women to establish any kind of feminine subjectivity. Indeed, there can be no possibility of subjectivity for women so long as their only value is as a ground for the construction of male subjectivity.

In the previous two chapters we have outlined some of the disciplinary mechanisms used to produce and enforce feminine behavior as envisioned in these authors' textual worlds. In the next chapter we will encounter another persistent trope employed to critique restrictive gender binaries—the "odd body," or alternate forms of corporeality that resist characterization as either male or female, masculine or feminine. These bodies not only expose as false the dichotomy that underwrites such binary distinctions, but further undermine this structure at its core by "queering" the male body that forms the theoretical standard for binary gender difference.

CHAPTER 4

Odd Bodies

The issue is not one of elaborating a new theory of
which woman would be the *subject* or the *object,*
but of jamming the theoretical machinery itself, of
suspending its pretension to the production of a truth
and of a meaning that are excessively univocal.

—*Luce Irigaray, "The Power of Discourse"*

As noted in the previous two chapters, women in the texts we have
analyzed so far can be said to be held accountable to norms of femininity, whether they identify with such constructions or not, based solely
on the fact that they inhabit female bodies. These norms are repeatedly
instilled by a masculine disciplinary gaze that continually reminds women
to "behave themselves" according to societal expectations. Women are
thus taught to embody and perform femininity so that men can define
themselves as masculine, according to gendered binaries that render these
two terms opposite and mutually exclusive. Masculinity can therefore be
understood as predicated on a profound disavowal of all qualities associated with the realm of the feminine, in order to transcend this abject
position of corporeal immanence for the elevated plane of intellectual and
spiritual superiority.

Luce Irigaray describes such binary distinctions as operating according to a logic of "sexual indifference," whereby femininity is defined
according to its difference from masculinity, embodying everything that
men (would like to believe they) are not. While this would seem to yield
two distinct genders, in effect it reduces conceptions of masculinity and
femininity to one model of gender—the masculine—whereby femininity
becomes "non-masculinity"—that is, incomprehensible without reference
to its conceptual opposite.[1] As we saw in chapter 1, this strictly gendered
binary division was underwritten by the exigencies of the high-growth

economy of the 1960s, whereby the masculine ideal of salaryman was possible only through the creation of a feminine complement, the housewife/mother who took full responsibility for the domestic sphere. Women's contributions to society were thus understood to encompass everything that had been excluded from the masculine sphere—reproduction, care of children and the elderly, domestic labor, and any other activities required to support the total dedication of men to the world of work outside the home. Women writers of the 1960s, particularly those whose works are analyzed in this study, resisted such ideologies of gender through fictional narratives that sought to expose such binaries themselves as fictitious, thus "jamming the theoretical machinery," in Irigaray's terminology.

In this chapter we will examine one trope that is frequently used to critique these binary models of gender—the "odd body," or a protagonist whose physiology fails to conform to gendered expectations of "normalcy." The bodies examined in this chapter are perversely reproductive (or nonreproductive), deformed, or androgynous, covertly or overtly defying prescribed patterns of difference between masculine and feminine norms. In the process, they underscore the mutual imbrication of human bodies and the societies that both produce and define them, highlighting the fact that even though binary gender distinctions are fallacious and constructed, society perversely insists upon enforcing compliance with artificially crafted gender norms by assuming a one-to-one correspondence between biology and behavior. These "odd bodies" therefore serve as a subversive challenge to the logic of "sexual indifference" that would confine women to the realm of the inferior so that men may envision themselves as superior.

In the first story under discussion, Kōno Taeko's "Toddler-Hunting," we see a protagonist whose perverse attraction to little boys entails a fantasy of violent inscription of "feminine" bodily characteristics upon a male body. This produces a narrative that not only subverts assumptions about the "naturalness" of maternal instincts, but furthermore calls into question the integrity of gender norms themselves. Next, in Takahashi Takako's story "Secret" (Hi, 1973) we meet a protagonist who defies normative standards of "beauty" by crafting an alternate model of femininity that is predicated on her own deformity. This new "feminine" ideal is then ironically superseded by a male character who more successfully embodies this combination of the sublime and the grotesque. Finally, in Kurahashi Yumiko's "Snake" (Hebi, 1960) we encounter a text that combines conventionally masculine and feminine characteristics in ways that frustrate any attempt to understand sexual difference through reference to a binary model of gender. In each story, the feminization of male bodies serves as a vehicle for the subversion of both feminine and masculine norms, further destabilizing conventional linkages between sex and gender.

"Toddler-Hunting"

Akiko, the protagonist of "Toddler-Hunting," is a self-supporting single woman with a fondness for little boys that goes well beyond what one might consider to be "normal" maternal instincts. Although motherhood was still very much the standard by which feminine maturity was judged when this story was written—with the image of women as "naturally" wives and mothers still definitive of "proper" expressions of feminine subjectivity—Akiko is childless and infertile and seems quite content to stay that way. Nevertheless, she is inexplicably drawn to little boys between the ages of three and ten, yet thoroughly repulsed by little girls of the same age.

Akiko's hatred for little girls is explicitly linked to her own unpleasant experiences of maturing into womanhood, evoking the abjection of femininity discussed in the previous chapter. In the very first pages of the story, we learn that the feelings of constriction Akiko herself felt in the process of developing into sexual maturity are displaced onto other little girls once she has passed this stage:

> Akiko could not bear to remember that she herself had once been a little girl.
>
> But in fact her childhood had been happier than other periods of her life. She couldn't recall a single hardship; she might have been the most fortunate child who ever lived, a cheerful thing when she was young. But beneath the sunny disposition, in the pit of her stomach, she'd been conscious of an inexplicable constriction. Something loathsome and repellent oppressed all her senses—it was as if she were trapped in a long, narrow tunnel; as if a sticky liquid seeped unseen out of her every pore—as if she were under a curse.
>
> Once, in science class, they'd had a lesson about silkworms, and with a scalpel the teacher had sliced open a cocoon. Akiko took one look at the faintly squirming pupa—a filthy dark thing, slowly binding itself up in thread issuing from its own body— and knew she was seeing the embodiment of the feelings that afflicted her.

And then for some reason Akiko became convinced that other girls her age shared her strange inner discomfort. Grownups, however, did not feel this way, and neither did little boys and older girls.

And sure enough, once she got past ten, the queasiness left her. As if she had stepped out of a tunnel into the vast free universe finally she could breathe. It was at this time, however, that she started to feel nauseated by any girl still passing through that stage, and her repulsion grew stronger as the years went by.[2]

These descriptions of Akiko's girlhood suggest that the sources of constriction she experienced derive simultaneously from both within and without. The girl-pupa is unquestionably surrounded by a cocoon-like shell that both protects and confines her during this critical period of development. Yet this protective enclosure is seen on some level as of her own making; the "threads" that form the prison are produced directly from her own body, an eloquent analogy to the way gender is internalized and produced through performance by the subject in question as much as it is enforced from without by societal forces.

It is interesting to compare this narrative of becoming-woman with that of Kurahashi Yumiko's protagonist in *Blue Journey*, discussed in chapter 1. In Kurahashi's text, the moment of initiation into puberty seems characterized as a kind of fall from grace, when the protagonist is first confronted with the "truth" of womanhood and wishes she could go back to the idyllic ignorance of childhood. Akiko, on the other hand, isolates an even earlier period of development as the source of discomfort. For her, the prepubescent years of three to ten are described as far more oppressive than the "freedom" that ironically coincides with a girl's first menstruation. The issue here seems to be not merely the process of biological maturity, but also the way a young girl's body is sculpted as feminine even before her menarche in preparation for that transition into womanhood: "The more typical a girl this age, the less Akiko could bear to be near her. The pallid complexion; the rubbery flesh; the bluish shadow at the nape of the neck left by the bobbed haircut; the unnaturally high, insipid way the girl would talk; even the cut and color of her clothes: Akiko saw in all this the filthy closeness she had glimpsed in the pupa" (46). The traits that are listed as most disagreeably feminine here evoke not merely a sense of an unfinished or immature physical form, but also the way the body in question is packaged, through grooming and sartorial regimens considered appropriate to a girl of this age. Even the child's "pallid complexion" and "rubbery flesh" seem to signify not merely immaturity, but rather a body that has been deliberately kept at a state of arrested development through overprotection or confinement indoors—that is, in the dark cocoon of the previous passage. It is perhaps not surprising then that to Akiko, this period of becoming may have been more arduous than the entrance into puberty that followed it; having struggled as a girl to internalize the self-disciplinary mechanisms expected of a proper young woman, she may well have seen the biological change known as menstruation as a fait accompli.

Little boys, on the other hand, are desirable to Akiko because they represent freedom from such restrictive confinement. Several scenes in the text depict Akiko's interaction with boys of the "target age" of three to ten, and in each case the child in question is charming precisely because he represents the possibility of active subjectivity that in Akiko's mind is denied to girls.

> She could just see a little boy, about four years old, pulling on this cozy, lightweight shirt, his sunburned head popping up through the neck. When the time came, he would definitely want to take it off all by himself. Crossing his chubby arms over his chest, concentrating with all his might, he would just manage to grasp the shirttails. But how difficult to pull it up and extricate himself. Screwing up his face, twisting around and wiggling his little bottom, he would try his hardest. Akiko would glimpse his tight little belly, full to bursting with all the food he stuffed in at every meal. (48)

The overwhelming use of active verbs—"wiggling," "twisting," "grasping"—signifies a degree of self-expression and aggressive conduct that contrasts noticeably with the depiction above of the "filthy closeness" that is said to confine young girls. This robustness is fueled by a voracious appetite, implied by the boy's full stomach, and it seems directly opposite to the situation of the girl-pupa, whose body seems on the verge of leaking away as it continually produces the threads of its own constriction. Note also that the boy is "sunburned," apparently through vigorous outdoor activity, whereas the world of little girls is dark, tunnel-like, and confining. If this is Akiko's perception of gender difference, then it is no wonder that she has a preference for little boys to match her aversion to little girls— they allow her to fantasize a possibility of transcendence of the restrictive subject position to which she has been assigned by virtue of her inhabitation of a female body that has forcibly been rendered feminine.

Akiko's attraction to male children is thus not due to any unfulfilled maternal instinct—which she claims not to have—but rather to a perception of masculine subjectivity as offering an alternative to the confinement of the gendered expectations placed upon women. On her inability to bear children, we are informed that even before Akiko learned that she was sterile, she balked at the notion of being tied down by the "long commitment" required of women who rear children:

> When she'd been younger, Akiko had been amazed by her body—by its strangeness. Every month, over and over, it made a little bed inside for a baby, unaware that none would be born, and then took it apart again. And it had seemed to her a grave matter that not one person on this earth was created yet out of her own blood.
>
> But she would always find herself wondering how, after giving birth to the baby, she could get someone else to take care of it— and whether there wasn't some way she could reserve the right to only occasionally oversee its care. She began to greatly envy men, who could avoid parental tasks so easily. All this surely proved how poorly she was endowed with natural maternal urges. (58)

A man's absence from the home and site of child rearing would have been considered socially acceptable at this time—even expected, given the gendered division of labor that was normative in Japan circa 1961, whereby men were assumed to work outside the home and support their families while women took sole responsibility for domestic labor. Akiko is keenly aware that her desire to evade the feminine side of this gender binary and adopt a masculine subject position renders her abnormal by the standards of common sense operative at this time. It is interesting that Kōno's protagonist never explicitly questions the naturalness of such maternal desire or the way it is defined as total absorption in the care of one's children to the exclusion of all else. However, the narrative itself places this "naturalness" under scrutiny by presenting us with an obvious counterexample—a character who not only is unable and unwilling to have children, but whose sexual proclivities in fact shock the reader by confronting him or her with an antithesis to the stereotype of the nurturing and loving mother.

In addition to enjoying sadomasochistic sexual play with her partner, Sasaki, Akiko experiences a recurring fantasy in which the beating and whipping she begs from her lover is instead administered to a young boy of precisely the "target age" that fascinates her so. While it is clear that the violent treatment is actually performed by a man, it is equally clear that the female witness to the beatings, a stand-in for Akiko herself, directs and orchestrates the performance. The text is quite graphic in its description of Akiko's fantasy, particularly with respect to the following two moments of interest for this discussion:

> *More punishment. With every lash of the cane, there are shrieks and agonized cries. The boy is sent sprawling forward, sometimes flat on his face, but he struggles to get up each time, ready to receive the next stroke, a course of action he carries out without being told.*
> *—Look. Look at the blood. The woman's voice again. There it is, the red fluid trickling down over the child's buttocks, over his thighs. The blood is smeared over the surface of his flesh by yet more thrashes of the cane.* (60)

> *—You haven't touched his stomach. The woman's voice again, insinuating. The child gets a few lashes on his belly, and suddenly, his stomach splits open. Intestines, an exquisitely colored rope of violet, slither out.* (61; italics in translation)

As Gretchen Jones has noted in her insightful study of sadomasochistic themes in Kōno's work, the little boy is twice feminized in his encounter with the punitive father figure—first when the blood runs down his buttocks and thighs, as if to evoke menstruation, and again when his stomach bursts open, which is reminiscent of childbirth. Jones further notes that "Akiko identifies with the little boy not only as a male, but, as the menstrual and birth scene overlays suggest, the boy's biology too is also reversed at times, allowing Akiko to identify with the boy as female. In a manner similar to the way in which a woman's body boundaries are frequently crossed or violated, in the fantasy, the boy's body becomes a site of transgression, of opening up—of blood, even of birth."[3] Thus, feminine characteristics are in effect inscribed upon the body of the boy, in a kind of hysterical parody of the gendering process to which young girls are subjected.

As noted above with respect to the girl-pupa image, the transformation into womanhood is depicted in this text as a product of two mutually imbricated processes—a combination of biological development and social training that genders a young girl as feminine. The goal of this process of socializing girls is to prepare them not just for the biological events of menstruation and (later) pregnancy, but also for the ways in which these biological processes will be contained and structured by society in order to craft them into future wives and mothers. Girls are therefore instilled with behaviors that will facilitate this social use of their bodies—obedience, docility, dependence, self-ingratiation—and learn to replicate them "voluntarily" through mechanisms of self-discipline. For Akiko, boys represent the absence of this exhortation to subsume oneself to the demands of society. Throughout this story they are portrayed as vigorous, active, expressive, petulant—and this behavior is accepted and considered normal.[4] Yet the little boy in Akiko's fantasy is not only corporeally but also behaviorally inscribed with signifiers of femininity—he docilely accepts the punishment meted out to him by his "father," not once but repeatedly, as he continues to rise after being knocked down to accept blow after blow. As a result of this process of (self-)discipline, his body faithfully replicates the physiological signifiers of femininity—menstruation and pregnancy—that are expected of appropriately feminine subjects.

Thus, in "Toddler-Hunting" we are presented with a highly conflicted narrative that upholds masculinity as a means of escape from restrictive feminine models, even as it perversely reinscribes this body with the very qualities it wishes to transcend. As noted above, though Kōno presents her protagonist as ostensibly unaware of the contradiction inherent in accepting maternal instincts as natural to women, the narrative clearly highlights this disjunction for the benefit of the reader. Though Akiko may perceive herself as abnormal for possessing desires that place her beyond the pale of normative femininity, the reader, through her narrative alignment with the protagonist, is encouraged to wonder about the naturalness of this standard. Likewise, the author pointedly presents us with an irresolvable contradiction in presenting masculinity, in the form of the little boy in Akiko's fantasy, as a transcendent state, on the one hand, while violently re-engendering this same character as feminine—an obvious parody of the process of gender production that highlights its artificiality.

Both Akiko and the boy in her fantasy, then, can be considered to be "odd bodies" in the sense that they defy normative models of femininity and masculinity respectively. That a woman can not only be diagnosed as infertile but revel in this status, and furthermore harbor violent thoughts against small children, is odd by the standards of normative femininity that define women as naturally maternal. That a male can be made to menstruate and give birth, through violent subjection to feminine disciplinary mechanisms that render him complicit in his own subordination is likewise odd by the standards of normative masculinity that define males as aggressive, inviolate, and penetrative (rather than penetrated). Though these narrative disjunctions go untheorized by the protagonist herself, they force the reader to question the "naturalness" of the logic of "sexual indifference" that underwrites such distinctions.

"Secret"

The protagonist of "Secret," Asako, has a large birthmark that covers the length of her back and upper arms, and she learns to hide it from the censorious eyes of society. The reactions of other people to Asako's "deformity" profoundly shape her self-image in an emphatically negative way; the boys across the street stare at her, a gang of boys at school bullies her, and another neighborhood child quotes her mother as declaring that Asako will never be able to marry because of it. She is very self-conscious about this defect until she meets a much older man with a penchant for oddities who helps her to see this abnormality as attractive rather than hideous.

While on the one hand the man's attraction to Asako helps to liberate her from her self-described misanthropy—the result of years of being made to feel ugly and deformed—her self-image becomes inordinately dependent on his approval, and she is able to feel confident about herself only to the extent that he validates this self-image. Excluded from the category of "appropriate" femininity—defined as inhabitation of a body that is conventionally desirable to members of the opposite sex and thus marriageable—Asako is to some extent able to craft an alternative femininity for herself that is attractive within a certain limited sphere, that of men with unconventional tastes in women. On the other hand, her dependence on the man's validation leads her to adopt a masochistic position that allows him to use her in rather degrading ways—along with possibly a large assortment of other "odd" women—and she learns to subordinate her own pleasure to his.

This text obviously echoes some of the corporeal dynamics we have seen in previous chapters. First of all, the role of the disciplinary gaze in structuring feminine subjectivity, noted in chapter 2, is clear in the way Asako is trained to see her body as freakish and shameful. She first learns that there is something wrong with her physical form in sixth grade, when the lady next door comes to inform Asako's father that her sons are inordinately interested in watching Asako from their upstairs window: "[Until that time,] Asako had wandered about outside in a thin chemise, frequently looking up with a puzzled feeling at the two junior high school boys staring down at her from the second-floor window."[5] It is interesting that the boys' desire to gaze at her body is apparently not questioned or identified as a behavior that must be sanctioned. Rather, the offense is Asako's, and she is therefore the one singled out for discipline, both because she is baring too much skin at an age when her body is beginning to develop and because the body in question fails to conform to the type that is most pleasing to the masculine gaze.

As a result of the negative reactions of those around her to her birthmark, Asako comes to disavow her own body (as discussed in chapter 3) by developing patterns of behavior that conceal the offending deformity from the disapproving gaze of others. It is therefore no coincidence that as the story begins, we are introduced to Asako as she is shopping for a blouse with sleeves long enough to hide her affliction. When accosted by a saleslady who insists that sleeveless tops are "in" this year and that a young lady should wear something more fashionable, she rebuffs the woman with a firmness that conceals the sadness within (63). She then catches sight of a mannequin wearing this summer's approved costume, and regarding the feminine perfection that this anything-but-natural figure represents, she again experiences a sadness concealed within an outward posture of strength (64). To add insult to injury, this icon of femininity is rendered in Western form, further emphasizing that this standard of beauty is thoroughly unattainable for her. At this point in the text, Asako's feeling of pathos is intimately linked with a sense of being alone in her "abnormality"—that is, in spite of the unrealistic standards of attractiveness to which women are trained to aspire, she believes that she is alone in failing to achieve the anointed status of "beautiful" because of her deformity. Asako therefore feels isolated not only because her body is unlovable to men, but also because she is set apart from other women by her difference—a feeling that is instilled by the reactions of those around her and perpetuated by her own insecurities.

This feeling of isolation is immediately undercut by a narrative flashback to a high school field trip, when Asako first encountered another girl who was likewise "deformed." Reluctant to bathe with her schoolmates for fear of their reaction to her birthmark, Asako sneaks into an empty bathroom in another part of the inn where her class is staying. Just as she settles herself into the tub and begins to relax, she hears the door to the changing area open. She is horrified when the interloper reveals herself to be another girl from her school, but then she is fascinated to notice that one of the girl's breasts is dramatically larger than the other. Their eyes meet briefly, and the girl quickly moves to cover herself by entering the tub with her back to Asako: "The girl, showing her back to Asako, and Asako, hiding her back from the girl, both sat in the tub facing the same direction, each observing the movements of the other. When Asako realized that she would definitely not turn around, she silently raised her body from under cover of the water and escaped by backing out through the door" (65). Asako is thus able to sneak away without having her birthmark noticed by the girl.

As she slips into the changing room, Asako notices her reflection in the full-length mirror and turns her back toward it in order to scrutinize her "deformity." She dresses and moves to leave, thinking about the girl in the next room who suffers from the same sense of sadness as herself: "In front of the mirror was a wet mark in the shape of Asako's foot. She had stood there with her back turned and her body twisted around, so the footprint was at a diagonal. She imagined the girl getting out of the bath and standing in the same place. She would probably face forward to gaze at her chest, so that would result in her leaving a wet footprint that intersected crosswise with Asako's. Asako thought vaguely about the sadness of those two footprints" (65). It is remarkable that although Asako clearly senses a similarity between herself and the girl, this does not seem to yield a sense of solidarity by virtue of their shared affliction. Rather, the crossed footprints, one girl facing forward and the other facing the opposite direction, echo the scene in the bath when each girl is so concerned with hiding her own abnormality that she avoids the gaze of the other. Neither has the courage to reach out to the other and attempt a connection, in spite of the fact that they share the same pain. Both girls have apparently learned to privilege self-protection above all else as a means of coping with the disciplinary gaze of society. Furthermore, the protagonist has clearly internalized the gaze to the point that she uses it against other women whose bodies are similarly non-normative; knowing that the girl will not turn around as long as she fears Asako's gaze, Asako uses this knowledge as a means of protecting her own secret from discovery.

Asako consequently learns to disavow her own corporeality, at least until she discovers, thanks to her older and rather unconventional lover, that this "odd body" itself presents her with an alternative to normative femininity. However, this alternative fails to offer Asako complete liberation from convention; it is at best a variation on the same gendered binaries that render women subordinate and passive objects of the masculine gaze. This much is clear during the episode that ostensibly signifies Asako's conquest over her self-consciousness about her birthmark.

In this scene, she visits her lover one day to find him conversing with a friend. This young man invites both Asako and her lover to attend one of his upcoming performances—an interpretive dance entitled "Androgyny"—where he will apparently perform in the nude. Asako's lover challenges her by asking if she would have the courage to reveal her own body in such a public way, and both men encourage her to take off her clothes. Asako speculates that her boyfriend might enjoy the "immorality" of "exposing the naked body of his own woman to another man." The young man, noticing a bronze cross lying on the table, further suggests that she arrange her body in that position.

> The room was filled with silence. Asako could feel on her skin that the man and the dancer were waiting. The mass of hesitation inside her unfolded layer by layer as Asako, basking in the gaze of the two men, removed layer after layer of her clothing.
>
> "It's not really a body worth showing to you. I have a really large birthmark," Asako said as she stood completely naked, held out her arms, and turned around once. Strangely, there was no trace of hesitation left. (74–75)

This scene could be read as a kind of liberation in the sense that Asako seems no longer paralyzed by shame at her own body. However, there is also a rather blatant undercurrent of masochism underlying Asako's willingness to expose herself as an object of visual gratification before the men. Her subordinate status is underscored by the fact that as she stands there, in the position of Christ on the cross, the men quickly lose interest in her and become absorbed in a totally unrelated conversation. She waits in that position, patiently, for them to take notice of her again, and they do so only when the young man realizes that the holes drilled into either end of the bronze cross are perfectly positioned at the same interval as her breasts. He has her hold the cross in front of herself as he pulls her nipples through the holes in the metal, which is sharp enough to cut her flesh, and she begins to bleed: "At this unexpected result, the men looked at her with a sublime glint in their eyes, but their expressions gradually returned to normal....Asako herself was moved by the phenomenon that her body displayed. But she was silent because she felt that if she were to raise her voice, it would destroy the pleasure of the men....She sensed that she was being enjoyed [by the men] as an object. Objects must remain silent. Asako rather enjoyed the fact that the men demanded this" (75–76). Asako has clearly submitted herself entirely to the desires of her male audience—by allowing them to manipulate her body as they please, by remaining passive and silent before their gaze, and by subordinating her own impulses and desires to theirs.

In addition to yielding to her lover's demands to subordinate herself to his gaze, Asako also clearly internalizes this gaze to the point of wielding it not only against herself, but against other women as well. Asako has long suspected that the man is having relationships with other "odd" women besides herself, yet rather than feeling jealous, she derives a kind of pleasure in imagining these other women and the types of deformities they have that might titillate him. She begins to scrutinize the crowds that cross her path each day in search of women like herself whose bodies harbor such secrets, and when she finds them, she subjects them to various fantasies of the ways "a man" (such as her lover) might take pleasure in their oddness. Adopting the point of view of her lover and identifying with his pleasures and proclivities, she even imagines her own type of "deformity" as projected upon these other women:

> Asako realized suddenly that she was searching for women with the eyes of a man. Looking at women with those special eyeglasses that the man had loaned her, she was now aware of previously unseen vistas. Walking alone through the streets where she passed innumerable women, Asako little by little became enthralled by visions of birthmarks. A birthmark in the shape of a butterfly in the middle of a woman's chest, its wings extending left and right onto each breast, fluttering whenever those breasts jiggled. Or if it's in the shape of a butterfly, one that extends left and right from the woman's crotch, so that you couldn't see it unless she opened her legs—that would be good....Asako walked along enchanted by the dark visions produced by the birthmark fantasy. She thought of such birthmarks underneath her own clothes and underneath the clothes of the women she passed by, and enjoying herself in this way, she felt as if the spring heat of the streets exuded the hidden pleasures of women. (72–73)

As with the crucifixion scene above, here the power dynamics governing the relationship between subject and object of the gaze are exceedingly complex. On one level, Asako is clearly objectifying these women, just as her lover and his friend have done to her, on the basis of the same standard of value—the eroticism of "oddness"—that they employ to judge her attractiveness. The passage even specifies "the man" as the authority who determines such criteria of desirability, and therefore Asako is merely "borrowing" his way of looking at women to achieve the same purpose. On the other hand, not only does Asako seem to take pleasure in this form of erotic ventriloquism, but also the knowledge that other women may harbor the same sort of "secret" as she does helps her to conquer her feelings of isolation. In a sense it is liberating for her to know that there may be many women like her who defy standards of normative femininity and are loved for it.

One might even construe this knowledge as a nascent sense of connection between Asako and these other women—except for the fact that as in the bath scene, any similarity she observes between herself and these other women remains tightly contained within her own mind. That is to say, it does not translate into friendships or support structures based on relationships among women who perceive themselves to have something in common. This is underscored in a scene in which Asako pursues a fellow "oddity" down the street, absorbed in fantasies about how a man might find the difference in length and size of the woman's legs to be erotically stimulating. Though her mind is abuzz with titillating visions throughout the "encounter," she never actually makes contact with the woman. Content with a single glance at the anonymous woman's face, Asako is satisfied and moves on, as if the woman merely provided an expedient vehicle or screen for the projection of her (lover's) desires.

What these women represent for Asako, more than anything, is a fantasized alternative to both the "properly" feminine physical form and to the kinds of pleasures and desires that are sanctioned within the conventional society that structures them. "Women with proper bodies probably experience proper forms of pleasure. Though in the past Asako had envied such pleasures, now she didn't care for them. Rather, she walked about searching for women with secrets hidden under their clothing" (72). While this attitude poses an obvious challenge to the oppressiveness of feminine training and gender role restrictions, it is important to remember that this alternative expression of femininity is itself still subordinated to the desires and pleasures of men and derives its legitimacy from the fact that (some unusual) men find it attractive.

The variant construction of femininity embodied by Asako and these other women is distinguished within the text itself from androgyny, which is defined as a state of being "both man and woman, neither man nor woman" and is clearly privileged as a superior form of transcendence of gender norms (81). It is furthermore implied in the conclusion of the story that only men, not women, are capable of attaining this privileged state. Women, by implication, are thus irrevocably bound by the limitations of a feminine gender identity that is grounded in their physical form, and even unorthodox versions of this feminine subjectivity are presumed to be inferior to the type of gender bending of which men are capable.

The androgynous ideal that is privileged by the text, and conveyed through the authoritative judgment of Asako's lover, is represented not by Asako but by his friend, the young male dancer whose triumphant transgression of gender brings the story to its climax and conclusion. As the final scene begins, Asako is on her way to meet her lover at the theater where the young man's performance is to take place when she discovers that she has started her period. She is supposed to spend that night at her lover's place, and remembering this, she sets off on a frustrating quest for a piece of vinyl sheeting. It is implied that capitalizing on his pleasure in the perverse, she intends to use this to display her menstrual blood for her lover in much the same way as she was able to titillate him with the blood from her nipples during the crucifixion incident. As in that previous scene, it is clear here too that Asako derives pleasure from displaying her body for her lover, reveling in his enjoyment of her as a perversely erotic "object."

At several points during this final episode, Asako's desire to objectify herself through erotic performance for her lover is contrasted with the onstage spectacle of the androgynous male dancer in ways that make the superiority of the latter type of performance abundantly clear. This linkage is first suggested when Asako notices the lurid color of the tickets for the recital: "The tickets were printed with red lettering like the color of fresh blood, against a gray background. There was also a photograph of the dancer, but it too was the same color of red. That color made Asako remember the blood that dripped from her nipples the other day, as well as the blood of her menstrual cycle" (77). This is also the moment when she remembers that she will stay the night with her lover and sets off on the quest for the vinyl sheeting; the connection is further underscored by the blood red costume worn by the dancer onstage. The young man has painted his body white and draped himself in a loose and flowing red cloth that does not conceal his nakedness underneath.

When Asako catches sight of the beautiful youth in full display, it excites fantasies within her of the possible effects on the dancer if a similarly scantily clad young woman should emerge as his partner. It is as if she is rehearsing in her mind the entertainment that she and her lover will enjoy that evening and anticipating the reaction that her performance might have on him. This impression is further underscored when the man seems to guess her intentions:

Asako then felt shame echo noisily throughout her body. It was because the man had articulated what she had only faintly sensed. Losing her composure, she glanced at the stage, and the red cloth that the dancer was waving about took on the color of blood and covered Asako's field of vision.

The red cloth danced above his head and seemed to separate from his hands and float in the air. Looking up at it, he seemed for a moment to thirst for blood and then in that moment melted into a frenzied dance, the red of the cloth and the white of his body delicately intertwined. Asako thought of a piece of vinyl sheeting painted with blood and thought that it had been prepared for her own pleasure tonight. She put her hand into her raincoat pocket and made sure the small folded piece of vinyl was still there. Then, as she stared at the dancer on the stage, who had converted the thing she had sought so insistently into a red cloth and was waving it about in a frenzy, she felt suffocated by feelings of oppression.

"It's all right." Asako heard the man's voice as if it emanated from some place far away.

"What is?" she responded vaguely.

"He wouldn't respond even if there were a woman there," the man said as if joking. Those words entered Asako's body like a foreign object. Stunned, she looked at the man and then looked at the dancer on stage. (80–81)

Asako then experiences a vision of the dancer flying higher and higher through the air, parting the layers of clouds stained red by the evening sun, "as if his life were nothing but the beauty of flight" (81). This vision of transcendence prompts her to remember her lover's claim that the most sensual type of beauty is "neither male nor female, both male and female" and that only men can convincingly pull off this sort of "self-intoxicated" performance (79). In the final lines of the story, as the dance comes to an end, Asako experiences a sensation of sinking down into the depths of herself, looking up at the heavens into which the dancer has ascended.

In the beginning of this final sequence, Asako at first seems embarrassed about having her secret fantasy discovered. But this embarrassment quickly turns to dismay and even oppression as she realizes that the dancer has not only stolen her idea—at this point she has to check and make sure the vinyl sheeting is still there—but has managed to turn it into a form of performance that is even more pleasing to her lover. While Asako had thought to excite her lover through the perverse display of her own menstrual blood, the dancer has transformed this crude literal interpretation of the man's desires into a highly aestheticized and artistic representation. Furthermore, he manages to achieve through this performance what Asako cannot—a beautiful and harmonious blending of masculine and feminine, symbolized by the white of his body as it mingles effortlessly with the red of the costume.[6]

In fact, there is no place at all for Asako in her lover's fantasy of androgynous perfection, as she discovers to her horror when her lover reveals the young dancer's "secret." Asako has fundamentally misunderstood the process by which this transcendence is achieved, according to the man. While in the beginning of the sequence she envisions a man and a woman in a dance that elevates both of them onto a plane of ecstasy, she learns to her dismay that women are in fact irrelevant to this process. Transcendence, as defined by the climax of this story, is embodied in a single "male" character that beautifully fuses both masculine and feminine in a purely self-contained performance of androgyny—what her lover refers to as a state of "self-intoxication" that requires no outside assistance. Asako, who has attempted to escape normative femininity by producing an alternative subjectivity that nevertheless depends on male validation, discovers in the end that her new persona is insufficient to this task.

As in "Toddler-Hunting," internal contradictions in Takahashi's text likewise create a space for criticism of the sexual politics espoused by its characters. Though Asako is clearly willing to subordinate herself to her lover's somewhat sadistic desires in exchange for the validation that promises to "liberate" her from normative femininity, the narrative makes clear that this strategy offers merely a false vision of transcendence. As in Kōno's story, much of the criticism of gender norms is inherent in the description of the process of engendering as a form of "discipline" that limits and constricts the protagonist. In Asako's case, the negative reaction of members of her community to her physical "deformity" is directly cited as the reason for her low self-esteem and consequent willingness to so debase herself before her boyfriend and other men. Takahashi's story, like Kōno's, therefore underscores the mutual imbrication of corporeality and society in creating and producing such restrictive models of gender—while the "oddness" of Asako's body is ostensibly the reason for such treatment, the birthmark itself has no significance outside of the meanings ascribed to it ("unattractive" equals unmarriageable), and these are determined by gendered norms.

In "Secret," Takahashi has therefore crafted a protagonist whose "odd body" renders her incapable of conforming to conventional standards of feminine beauty. Yet as Irigaray's "law of the same" would suggest, she is still held to this feminine standard since by virtue of being not-male she must represent everything the not-male side of the gender binary represents. In the course of her narrative, Takahashi exposes the way normative concepts of feminine beauty render women dependent on the approving gaze of the Other, thereby constructing feminine subjectivity as opposite and complementary to an autonomous masculine subjectivity that is indifferent to the responses of others. This is represented within the story by a second "odd body," that of the young male dancer whose triumphant performance brings the story to its conclusion. Disciplinary regimes of beauty therefore conflate the terms "female" and "feminine," "body" and "gender," defining both as not-male according to a logic of sexual indifference that allows men to rhetorically transcend all of the above in favor of an autonomous existence.

But even as she highlights the oppressiveness of this logic of sexual indifference, Takahashi narratively undermines it by presenting the "transcendent" vessel of masculine superiority as corporeally and sexually ambiguous. As in Kōno's story, we are met with two "odd bodies," one male and one female, and in this case too the male body is privileged as the site of transcendence of gender norms, even as it is inscribed with signifiers of femininity that yield an eerily androgynous form. If the goal of androgyny is the harmonious combination of both masculine and feminine qualities, then why should male bodies alone be characterized as privileged sites of transcendence? By underscoring the hypocrisy of this illogical set of standards, Takahashi's narrative performs a powerful critique of the gendered discourses that render women inferior.

It is also striking that in both stories, menstrual blood serves as a prime signifier of femininity, even as it is ironically attributed to male bodies. In Kōno's story it is produced through physical violence, albeit only in the fantasies of the protagonist. In Takahashi's story it is transformed from (fantasized) literal display to aestheticized performance in the form of the red gown worn by the dancer. But in each case, the ascription of such a quintessentially "feminine" physiological phenomenon to a male body radically destabilizes conventional distinctions not only between "masculine" and "feminine" (that is, binary gender), but also between the sexed bodies that are said to ground such distinctions. We will see much the same process at work in the next story, wherein not only menstruation but also pregnancy is parodically attributed to male bodies in ways that thoroughly subvert gendered binaries on multiple levels at once.

"Snake"

Kurahashi Yumiko's "Snake" is an absurdist farce that begins with a male university student, K, waking from a nap to find a giant pink snake attempting to enter his body through his open mouth. The snake takes up residence inside K's belly, and the story centers on the reactions of various sectors of society as they try to find some way to account for this bizarre incident according to their own prejudices and presumptions of "normalcy." While on one level this story can be read as a thoroughly irreverent portrayal of the ANPO-era political landscape[7]—Diet politicians, student activists, university administrators, academics, members of the medical establishment, and business moguls are only some of the authorities that come under fire in this text—there is also a distinctively gender-bending subtext. This particular narrative produces an "anti-world" that consistently blurs the boundary between sex and gender by reassigning or subverting many of the "commonsense" distinctions between male/masculine and female/feminine subject positions.[8]

The protagonist, K, is napping in his dorm room when he awakes to an uncomfortable sensation and discovers the snake in the process of inching its way down his throat. By the time his friends notice the problem, it is too late and they are unable to remove the snake, which lodges itself inside his digestive tract. Fellow dormitory residents, led by a student activist, S, who has recently been released from police custody, insist on viewing the invasion by snake as part of an evil plot by the "powers that be." Though S and other dormitory residents clearly witness K in the process of "swallowing" the snake, they need to find some way of presenting K as the victim of government oppression in order to be able to use this episode to "mobilize the masses." They spread the word that K has in fact *been swallowed* by the snake because the alternative cannot be theorized and fails to yield a viable strategy for revolution. When K attempts to argue the facts of the incident with S, he is accused of "false consciousness" for failing to see society as the agent of his victimization and for neglecting to recognize the revolutionary potential of his situation.[9]

Subsequently, Okusan, the housewife who employs K to tutor her children, notices his distended belly and worries that he might be pregnant. While at first K reasons that there should be no "scientific basis" for this theory about his condition, his certainty soon wavers and he begins to worry about the question of "legal responsibility" and whether or not he would be able to afford an abortion (88). He even refers to himself as pregnant later in this scene (90), and when it becomes clear that his "condition" has begun to interfere with his job, he is informed that his services are no longer needed. Apparently he has proved himself thus far to be more useful to the housewife as an unwitting sex toy than as a music teacher for the children. She has evidently been drugging him and taking advantage of him after each lesson, but this time the usual plan goes awry as the snake, whose head has lodged itself in his throat, consumes the "hormone" cocktail meant for K, and he is unable to perform because of the heavy weight in his stomach.

A visit to the hospital to determine the exact nature of K's condition results in further confusion, as none of the medical authorities seem able to determine how best to deal with the "foreign body," much less the question of whether or not K might be pregnant and what if anything can be done about that. The first doctor K sees is determined to gut him like a fish in order to remove the snake, until the nurse reminds him that there would be legal implications attendant upon performing surgery on a pregnant patient, should that turn out to be the case. The second doctor uses an X-ray-like machine to produce an image of the patient's condition, only to blur the boundary further between "foreign body" and host:

> "Don't move. I see. It's definitely a snake. However it seems there's still quite a bit of human remaining. . . . That means that the snake hasn't completely digested the human yet. Hm, it looks as though humans are difficult to digest."
>
> "What's happening? Certainly it seems that the snake hasn't dissolved completely. Sometimes it moves, so it's probably still alive," K started to say.
>
> "Of course," the doctor said in an irritated tone of voice. "The snake is still alive. What's strange is that there is any human left." (100)

In spite of the fact that K seems to all observers to be intact and functioning and by all scientific logic should be in the process of digesting the snake, the doctor's diagnosis "demonstrates" that it is in fact the other way around—K has been "assimilated" by the snake, which has irrevocably fused itself to his skeletal structure and is in the process of "digesting" him from within.

K's unfortunate condition further complicates his engagement to his fiancée, L, as she refuses to take "responsibility" for the fact that he might be pregnant, and both are concerned about the impact the snake incident may have on the process of negotiating the marriage contract. K is taken to the headquarters of a large corporation to talk to someone whom he assumes to be L's father, although L refuses to acknowledge a blood relationship and persists in calling him her employer. K's largest faux pas in the course of the discussion, however, turns out to have nothing to do with the snake—he insists on discussing his feelings for L, which both she and her "employer" consider irrelevant, and they cannot seem to make K understand that L is nothing but a "proxy" in the negotiations that should properly be conducted between K and the "boss" himself (102).

The snake in fact turns out to be useful to the discussion, serving as K's only collateral—though not a very stable form of capital, as the "employer" sympathetically explains (103). While K manages to conclude this stage of the negotiations successfully—with the snake in fact according him a kind of celebrity status due to the fact that it has attracted the attention of the authorities and earned K an invitation to testify before the Diet—it ultimately puts an end to his relationship with L when it eats her during the course of their lovemaking.

The story climaxes with K's visit to the Diet to testify, accompanied by his academic adviser, a very large, hairy, and pregnant man known as Professor Q. They travel to the legislative assembly via a long, snake-like pneumatic tube that drops them into the mail room, whereby they are whisked into the main hall and K is immediately taken into custody. Various "experts" are called to give their opinions on K's condition and what, if anything, should be done about it. However, as each "expert" tends to approach the problem from a radically different set of presumptions and concerns, their testimonies diverge into an incoherent cacophony that produces no real conclusion. The legal scholars question the legitimacy of the proceedings themselves, the biologists stress the need to study K as an example of the future of human evolution, the sociologists are concerned about how they might craft a new set of policies to account for such an eventuality, and so on.

The proceedings are interrupted twice—once when the snake, which has not been fed since digesting L, swallows the microphone, forcing them to wait until the laxative K is given has produced the object (along with a shiny black piece of excrement). The second time, student activists storm the building, and the scene descends into a free-for-all. This seems to antagonize the hungry snake, which emerges from K's throat once again and frightens the assembly before consuming the protagonist and ending the narrative, a neat resolution to a messy problem that seems to satisfy everyone concerned.

It is tempting to read the invasion by snake as a metaphor for pregnancy; such a reading would imply that the male protagonist is subjected to a straightforward experience of gender role reversal. In some ways Kurahashi encourages this interpretation, portraying K as increasingly identifying with the "invader" to the extent that by the end of the story, he appears to be a nurturing and loving parent who is so concerned with the welfare of his "child" that he willingly allows the snake to feed on him. However, a clear distinction is drawn in the story between "male pregnancy"—which is taken for granted to be "normal" (that is, within the realm of possibility according to the laws of Kurahashi's alternate universe)—and the unusual experience of K as he is "penetrated" by the snake. Other male characters, such as Professor Q, are said to be pregnant or potentially pregnant, and this is not treated as aberrant in any way. Only K's body is invaded by a snake, and this invasion is depicted as so extraordinary that a special Diet session must be called to investigate it.

In fact, the snake image itself seems to signify different things at different points in the story and is portrayed alternately as embodying consumptive, excretory, sexual, and reproductive functions. The snake rises from K's throat whenever he becomes excited, as if to signify erection, and the description of it within the text as long, pink, and penetrative gives it a distinctly phallic character. On the other hand, several characters in the story make a point of noting that K is "penetrated" not genitally but orally, and the snake attaches itself primarily to K's digestive tract while consuming people and things in place of K. Toward the end of the story, though, when the snake swallows the microphone during the Diet session and is forced to expel it with the aid of laxatives, its function is clearly excretory, as its tail end protrudes from K's anus. And yet K's fascination with the shiny black ball of excrement it deposits alongside the microphone—he is so absorbed with it that he polishes it lovingly and to distraction, completely oblivious to the proceedings that will supposedly decide his fate—once again evokes an impression of a doting parent.

Obviously, then, the implications of K's relationship to the snake are more complex than a simple gender role reversal that "feminizes" a male protagonist by rendering him pregnant. In fact, "Snake" features a subversion of gender roles that does far more than merely reverse the masculine and feminine sides of a simple binary opposition; rather, it destabilizes the very foundation upon which such distinctions of gender or sex are predicated. Through the creation of a bizarre "anti-world" that nevertheless operates according to surprisingly familiar human dynamics,

Kurahashi deliberately subverts an array of gendered binaries—subject/object, active/passive, masculine/feminine, and even male/female—in ways that call into question the "logic" according to which women and men are seen as differentiated into opposite and complementary roles in contemporary Japanese society.

From the beginning of the story, the boundary between subject and object is rendered indeterminate by the question of K's relationship to the snake. In the opening pages of the story K clearly resists the snake's attempt to forcibly enter his body; however, the incident is so absurd and unexpected that those around him—even the roommates who witnessed the event—have trouble describing what actually occurred. The problem of whether K should be understood as an active agent or passive victim of this incident is openly discussed among the dormitory residents. While K consistently uses the active voice "I swallowed" to describe his role in ingesting the snake, his friends seem unable to accept this explanation and at first refer to him in the passive voice as having "been swallowed" *by* the snake. However politically expedient the friends' viewpoint might be as an explanation, it unfortunately fails to correspond to observed reality, so they eventually arrive at the conclusion that K has instead *become* a snake:

> "Oh, that was you, the one who became a snake yesterday?"
> "No, he's the one who was swallowed by the snake."
> "Same difference. Essentially, he *is* a snake." (94)

By positing the ontological unity of K and the snake, they are able to avoid the thorny problem of who swallowed whom and furthermore are able to characterize both K and the snake as being "sacrificed" to established authority structures. However, K objects to the use of this term to describe his situation:

> "Actually, I don't think of myself as a sacrifice. Since, after all, I swallowed the snake." However, his explanation was drowned out by the overwhelming power of S's voice.
> "No, he's not a sacrifice; he's a victim—the snake, I mean."
> "The snake?" K cried, confounded.
> "Right, the snake. K is a victim who was swallowed by the snake, and that makes it clear that he is essentially a snake. He *is* a snake, and therefore that means that we have to call the snake a victim." (106)

Through this simple mathematical substitution, S has apparently "logically" concluded that if K = victim and K = snake, then it must also be true that snake = victim. This not only rationalizes K's usefulness to the student movement, but also reduces what might pose a difficult philosophical problem of agency and heterogeneity to a matter of simple equivalency. If K and the snake can be considered to be one and the same, then both can be construed as "victims" of a near metaphysical system of authority without a need to grapple with the politically uncomfortable possibility that one might be seen as "victimized" by the other. Not surprisingly, the elegant simplicity of this explanation catches on, and other characters come to the same conclusion that K's uneasy coexistence with the snake within can be most expediently dealt with by assuming that he must "essentially" *be* a snake.

The tendency of the characters to paper over questions of agency is underscored by the fact that the invasion by snake can be envisioned only according to a binary choice between "swallowing" or "being swallowed." Either K has swallowed the snake or the snake has swallowed K; there apparently is no other logical alternative that can be understood by these characters. But since both terms prove inadequate to describe the complexity of the phenomenon in question, the subject/object dilemma is ultimately reduced to a metaphysically vague notion of "becoming." It is interesting that the causative-passive form, "was made to swallow," is never once used in this text to describe K's condition. By withholding this option, which would seem to blur the line between victim and oppressor relative to the neat passive/active binary of "swallow/be swallowed," Kurahashi highlights the tendency of her characters to subordinate the delicate indeterminacy of power dynamics in this "anti-world" to a false dichotomy-cum-unity. On an extradiegetic level, then, the narrative makes it clear to the reader that these binary simplicities are inadequate to describe K's condition, creating an implicit tension between narrative inside and outside that opens a space for critique of the characters' reductive logic.

In other words, the language employed by the characters throughout creates a set of binary options that oversimplify the "reality" of K's dilemma. The two possibilities offered by the text effectively mirror each other, such that one may be seen as the precise opposite of the other—K either "swallows" or "is swallowed" by the snake. Given that one alternative essentially defines the other through a relationship of pure opposition, one might say that "swallowing" and "being swallowed" are therefore two sides of the same coin—one cannot exist without the other and derives its identity from the necessary presence of the other, to the extent that they might even be reduced to the same basic process known as "swallow," which encompasses both subject and object. It is no wonder, then, that in Kurahashi's text the two entirely different entities of K and the snake are ultimately reduced to a simple mathematical unity (K = snake).

Luce Irigaray has traced the same process at work in Western philosophy with respect to our conceptualization of gender, and she attacks it as implying a "logic of the same" that reduces gender difference to a single model that cannot understand femininity without reference to masculinity. In other words, masculine subjectivity is taken as the norm against which femininity is defined and understood to represent all that masculinity is not. In her critique of Freud, and by extension the Western philosophy upon which his theories of sexuality rest, Irigaray writes as follows:

> Himself a prisoner of a certain economy of the logos, [Freud] defines sexual difference by giving *a priori* value to Sameness, shoring up his demonstration by falling back upon time-honored devices such as analogy, comparison, symmetry, dichotomous oppositions, and so on. Heir to an "ideology" that he does not call into question, Freud asserts that the "masculine" is the sexual model, that no representation of desire can fail to take it as the standard, can fail to submit to it. In so doing, Freud makes manifest the presuppositions of the scene of representation: *the sexual indifference* that subtends it ensures its coherence and its closure.[10]

By "sexual indifference," Irigaray implies that to the extent that we are dealing with a model of gender that envisions femininity merely as the antithesis of masculinity, we are able to envision only one gender rather than two: masculinity and non-masculinity, both of which take the male subject as their model and point of reference. Feminine difference is therefore subsumed beneath an "indifference" to femininity as a separate and distinct category.

Irigaray is frequently attacked by critics for forwarding an "essentialist" model of femininity that places unwarranted emphasis on women's "difference" from men. It is important to stress here, though, that positing women as "different" from men (in the sense meant by Irigaray) is not the same thing as characterizing women as opposite to men in every way. In fact, this misunderstanding of woman as man's opposite is clearly something that Irigaray wishes to correct. Rather than understand femininity through contrast with masculinity, she is effectively arguing that women should be understood on their own terms without reference to some sort of spurious conceptual opposite. In the sense that Irigaray wishes to discredit the binary model of masculine/feminine as opposing and mutually exclusive terms, her theory has much in common with Kurahashi's attempts to subvert any conception of gender as a stable and neatly bifurcated category.

In her pathbreaking dissertation on Kurahashi's narrative style, Atsuko Sakaki demonstrates that a subversion of binary models of gender was a conscious and deliberate part of the author's literary agenda. Sakaki sees the relationship between the "anti-world" of Kurahashi's literature and that of the "real" world as analogous to that between women and men in society in that while the former is subordinated to the latter, it also serves as a potent site of critique. She further quotes Kurahashi as follows:

> This world has the sign of sex. Just as we forget that the numbers we deal with in our daily life have a positive [plus] sign, so we forget the sexual sign, the male sign, which exists in this world. Women are shut in the world of the negative [minus] sign, or the Anti-world in the [actual] world, so to speak. In short, this [actual] world belongs to men. In it, women are regarded as nothing but those who have the other sex of female, as *opposed to* male. As Beauvoir points out, women belong to the category of "the Other."[11]

Thus by narrating the "anti-world," Kurahashi in effect envisions herself as giving voice to an alternate (feminine) logic that questions the legitimacy of subordinating women as man's "Other."

Kurahashi's project in "Snake" thus seems to be to force her audience to question binary models of gender by presenting the reader with an "anti-world" that subverts the reader's desire to make sense of the distinctions between male and female, masculine and feminine, as portrayed in the text—either through direct analogy with the "real" world or through relationships of clear contrast with what is familiar. In spite of the term that the author herself uses to describe her narrative universe, Kurahashi's "anti-world" does not seem to operate according to a logic that functions in direct opposition to that of mundane reality. In fact, it is striking how much her "anti-world" resembles what we know as "reality" in terms of the sociodynamics of the relationships among characters and the organizations that structure their lives. In fact, the dynamics of her "anti-world" seem less a contradiction of everything we know to be "true" than a hysterical mimicry of the "real world" that highlights its hypocrisies and logical fallacies.

Thus, the gender roles in Kurahashi's narrative universe are inflected by power dynamics that seem remarkably consistent across the "anti-world"/"reality" divide, even as the author deliberately frustrates our desire to understand the gender difference between her characters according to a coherent set of rules that either replicate or contradict conventional models of gender difference. She does so primarily by reinscribing traits characteristic of one sex or gender upon the other yet refusing to do so in a consistent or fully reciprocal fashion. In other words, men are "feminized" but not entirely so, while women embody some masculine traits yet preserve something of conventional femininity, yielding a dizzying array of possible gendered and sexed subject positions that refuse to conform to any predictable pattern.

Bodies are rendered sexually indeterminate particularly by ascribing ostensibly "feminine" bodily functions to men. For example, the young male pupil that K tutors is described as feeling listless because it is "that time of the month" for him (89). K routinely worries that he might become pregnant in scenes where he is sexually involved with a woman, and this concern is taken seriously by both the medical establishment and other characters within the text (91, 96). I use the expression "feminine bodily functions" advisedly because although the term "feminine" is conventionally used to refer to behavior rather than physical sexual differences, facile distinctions between gender and sex are refuted by Kurahashi's subversive narrative tactics. Although the bodies in Kurahashi's "anti-world" can apparently perform some functions conventionally attributed to the opposite sex, men are not exclusively "feminized" or women exclusively "masculinized" on the plane of either sex or gender. Men may become pregnant, but they still exhibit some physical and behavioral characteristics associated with "masculinity." Professor Q, for example, is pregnant yet described as a large man with a hairy chest who physically overpowers K during their first meeting (113) and conducts himself authoritatively in official situations, such as the Diet testimony scene.

Likewise, both women in the text, L and Okusan, are described as conventionally feminine in some ways, yet both serve as active agents in their sexual involvement with K, in contradiction to the "feminine" passivity expected of women in contemporary 1960s Japan. The housewife who employs K to tutor her menstruating son is sexually aggressive toward K and physically subdues him (with the help of a spiked cocktail) in order to take advantage of him, yet she is described as otherwise conducting herself in a deferential manner by serving him at dinner and adorning herself in a very feminine dress made of exquisitely thin material (89). L also treats K primarily as a sexual object; when they meet, she is so eager and forceful in her desire for sexual relations with him that she mostly ignores his attempts to make conversation. However, K is expected to take the lead in negotiating with her "boss" for her hand in marriage, and the fact that K is expected to produce evidence of financial solvency as the primary basis for legitimating the contract sounds very similar to what is conventionally expected of a young man attempting to establish his readiness for marriage to his fiancée's family.

In other words, "traditional" signifiers of masculinity and femininity are combined and subverted with wild abandon in this text to produce a narrative that not only troubles the distinctions between these gendered ideals, but furthermore radically destabilizes any attempt to link gendered behaviors with the sexed bodies to which they purportedly correspond. Male bodies are alternately feminized and re-masculinized, both through atypical sexual characteristics and behaviors, whereas female characters are likewise presented as both "feminine" and "masculine" at the same time. It is interesting that the author of "Snake" seems more intent upon disturbing commonsense notions of masculinity than femininity, if the amount of attention devoted within the text to male bodies and genders is any indication. Only two female characters receive any significant attention in this story, and L and Okusan are marginal entities in comparison with K and his comrades.

In fact, as noted in the discussion of the previous two stories, all of these authors seem particularly interested in depicting the male body as a site for troubling gender norms. This fascination with "queering" male bodies is intimately related to the ideological struggle that was taking place in Japanese society during the 1960s, when conventional models of femininity came increasingly into conflict not only with the forces of social and historical change, but also with an emerging second-wave feminist discourse that sought to destabilize the logic of sexual indifference that underwrote such binary models of gender.

While we have seen a variety of "odd bodies" in this chapter, it is striking to note the frequency with which *male* bodies are chosen to signify transgression of gender norms. The hyperbolic and violent feminization of the male child in Kōno's text dramatically underscores the artificiality of the process of engendering female bodies and problematizes "natural" linkages between sex and gender. Takahashi's text also troubles the sex/gender divide by presenting the reader with a male body that supposedly transcends gender entirely, even as his "male" body is inscribed with markers of feminine corporeality. In the process, Takahashi further critiques the hypocrisy of standards of beauty that render women dependent on male validation so that men may view themselves as having transcended gender altogether in favor of an autonomous subjectivity. Kurahashi goes even farther, frustrating any attempt to impose a logic of sexual indifference upon the constellation of bodies, genders, and sexualities that coexist within her literary "anti-world." But why this obsessive focus on male bodies?

The remarkable prevalence of this literary trope had much to do with the tension between conservative pressures on women to conform to a strictly gendered division of labor and legal and societal transformations that opened a space for transgression of conventional gender roles. The process of renegotiating feminine identity was already well under way in Japan during the 1960s, with women increasingly venturing into the public sphere in various capacities as students, workers, and political agents even as they continued to perform the "traditional" roles of wife and mother. On the other hand, masculine gender ideals remained stubbornly fixed around the model of salaried work, which contributed to the process of national rebuilding and reinvention of the corporate society known as "Japan, Inc."

While women's roles and identities were undergoing a rapid process of change as the result of the new opportunities that were just beginning to open to them, men were resistant to such changes not only because change would require them to accept new roles for women, but also because it would require corresponding alterations to male gender identity. The authors represented in this study seem to have sensed that redefining femininity would require a reinvention of masculine gender roles as well. If male subjectivity is the ground upon which conventional gender norms are based, as Irigaray and others have argued, then destabilizing the conceptual foundation of masculinity would offer the most effective challenge to the existing structure of gender roles. This seems to be precisely what these authors had in mind.

In this chapter, we have seen how these authors have attempted to problematize the binary logic that underlies the strict policing of gender norms. Having attacked the disciplinary mechanisms and the logic of normative gender that undergird relationships between women and men, these authors further turn their attention to relationships among women.

One common thread in the literature of these writers is a profound pessimism about the possibility of solidarity among women, and women in these texts tend to serve variously as figures of longing as well as fear or resentment. In the next chapter, we will explore the function of the body of the Other Woman as a trope for expressing this highly ambivalent attitude toward intimacy among women.

CHAPTER 5

The Body of the Other Woman

"When I first saw you on the street, I had this nostalgic feeling like I'd seen you somewhere before, or rather I had the impression that there was no one in my life more familiar than you. The person I feel closest to, the person I know better than anyone, for some reason that was how I felt about you. Who are you?"

—*Takahashi Takako, "Majiwari"*

In previous chapters, we have explored the ways Kōno, Takahashi, and Kurahashi used literature as a means of exposing, critiquing, and then subverting binary models of gender that sought to confine women within restrictive stereotypes of femininity. In chapter 4, we saw that this binary structure is problematic in part because it is predicated on a logic of "sexual indifference." In other words, this model of gender difference is able to conceptualize femininity only as masculinity's logical opposite so that women are assumed to embody only those qualities that men lack (or disavow as "unmasculine"). Aside from the psychological violence such a model inflicts on women, who must strive to excise those proclivities deemed unnatural for their sex, it also presumes a consistent and uniform set of characteristics that "naturally" define "woman." That is, it is predicated on the assumption that women everywhere are similar to one another while being radically different from men.

As we will see in this chapter, the authors addressed in this study took issue with this presumption, and many of their narratives work to highlight the differences *among* women as a counterweight to hegemonic discourses of gender that emphasized the differences *between* women and men. In light of their personal histories, this should not be surprising. We saw in chapter 1 that each of these authors' educational experiences and life trajectories set them well apart from the mainstream model of postwar wife and mother and that these experiences may be seen as motivating not only their attacks on normative discourses of femininity, but also their refusal to adopt an appropriately "feminine" style of writing. In short, they were exceptional women for their time who found it difficult to identify with women who complied with gender norms, yet they also found themselves to be outsiders vis-à-vis the male homosocial networks to which they sought entry.

In this chapter, we will discuss three works of fiction that explore the loneliness of such a position through narratives of female homoerotic desire that is fraught with conflict due to incommensurable differences among women. These authors seem highly ambivalent about the potential for true intimacy between women, even as their narratives express a clear desire for such closeness. The stories discussed in this chapter all employ the trope of the body of the Other Woman as a means of working through the problems and possibilities of relationships between women, embedded as they are in networks of power and disciplinary regimes that operate according to a patriarchal logic that divides women against one another and against themselves. The notion of a member of one's own sex as a kind of constitutive Other that is radically different from oneself serves as a direct challenge to discourses of gender that treat Woman as a singular and coherent ontological category.[1] These stories highlight the fact that the differences among women may be just as insurmountable as the differences between women and men, and in doing so, they fundamentally question the integrity of the category of "woman" itself as a coherent and unitary signifier.

It is important to keep in mind that due to the specific sociohistorical context for expressions of homoerotic desire in modern Japan, these narratives would not necessarily have been understood as "lesbian" in the sense of implying the expression of a specific type of sexual identity. In fact, these authors are commonly understood to have been "heterosexual," meaning that they are known only to have been erotically interested in men in their personal lives, and indeed the vast majority of their literary works are concerned primarily with heterosexual relationships.

In fact, in Japan during the time these women were growing up, passionate friendships between young girls were tolerated as more or less normal and did not indicate the expression of any sort of identity (sexual or otherwise) that would preclude future heterosexual attachments.[2] Both fictional and autobiographical writings by these women indicate that such homoerotic friendships were a familiar part of the landscape of their personal experience. Subsequently, the first decade following World War II witnessed an explosion of narratives that explored various sexual desires and activities, including female homoeroticism. As documented by Mark McLelland in his study of the "perverse press" at this time, readers were able to enjoy a wide variety of erotic pleasures in fictional form without identifying themselves as possessors of a specific "type" of sexuality.[3] It seems that it was not until the "women's lib" movement of the 1970s that awareness of "lesbianism" as a politicized sexual identity permeated mainstream Japanese consciousness.[4] The 1960s may therefore be seen as a time of flux, when in spite of increasingly conservative social mores, a variety of possible sexual behaviors and desires might still be imagined without necessarily identifying the subject of those fantasies as possessing a specific "type" of sexual identity.

In each of these texts, the protagonist and the Other Woman are bound together by a complex of emotions that blurs the distinction between desire and identification. Whether this is expressed through the protagonist's envisioning of the Other Woman as a surrogate or replacement, as a complement to oneself, or as a more perfect vision of the self that one might have been, the protagonist simultaneously sees herself in the Other Woman even as she desires her as an Other that is external to the self, and in no case is she successful in either possessing or internalizing her. The Other Woman therefore serves as a figure of desire that can never be fully satisfied, a fantasy of wholeness and fusion that is perpetually frustrated, highlighting the boundaries that separate women even as they struggle to bridge the gaps between them.

In the literature of Kōno Taeko, homoerotic desire frequently takes the form of erotic substitution of one woman for another through partner-swapping arrangements that allow for women to experience physical intimacy indirectly by sharing the same man. We will see this dynamic operative in the short story "On the Road" (Rojō, 1964), where the protagonist's fantasy that her sister might take her place as her husband's sexual partner is just one example of the kind of substitutional logic that governs relationships among women. Kurahashi and Takahashi also have produced texts that employ themes of erotic substitution of one woman for another in relationships with men in ways that involve an identification of one woman with another through a merging of their sexual subjectivities.[5] However, in other texts they take the homoerotic trope one step further by portraying the sexual desire of one woman for another more explicitly through scenes of erotic gratification between women that do not involve the mediation of a man. In these texts, too, the Other Woman frequently appears in the guise of a doppelganger or alternate self for the protagonist, once again highlighting the mutual imbrication of identification and desire in these narratives. The two examples we will see of this type of story are "Intercourse" (Majiwari, 1966), by Takahashi, and "Bad Summer" (Warui natsu, 1966), by Kurahashi.

"On the Road"

This story begins on an ostensibly auspicious note with the marriage of protagonist Tatsuko's younger sister Kimiko, yet fissures soon develop in this picture of perfect happiness as we learn that the bride would have preferred another groom. Kimiko's confession, just before her wedding, that she wanted to marry "a man like [Tatsuko's husband] Kanō" sets the tone for the rest of the story, told mostly in flashback; it chronicles the complex web of relationships between the protagonist and various other women who present themselves as potential replacements. From her mother to her sister to a stranger on the train, these other women serve variously as figures of desire, fear, and identification, threatening to destabilize Tatsuko's existential integrity in ways that are alternately pleasurable and frightening.

This principle of substitution seems to operate with alarming regularity in Tatsuko's family, beginning with her mother's early death and replacement by the stepmother who raised her. Tatsuko was six when her birth mother died and has few clear memories of her. Although she claims to have grown up in this household without feeling overly sentimental about the early loss of this parent, she clearly felt a bit of an outsider in her new family, in spite of the efforts of her parents and half-sisters to include her.

> She only vaguely remembered her [mother's] face. When she looked at a photograph, all she felt was a sense of "Right, that's what she looked like." She never felt like going out of her way to look at such pictures either. As a girl, when she would finish her homework and go downstairs, upon hearing the loud laughter of her parents and sisters coming from the living room, she did feel a stepchild's hesitation to open the door, but it wasn't so bad that she wanted to cry before her mother's photograph.[6]

While Tatsuko claims not to have suffered much from her family situation, it is obvious that she has never felt herself to be an equal member of the household and that this feeling of alienation from her family has stayed with her until the present. Early in the story, when her husband encourages her to stay overnight with her parents the night of Kimiko's wedding, thinking that they might want one child nearby to console them in light of this new empty-nest situation, Tatsuko at first demurs because she does not think her presence would be as welcome as that of her other half-sister (8). From the beginning of the story, then, it is clear that Tatsuko views herself to be easily replaceable, just as her own mother was replaced by the stepmother who raised her.

Tatsuko's sense of being superfluous to her family only increases as she grows up and at last begins to feel an increasing sense of connection to her own mother. She recalls that a year after her marriage, on a visit home to see her stepmother, she had been given a photograph of her birth mother in her early twenties, before she fell ill. Seeing the photo, Tatsuko is shocked not only to recognize herself in her mother's image, but also to realize that she would soon be the age her mother was when she died. Examining the woman in the picture carefully, Tatsuko reflects:

> She must have been about twenty. Maybe it was because Tatsuko herself had already lived well past that point, but in the image of her mother in the photograph, Tatsuko unexpectedly felt the youth of that age. When she thought that her mother had that photo taken at an age that she herself had experienced and remembered clearly, Tatsuko had the sensation of being able to touch the fabric of the old-fashioned parasol [that her mother held in the picture]. She realized that until now, even when she had occasion to think about the fact that her mother had died long ago, she had never really felt that she had once had a real mother. When she realized this, for the first time she longed for her dead mother. (19)

From this point on, Tatsuko begins to fear the possibility that she too might die young, as though the emotional connection that has been established between them creates a channel for inheriting the woman's fate. Tatsuko grows to identify with her mother, but this is initially experienced as a fearful and inauspicious sense of foreboding.

The situation changes, however, with Kimiko's sudden confession of feelings for Kanō. In the first pages of the story we learn that Kimiko, the youngest of the three sisters, has been unlucky in love. After two of her suitors die within a year of one another, she gives up on dating and then eventually consents to an arranged marriage after coming dangerously close to becoming "Christmas cake."[7] While she had not particularly cared for the first man who proposed to her, the second was a boyfriend whom she very much hoped to marry, but her family's disapproval prevented their engagement, and eventually she broke off the relationship. Although by the time she learns of his death she seems unaffected by it, when she realizes that both men died in such quick succession, she begins to believe she is cursed and will never marry happily. While she consents to the match arranged for her out of a sense of responsibility to her parents—they require one daughter to bring a son-in-law home as successor to the head of the family home—her outburst just before her wedding makes it clear to Tatsuko that Kimiko is not entirely happy with her choice.

As Tatsuko lies in bed the night after the wedding, thinking about her younger sister's unfortunate situation, she begins to wonder if perhaps Kimiko's words might not have been prophetic. If it is true that Kimiko has been cursed to find marriage partners with early expiration dates, then what might happen to the man she just married? And what if Tatsuko herself has been cursed with the misfortune of carrying on her mother's legacy of early death? In that case, might not her younger sister and Kanō have the opportunity to marry after all? Curiously, Tatsuko seems neither jealous nor disturbed by this prospect. The more she thinks about it, the more she even seems to relish the idea, and she lies awake that night fantasizing about Kanō killing her during a violent bout of lovemaking before taking her younger sister as a second wife:

> Tatsuko often dreamed of death. Bound ever tighter by the rope, when her body would fall over with a thud, or when she felt her fingertips—the only part of her body that she could still move— grow cold behind her back, she felt as though she experienced the pleasure of death.... She lost herself in dreaming of the pleasure of a death bestowed upon her by Kanō. She would definitely die young. Then perhaps Kimiko really would marry Kanō. But the only way Tatsuko would set him free would be if she met that kind of end. Thinking about that, Tatsuko felt warmly towards Kimiko. But if Kimiko knew how she had died, she might hesitate to marry Kanō.... Pursuing such thoughts endlessly, Tatsuko's eyes glinted ever more fiercely in the dark. (20–21)

Tatsuko and Kanō, it seems, have long enjoyed sadomasochistic sex play, and this fantasy is depicted as not atypical of their usual bedroom antics, with one important exception—the addition of younger sister Kimiko.

This seems only to add to Tatsuko's pleasure in the anticipation of death at the hands of her husband. It is implied that they have enacted this scenario together many times, coming close to the ultimate climax of death but stopping just short of satisfaction. The fantasy of a substitute allows Tatsuko to imagine having it both ways, attaining the objective of death yet not really dying. The possibility that Kimiko would take her place therefore gives her the sense of endlessly renewable pleasure.

In the final pages of the story Tatsuko meets with yet another doppelganger, who gives her a prescient glimpse into her own possible future. On the train as she is returning home from her parents' house, Tatsuko encounters a pair of older ladies chatting together and pays little attention to them until she overhears one remark, perhaps in the context of a conversation about health care remedies: "I wouldn't worry about it if I were you. Look at me. I didn't even think I would make it to forty. My mother died young, you know" (22). From this moment on, Tatsuko becomes fascinated with the woman and cannot stop observing her, carefully noting her clothing and hairstyle, trying to imagine her daily activities and her destination, and repeating her words over and over in her head. When the woman gets off at Tatsuko's station, she follows her, trying to determine if she lives there or is simply visiting someone she knows and feeling an eerie sense of connection with her as strangers who might possibly share the same fate. Just then, in the final lines of the story, the woman is run over by a speeding truck right before Tatsuko's eyes.

The interlocking set of substitutions—Tatsuko for her birth mother, Kimiko for Tatsuko, and even Tatsuko for an anonymous stranger—implies a complex web of emotional investment by the protagonist in the body of the Other Woman. Her encounter with her mother, mediated by the photograph that she receives from her mother's surrogate, is bittersweet. As Tatsuko searches the picture eagerly for clues to her own forgotten past, her mother's image evokes recollections of her own experiences at that age, as Tatsuko begins to identify with her even to the extent of imagining herself in her place, holding the parasol in the photo. While this sense of identification with an intergenerational body double is pleasurable in that for the first time she is able to feel a sense of connection with this long-lost member of her family, it also provokes feelings of dread at identifying so closely that she might literally repeat her mother's unfortunate history. Even a stranger on the train can apparently serve this dual function—proffering a kind of privileged self-knowledge, only to threaten the transmission of a horrifying fate. The desire for intimacy with the Other Woman here is therefore tempered by a fear of the same.

Ironically, though the protagonist is able to resolve these fears on one level by shifting the object of identification to younger sister Kimiko, this strategy is likewise fraught with pain and danger to self. While Tatsuko thinks of this shift as an opportunity to satisfy her rather unconventional sexual desires, implicating Kimiko in an erotic triangular relationship with herself and her husband, such a scenario can obtain only so long as it is preceded by the protagonist's own physical experience of pain, and death, at the hands of her husband. But why would Tatsuko consent, or rather insist, on such an outcome? Why would she wish to be replaced by her younger sister?

Just as with her birth mother, intimacy between women here too seems permeated by a logic of substitution that punishes as much as it rewards. In addition to an obvious wish to see her younger sister happy after so many disappointments in love, it is also implied that Tatsuko feels superfluous and inferior to the members of her father's family. She even begins to feel that after learning of her sister's desire for her husband, she no longer has the "right" to feel frightened of her mother's legacy of death, and it is this thought that prompts her violent fantasy of dying at Kanō's hands in order to be replaced by Kimiko (20). The baby of the family, Kimiko has always been indulged by her parents and sisters, and it seems that Tatsuko here feels obligated to continue this tradition not only out of feelings of love for her sister, but out of a distinct sense of inferiority as well.

Rather than warm havens of emotional support, families in Kōno's literature seem more like unsympathetic machines composed of a set of interlocking yet easily replaceable parts, and "On the Road" is clearly no exception. Women are particularly susceptible to the logic of substitution, as they seem continually to replace or be replaced by other women through adoption, remarriage, and even death.[8] Kōno's female protagonists are thus haunted by a sense of existential instability, and they struggle to establish a basis for autonomous subjectivity. Other women thus serve to both facilitate and impede this process of subject formation, acting as sites of privileged self-knowledge even as they also present themselves as potential rivals or threats.

"Intercourse"

The first-person protagonist of this story, known to the reader only as Watashi ("I"), is fond of wandering aimlessly through the streets of unfamiliar places. She is evidently experiencing some sort of existential crisis because she says this type of activity is "her only consolation." She finds the visual stimulation of these unknown environments to be pleasurable because it overwhelms her sense of self in a kind of flânerie-induced oblivion that "numbs her soul."[9] One day, as she is walking through the dingy back streets of the old part of town, she encounters a mysterious woman, roughly the same age as herself, and is convinced that she somehow knows this person but cannot remember how. Watashi is attracted to the woman because in spite of her shabby appearance, she seems to harbor a light within that is invulnerable to the ravages of time: "Her dark kimono was made of silk but seemed to be more than ten years old, terribly threadbare, and the sleeves were ragged. Her whole appearance gave off the shadow of decay, the mark of erosion of forty years of life. But somewhere inside her there appeared to be a core that glowed dimly, emitting a faint light from the depths of her existence" (149). Watashi decides to follow the woman but then loses sight of her as a strange dark fog suddenly descends upon her.

The next time she encounters the woman, it is in the thoroughly different environment of brand-new high-rise apartments in a more modern section of town. The woman's dark and dingy appearance contrasts shockingly with the clean white concrete walls of the maze-like apartment district, and yet Watashi feels the same eerie nostalgia as before. The woman seems to remember her from their previous encounter and speaks to her. This startles Watashi because the woman had not seemed to notice her that day or even look in her direction. On the other hand, her intuition tells her that she has known this stranger from somewhere else, even though the woman seems to refute this by suggesting that they had only met that one time. Just as confusion begins to set in, Watashi's doubts are abruptly erased by the woman's touch: "Her thin dry hand extended out from her threadbare sleeves and rested on my shoulder. Something like a pleasant electric sensation flowed from her hand, and my body tingled slightly. The atmosphere enveloping us instantly sparkled and gave off a clear light" (151–152). They begin to reminisce about their earlier meeting, and the woman again surprises Watashi by appearing to know things about her that she should have no way of knowing. However, the woman remains a mysterious figure to Watashi, one who thwarts her attempts to know more about her. When Watashi asks questions about her life, the woman merely smiles and gives her a coral hairpin as a token of remembrance. The two begin to walk together through the "hypnotically white" landscape, which seems to have something of a trance-like effect on Watashi, and she eventually loses sight of the woman again. Returning home, Watashi tries on the hairpin and discovers that it suits her perfectly, as if it had been hers all along (154).

In subsequent encounters the woman continues to deflect Watashi's desire to know more about her and their strange connection. When Watashi presses her on the question of whether they had known each other from before, she merely responds that the question is unimportant because "lovers" always feel that way, and she adds, "As long as we are able to share this happiness together, isn't that enough?" (155). When Watashi persists, the woman again distracts her with physical intimacy:

> My voice that had questioned her single-mindedly faded and was overcome by the force of the sensation that communicated from her to me. Even though we were linked by nothing more than her thin hand placed on my shoulder, we experienced a deep intercourse during which our whole bodies were abuzz in a confusion of sensation. In that moment, the signs of decay that had covered her disappeared, the shadow of decline that had clung to her fell away, and the dim flame that had until now burned faintly deep inside her flared up suddenly. That faint glow within that had been her hallmark ascended vibrantly to the exterior of her being, became pure light and shone brilliantly. (156)

From this point until the end of the story, the woman becomes Watashi's frequent companion on her walks through the cityscape, a journey that takes them alternately through the "land of shadows"—their name for the dark back streets—and the "land of light," or the sparkling new high-rise district. While Watashi had been accustomed to wandering about in isolation, she seems gratified by the intimacy and companionship the woman offers her, though she is still disturbed by her frequent disappearances and eerie familiarity and is curious to know more about her—a curiosity that is never satisfied.

Whether they are wandering through the land of shadows or light, the space the women traverse during the course of their walks together is portrayed as occupying a different plane of existence from the mundane world. These worlds of shadow and light in fact seem more like states of emotion or sensation rather than physical spaces per se—modes of experience whose undulating rhythm gives structure to the narrative and mirrors the tension between youthful purity and physical decay that the women embody. Watashi and her companion seem strangely insulated from contact with other people so long as they inhabit this psychic space, and indeed at one point Watashi wonders aloud why no one has appeared to intervene in their relationship. In fact, they have become so absorbed in one another that other people have literally become invisible to them.

There is only one point in the story where the two women, while wandering together in their isolated haven, are forced to "turn their eyes to reality" (157). They encounter a ferocious bulldog that threatens to attack, and though they pass some scary moments as they walk by him, they are able to escape without incident. This experience reminds the woman of something that happened to her when she was a girl, and she tells Watashi the story about a "big, ugly man" who once attempted to take her pet dog. She successfully beats the dogcatcher off with a stick, but in the process he swells to "three or four times his size" and takes on a monstrous appearance. This story sounds familiar to Watashi, and this collective memory functions as another clue to the unusual bond between the women.

In spite of the fact that the women seem to present a picture of perfect harmony, Watashi cannot help but be suspicious about the woman's origins and identity, and her desire to solve this mystery intensifies even as their intercourse reaches ever greater heights of intimacy and sensation, ultimately propelling the story to its disastrous conclusion. During one erotic encounter the scent the woman gives off smells just like the new perfume that Watashi is wearing for the first time, and Watashi again cannot resist asking her why she seems so familiar. As the woman appears to achieve some sort of climax, Watashi presses her for an answer:

> "When I first saw you on the street, I had this nostalgic feeling like I'd seen you somewhere before, or rather I had the impression that there was no one in my life more familiar than you. The person I feel closest to, the person I know better than anyone, for some reason that was how I felt about you. Who are you?"
>
> I pulled out a knife I had slipped into the sleeve of my kimono. "At least let me tell you my name. Let me carve my initial into your brilliant white shoulder with this knife." She was still trembling with pleasure. I cut the letter F deeply into her white left shoulder. The pleasure of giving and receiving pain converged beneath the tip of the knife as if inscribed there. Instantly blood spurted out, coloring the letter and the woman's skin red. Before my very eyes a mist the color of blood rose and quickly grew dense. As my vision grew foggy, our friendship dissolved like a receding tide. (163)

The last lines of the story leave Watashi wandering aimlessly through the streets, isolated and alone, with a wound in her left shoulder to match the one inflicted upon her companion and a knife "weighing heavily" in her sleeve. Her desire to define her relationship to the Other Woman—either through knowledge of her identity or by ascribing her own identity to the woman—has not only destroyed their relationship, but has also resulted in a self-inflicted wound that mirrors the psychic damage done to the protagonist through the loss of her "lover."

The conclusion of the story, in addition to the various similarities between the women that are underscored throughout the text, strongly indicates that the Other Woman may simultaneously be read as a doppelganger for the protagonist. Watashi's persistent sense of nostalgia upon seeing the woman, as well as the woman's eerie knowledge of aspects of Watashi's life history to which she should logically have no access, suggests a series of encounters that verge on self-knowledge or recognition of suppressed aspects of her own personality. But in spite of the many textual clues that indicate the identity of protagonist and Other Woman, the woman nevertheless remains Other until the very end. Watashi's attempts to force a convergence of self and Other, first through the relentless pursuit of knowledge about her double and then through the inscription of her own identity upon the body of the Other Woman, irrevocably destroys the harmony between them. Maintenance of this tension between self and Other would thus seem crucial to the preservation of the intimacy between them. So long as Watashi is able to accept the otherness of her companion, she can continue to enjoy the feeling of nostalgia for the second self that the woman represents for her, but the moment she attempts to resolve this dichotomy by enforcing a kind of totalistic identification with her double, the bond between them is broken.

From the first lines of the story, Watashi seems to identify strongly with the Other Woman. They are roughly the same age, around forty, and Watashi appears profoundly moved by the woman's aura of having suffered through accumulated years of struggle and decline. The light that she senses within the woman, which is likened to a core of youthful purity that has resisted the ravages of time, is echoed in Watashi's own bodily experience: "My face and hands had grown dark with decay, but for some reason only my shoulders preserved a youthful whiteness, and as if she had known this already, she [slipped my kimono off and] stroked my bare left shoulder, saying 'Just this part is pure white'" (161). The women seem instinctively to sense and seek out this inner beauty in one another, and their "intercourse" serves to release this light within, as the erotic climax of the Other Woman is always accompanied by a moment when this hidden light emerges to the surface and permeates her being. In bringing forth the light deep within her companion, Watashi is also able to access her own inner beauty through the body of the Other Woman. In recognizing and drawing forth the beauty of the Other Woman, Watashi is rewarded with recognition of her own beauty, such that knowledge of and communion with the Other provides a channel for expression of one's own inner self.

This sense of communion with the Other Woman is facilitated by their isolation from "reality," as their bond is described as creating a world of two that is immune to outside interference. The Other Woman declares that there is "no greater love" than the one they share, and until the very end of the story, their intimacy seems to offer the purest and most complete type of love imaginable between two people: "In any relationship between lovers, one person loves and the other is loved, one loves more and the other less, but between us there was absolutely none of that sort of discrimination. It was all intoxication and no anguish whatsoever. It was just like she said: 'There is no greater love than this'" (161). Their relationship is therefore characterized by a remarkable degree of harmony and equality that is predicated on a delicate balance between the two women, and they marvel that no one has attempted to come between them to disturb this balance. The Other Woman surmises that this is because their love is of a "special quality" and that the rest of the world seems to have disappeared because their love "shines so brilliantly" that other people are no longer visible to them. Furthermore, because their intimacy can be achieved through such unobtrusive means as the touch of a hand on a shoulder, they can have "intercourse" wherever they like without arousing the suspicions of passers-by (160).

Though Watashi says that their "intercourse" consists only of this kind of slight physical contact, it is obviously and explicitly erotic. The woman even refers to their relationship as *koi*, a word denoting erotic feeling as opposed to spiritual love, and she refers to the two of them as "lovers."[10] This aspect of their intercourse is evident through its electric effect on the protagonist and the feelings of intimacy that arise as a result of their mutual response: "Our intercourse was complete with just the touch of her thin dry hand on my shoulder. Her total existence was directed toward me, and my total existence was directed toward her, and since her existence and mine were each like a delicate chord waiting fervently for the hand of that one person to play us, just a slight touch was enough to make our total existences tremble in response to one another"

(160). Yet it is interesting that the eroticism of these encounters between the women is not expressed in genital terms but rather through a diffuse sort of sexual expression that can be achieved through any kind of physical touch.[11] In fact, bodily contact seems secondary to the mutual response of each woman's "total existence" toward that of the other. By the end of the story, it is implied that they are able to feel the electric current that presages such encounters without even being in the same place, indicating that the two women's intimacy has intensified to the point of near fusion between self and Other.

In fact, given that we may read the Other Woman in this story as a doppelganger for the protagonist, these encounters may be understood as simultaneously homoerotic and autoerotic. The references to the notion that there is "no greater love" than the type they share can of course be read as indicating self-love rather than feeling that is other-directed. This tension between self- and other-directed love mirrors the tension between identification with the Other and desire for the Other that structures the relationship of these two women. One may of course read the Other Woman as a double for Watashi, but this does not mean that they are the same person, and to the very end of the story aspects of the Other Woman (most prominently her identity) remain inaccessible to Watashi. She is similar, but she is not the same, and she cannot be made to be the same, as Watashi unfortunately discovers in the final lines of the narrative.

One might say the same is true of all relationships between women, erotic or otherwise. There may be as many differences among women as there are between women and men—and this seems to be precisely Taka-hashi's point. Though women may long for the kind of total intimacy that bars all outside intervention, in reality there are many barriers that serve to keep women apart—among them class, race, age, experience, and edu-cation, not to mention rivalries over men and the access to power or privi-lege that they represent.[12] Takahashi's protagonist, isolated and lonely at the beginning of the story, encounters another woman with whom she feels a profound connection. Through this relationship each woman is able to bring out the beauty in the other, in the guise of the light within, and Watashi cannot help wanting to push that feeling of connection to its logical extreme through possession of her "lover," expressed through a radical desire for total identification between self and Other. Yet she finds at the end of the story that this only exacerbates, rather than cures, her sense of loneliness as the Other Woman literally evaporates before her eyes.

"Bad Summer"

The protagonist of this story, known only as L, is an established novelist at the pinnacle of her success who is suffering from an unnamed illness.[13] As the story opens, she is on her way to a party in honor of the publication of her collected works, where she meets M, a young girl of seventeen or eighteen who has just made her debut on the literary scene. Even at such a young age she is considered by the literary world to be a genius, and L soon becomes attracted to her. After the party she sends M signed copies of her collected works but is disappointed to find that M is out of town and unable to receive them. Overdue for a change of scene, suffering from writer's block, and wanting to evade the doctor's diagnosis of her medical condition that is expected the following week, L decides to journey to a remote island resort that is, not coincidentally, near M's birthplace.

Although L hopes that this island sojourn will pull her out of her artistic impasse, she instead finds that each time she attempts to produce "fruit of her creativity," it fails to "implant itself in her womb."[14] Even the "orthodox novel" she has grudgingly agreed to write, after years of avoiding what she sees as a hackneyed genre, fails to come to her. Though she has built her career on writing avant-garde fiction that some critics consider brilliant and others eccentric or downright disturbing, writing only during the wee hours of the night "like an insect excreting poison," here she finds herself sleeping and waking early like a normal person (155). Ironically, while her physical health seems to have returned, she now suffers from an indefinable spiritual illness. Since she cannot work, she instead begins writing love letters to M at her home address, confessing her desire to "consume" her and, failing that, to read her work. After many weeks pass and she still has received no response from M, L decides to travel to her hometown on the chance that she might be visiting her family there. Though she thoroughly exhausts herself in looking for M, no one seems to have seen her or know her whereabouts. Then one day, about a month after their first meeting, M unexpectedly turns up at the hotel where L is staying. L immediately has M move to the room next to hers and takes upon herself the dual role of M's "guardian" and "lover."

The majority of the story, then, is devoted to L's unsuccessful pursuit of M, and even when she finally finds her and manages to keep her close, L is frustrated by her inability to completely possess the girl. Rather, L is described as the one who is "captive" to M's charms, as in a scene where L watches her brush her hair: "M faced the mirror in her pajamas, brushing her long hair as if to deliberately tease L, and turning around, once more gave L a meaningful smile. But it was a cruel smile, the kind a person gives when she is certain that she is loved, a smile as if to lightly claw at prey that has already been captured" (170). The text is quite clear on the homo-erotic bond between the women, as they are explicitly described at various points kissing and caressing each other. L's description of her feelings for M includes references to love both in a spiritual, idealistic sense and as physical, carnal desire. However, it is equally clear that L's feelings are more intense than those of M, and it is even implied that M deliberately manipulates L and toys with her affections. Furthermore, in a conversation between the two women where they compare their love to the love of men, M is emphatic that what L has to offer her is vastly inferior to the heterosexual alternative (172).

Complicating this tale of unrequited love is the fact that with the exception of M and apparently herself, L obviously has a very low opinion of other women. In a familiar conflation of women with the body and men with the mind, L eschews anything that relates to bodily necessity in favor of intellectual pursuit. This is explicitly stated in the text as follows: "In her opinion, womanly things were lacking in absolute beauty; they were nothing but elements plucked down from the altar of spirituality to the marketplace of the terrestrial world" (167–168). In comparison to the transcendent standard of "absolute beauty," femininity thus occupies a substandard position as denizen of the mundane world. If spirituality is visualized as an "altar" that is literally elevated above this mundane world, then its opposite, the corporeal realm to which women are relegated, is implicitly inferior, having been "plucked down" to a position that is beneath this exalted world of the spiritual. Such a conclusion suggests that the body, coded as feminine, is little more than a commodity to be traded in the terrestrial "marketplace" and that in order to transcend this realm of crass materialism, a woman must deny her corporeality in favor of purely intellectual or spiritual concerns.

L therefore suppresses her physical needs and nurtures her intellect. She eats sparingly and sleeps less, staying up late into the night to devote herself to her writing, which she describes tellingly as a kind of creative process of impregnation and birth. However, she is careful to distinguish this from the kind of biological pregnancy that other women experience—indeed, anything associated with the female reproductive system is described as "vulgar," distasteful, and "empty" (143–144). She even despises other women writers, scorning them for being no different from ordinary middle-aged women in their concern for clothing and makeup and implying that they are worse than prostitutes (135–136). Clearly, L perceives herself to be different from other women, and M even asks at one point if she might not in fact be a man (173). Yet L seems profoundly drawn to M, who is described throughout the narrative as thoroughly feminine and seductive in all the ways that L appears to despise.

In fact, there are clues throughout the story to suggest that M can easily be read as a doppelganger for the protagonist. Having reached a plateau, or perhaps even a stumbling block, in her career at the age of forty and further suffering from physical deterioration in the form of an unnamed and possibly fatal illness, L seems to see in M a younger, healthier, more vibrant version of herself. There are physical similarities, such as the fact that M's hands are identical to those of L, in addition to a revealing conversation between the two women where L asks M to "become her" when she dies. M demurs, reminding L that if she dies, they both will (169–170). This "second self" motif is further underscored by Kurahashi's playful mention of titles published by both women that are identical to titles of works published by herself. This opens up the possibility of reading M and L as younger and older versions of the author, even as an autobiographical reading of this story is deliberately refuted within the text itself.[15]

Taking into account this doppelganger motif opens up the possibility of reading L's obsessive desire for M as an attempt to recuperate the femininity that she has discarded in order to pursue the path of pure intellectual creativity. While L is clearly ambivalent about her gender identity, if not downright misogynistic, M seems to have been able to establish herself as a writer of great reputation without casting off her feminine traits or conducting herself in a "vulgar" manner like the other women writers that L so despises. While L seems to be something of a shut-in, isolating herself in order to concentrate on her craft and avoiding contact with others, M is able to come and go freely between L's claustrophobic world of introversion and the outside world of everyday life. M represents what L has lost in the process of becoming an androgynous intellect, and her elusiveness frustrates L, who attempts unsuccessfully to possess her.

In a pivotal scene of conflict between L and M, we learn that L has rejected heterosexual love in the course of denying her own femininity, as part of the process of becoming the androgynous intellectual that she is now. In her youth L had fallen in love with a male artist who insisted on turning their relationship into a "game of imagination," apparently in spite of her own desire for physical intimacy. While she had experienced this initially as a kind of loss, she eventually internalized this way of thinking and in doing so, she completed her own "transformation" into an artist. The text then contrasts her situation to that of other women as follows:

> L was aware that women tried to become artists not through love of art but through love of artists, which in the end came close to the common opinion that women could not become real artists. Certainly L had become a poet through her discovery of love for a poet. But this love was not directed at those parts of man that were made from clay. If L had not succeeded at stripping her spirit from her flesh through love—and this was something that was essentially difficult for the female sex to accomplish—her "transformation" [into an artist] would probably have failed. By renouncing her sex, she had liberated her spirit and her imagination. From that time on L had not loved another man....
>
> However, now circumstances had changed. At a time when L had neared the end of her life, she had begun to love M. Of course, given that M was not a man, this didn't really constitute a sudden and inexplicable change in the fact that L could not love men. And what about M, who was bundled up in L's love? One afternoon, M lay her head on L's back, who was lying face down on the beach, and suddenly declared, "Hey, are you really a woman? I wish you were a man." Chewing on her own hair, M turned her head to peer at L's face. Clearly she realized that she had wounded L's love, and her posture indicated that she was prepared to flee quickly if L lashed out in anger at her.
>
> L asked gently, "What do you mean?"
>
> "If you were a man, I would let you inside of me. It's a shame you aren't a man."
>
> L resolved never to speak to M again. (171–172)

This passage begins with a meditation on L's own personal history, as a woman who learns to idealize her love of men into a purely intellectual form and of her eventual transformation into a "woman writer." The two parts of this term are seen to be inherently in contradiction to one another, requiring the female subject who aspires to a life of the mind to make a choice between the two. Most women, in L's opinion, are inadequate to the task of "stripping spirit from the flesh"—that is, renouncing one's corporeal femininity in favor of pure intellectualism—that is required to resolve the contradiction. In successfully navigating this difficult challenge,

L clearly sees herself to be exceptional vis-à-vis ordinary women, who are unable to embrace art in its pure form and therefore settle for the sexual embrace of artists—a love that is "directed at those parts of man that [are] made from clay." In contrast to ordinary women, who settle for a relationship to art that is mediated by heterosexual desire, L has bypassed this form of embrace for a "love" of male artists that is expressed as purely intellectual. She has therefore successfully cast off her feminine gender identity, which is intimately imbricated here with heterosexual desire, for an androgynous subjectivity that allows for the love of men only insofar as these feelings are abstracted into an idealized and disembodied form of intellectual admiration. Consequently, she learns to despise other women precisely because they represent the subject position of corporeal imma-nence that she has worked so hard to transcend.

The text then quickly turns to a meditation on L's relationship to M and how this fits in with L's refusal of heterosexuality, strongly imply-ing that both phenomena are linked to her existentially unstable status of "woman writer." Her love for M is clearly differentiated within the text from heterosexual desire, but from L's perspective this is a positive thing. Heterosexuality, which in this text is intimately bound up with "femi-ninity" as an inherently inferior subject position, clearly endangers the persona of disembodied intellectual that L has crafted for herself. In L's mind, for a woman to take up a place in the heterosexual matrix means to accept a position whereby one cannot produce art and must settle for loving it indirectly via the body of a man. By refusing the love of men, L has cast off her feminine gender identity and resolved the contradiction between "woman" and "writer," terms that come laden with an enormous amount of cultural baggage that implies the gendered and mutually exclu-sive nature of these subject positions.

Yet L's renouncing of her femininity is clearly accompanied by feel-ings of loss, judging by the way she arrived at this decision in the aftermath of a troubled and unsatisfying heterosexual relationship and by the way she is clearly drawn to M because she embodies those qualities that L was forced to reject. By loving M, she is able to recapture something of her lost femininity while remaining safely distant from those elements of it that threaten her status as androgynous intellect. Therefore, while many clues within the text suggest that M serves on one level as an extension of self, it is simultaneously crucial for L that M remain Other, preserving the tension between auto- and homoeroticism within the text. This ten-sion cannot and must not be resolved in order for M to fulfill her role as surrogate feminine self, embodying those qualities that L has had to reject in herself in order to complete her "transformation" into a disembodied intellect. The homoerotic relationship with M therefore offers itself as a solution to L's dilemma between complying with normative constructions of heterosexual womanhood, which would force her to abandon her status as artist, and renouncing femininity entirely by accepting a subject position that is implicitly masculine.

However, it is clear that while L seems satisfied with their arrangement, M is not, apparently because she has not experienced her own status as woman writer to be riddled with contradiction. M seems thoroughly comfortable with her own femininity even as she has established her credentials as an up-and-coming artistic phenomenon. Though she acquiesces to L's desire for her, perhaps for the strategic advantage of having an established writer's support—and in fact L does offer her professional backing—M still seems to be sexually interested in men and obviously believes L's love to be inferior to that of men. The generation gap in self-perception between these two women, such that L sees a contradiction between femininity and professional goals whereas M does not, is evocative of the actual differences in experiences of Japanese women born before or after the war. The former group, having had to navigate a sea change in expectations of their purpose in Japanese society due to post-Occupation changes in educational, legal, and social structures, seems to have struggled with questions of gender identity in ways that the postwar generation of women, who grew up taking these new opportunities for granted, did not.

Because L's longing for M is motivated by both personal and professional desires and because these desires are experienced by L as inseparable impulses, she experiences M's rejection of her love as a rejection of her as both lover and mentor. After the fight discussed above, L goes to some trouble to order a copy of M's collected works and finds that the young woman's vibrant and powerful literary style only heightens her erotic desire for the girl. Inspired by admiration for M's intellectual gifts, L presents M with a volume of her own literature but is wounded to discover that the girl is unacquainted with her work and finds her expression of enthusiasm for the gift to be perfunctory and shallow (174–175). This merely adds insult to the injury inflicted in the scene described above. M's suggestion that L is not a proper woman yet simultaneously lacks the qualifications to perform satisfactorily as a man can thus be interpreted as both an attack on her suitability as a lover and a suggestion that her "transformation" into a genderless intellect is incomplete. Depressed at the personal and professional impasse at which she has arrived, L begins to feel as though what she intended to be a short island vacation has in fact committed her to a path that can end only with her death and that perhaps the only way to avoid this fate is to kill M first (181–182).

The ending of the story highlights the contradictions between feminine and masculine that L embodies in a surreal and shockingly violent denouement. One morning, while M is still asleep, L gets a ride on the hotel motorboat out to a deserted island nearby where she and M had previously shared many intimate encounters. She takes with her a volume of M's collected works, reading it with a bittersweet combination of admiration for the girl and painful feelings of unrequited love. She begins to feel drowsy and experiences a sensation as if her "existence" were melting away into the ocean, and she likens it to the feeling of "blood like blackness itself flowing ceaselessly out of her womb." She feels "pinned down" by an intense feeling of lethargy. The story ends as follows:

> Just then, the world became tinged with an inauspicious shadow and filled with a roar like a large flock of birds flapping their wings. These strange birds, flocked together in the sky, had long, bald, pink heads, and just like so many phalluses, they descended upon L in unison. Their lewd cries resounded terrifyingly in her ears.... L screamed just as the naked boys leapt at her. Countless sharp nails ripped off her clothes, and L's body, thin but retaining the form of untarnished sex that belied her age, was exposed to the sun. Her face was covered with a straw hat as her body was rent apart by their evil blades....
>
> It was just before noon when M arrived by motorboat. Strangely, L's consciousness was floating above the ground at a height that allowed her to look down on everything. For example, she could clearly see her own body lying on the sand like a weird hieroglyphic. L understood it as her own dying body gushing blood from where it had been rent apart. M removed the straw hat covering the face of the corpse. The small ivory face was contorted as if in pleasure, its upper lip curled. She could hear M's sweet voice calling, "Sensei, sensei. The results of your medical exam came just a little while ago from a Tokyo hospital." Above her own face, L saw a face like a sunflower with a row of cruel teeth. (182–183)

It is unclear whether L's experience is real or a dream or some kind of hallucination. She seems to be dozing off just prior to this event, and despite the fact that after the attack her perspective hovers above the scene like that of a spirit leaving the body in its death throes, in the final line of the story L is once again gazing up at M while lying on the sand, suggesting that she does not actually die.

The nature of the "attack" she experiences on the island is as unclear as whether or not it actually occurred. Prior to this scene, a gang of malevolent-looking teenaged boys had arrived at the hotel, and L sensed trouble the moment she saw them. Several times their potential for dangerous or malicious mischief is hinted, including one scene in which they show up to a musical concert and appear to L to be wielding knives. These scenes foreshadow the final attack on L, and it bolsters an interpretation of the ending that indicates that actual violence was done to the protagonist. On the other hand, L's altered state of drowsiness just beforehand and the fantastic nature of her perception of the incident, whereby a flock of birds turns into a gang of attacking phalluses, creates the possibility that this was simply a dream or hallucination. Nor is it clear whether they raped her or stabbed her or perhaps both—the blood flowing from L's body, assuming it is in fact real, may emanate from one or more unspecified wounds, depending on how one reads the original text.[16] The "blades" in this passage may refer to the knives that L thinks she sees them carry earlier in the story; alternately, they may be a metaphorical expression for the male sexual organ that is more explicitly referenced as a "phallus" elsewhere in the passage.

Regardless of how one interprets this final scene, the imagery employed further elucidates the conflicted relationship between L's professional and gender identities. Having renounced heterosexual femininity in favor of an androgynously intellectual subject position, L has created a tenuous position for herself between genders that is perhaps impossible to maintain. Though her love of M hints at the possibility of resolving this tension between her desire for femininity and her desire for art, M's failure to return her affections suggests the fragile nature of such a compromise. M represents for L all the feminine qualities that she desires but cannot allow herself to express, and while attributing these traits to the body of another woman allows her to protect herself from the cultural baggage they carry, by externalizing them onto the Other Woman, she has placed them outside her own control. M may represent what L desires for herself, but though L sees something of herself in this Other Woman, in the end she remains Other and therefore outside the realm of L's control.

L's strategy of abjecting her own feminine qualities onto the body of the Other Woman apparently solves one problem only to create others.

The final scene, in which L is raped either literally or metaphorically by a gang of young men who wield knives like phalluses—or perhaps phalluses like knives—therefore suggests a forcible reintegration of L into the heterosexual economy. Her untenable compromise between femininity and masculinity is clearly aberrant and societally unacceptable, and from the perspective of normative structures of authority, it must not be allowed to continue.

While the denouement of this story is shockingly violent, the strange smile of pleasure on L's "corpse" indicates that it may on another level represent a welcome reprieve from the tension of attempting to maintain this impossibly androgynous subject position. In Kurahashi's text, then, the body of the Other Woman may be understood not only as a physical embodiment of feminine qualities that intellectual women of her generation were forced to renounce, but also as a metaphor for the problem of oppressive structures of binary gender norms themselves. "Bad Summer" may be read as a critique of these structures, highlighting as it does the impossible position in which women who attempt to encroach upon traditionally masculine fields of endeavor are placed.

It is striking that all of the stories discussed in this chapter feature protagonists whose subjectivity is predicated on a profound sense of existential instability. Kōno's protagonist feels only a tenuous connection to her own family, given her status as stepdaughter and half-sibling, and she consequently feels that her place in that fundamental institution is insecure. Furthermore, her preoccupation with her birth mother's early death appears to threaten not only her position in the family but also her life itself, as she lives with the constant sense of foreboding that she will inherit her mother's fate. Takahashi's main character clearly suffers from some sort of psychological distress, and her engagement with reality is questionable, as she spends most of the story insulated in a world of two that allows no outside interference, obsessed with her relationship to a mysterious Other who seems to offer access to a privileged sort of self-knowledge. Kurahashi's L is fractured from the beginning, having pared away elements of herself in an effort to deny her own femininity, yet determined to reclaim these qualities through physical possession of a younger woman who reminds her of what she has lost. Each of these characters, feeling her connection with the world around her to be shaky and unsatisfying, seeks in another woman what she perceives is lacking in herself.

Although there is a strong sense of identification between the protagonist and her double, the doppelganger must remain Other to the self.

The Other Woman in each case serves as a screen for the projection of the protagonist's hopes and fears regarding her own identity and therefore must be held at a distance to be of any use in this quest for self-knowledge or exploration of her inner fantasies and desires. Maintenance of the tension between self/Other and desire/identification is therefore crucial both to the protagonist's quest and to the structure of these narratives, even as this distance creates frustration in the main character, whose desire for the Other is continually deferred.

The tension between self and Other (or identification and desire) is one reason that these narratives of female homoeroticism are permeated by an undercurrent of hostility toward other women. Tatsuko of "On the Road" clearly feels warmly toward her sister when thinking of her as a medium for her own desire, and this identification between self and Other creates a pleasing sense of intimacy. Yet this fantasy of homoerotic fusion requires distance between self and Other to be preserved, through a triangular relationship that is mediated by Tatsuko's husband. Furthermore, this fantasy is predicated on a structure wherein Kimiko takes her place in a masochistic and potentially fatal relationship to her husband—an experience that she senses would be unpleasant or shocking to the girl, given her worry that Kimiko would refuse if she knew the truth of the situation. At least some of Tatsuko's pleasure in this scenario seems to come from envisioning the girl as object of the same potentially painful and humiliating treatment that is meted out to her by her husband.

Likewise, "Intercourse" ends with a violent climax wherein the protagonist literally destroys her doppelganger in a failed attempt to possess her completely. Fusion of self and Other, figured here as a "convergence" of the woman who inflicts pain with the woman who is the recipient of it, results not in a sensation of wholeness or healing of the division within herself but rather in a sense of loss of a beloved companion whose very otherness alone preserves the integrity of the relationship.

Finally, L of "Bad Summer" learns to despise not only other women but the woman within herself as well, and her efforts to reconcile the contradiction inherent in her status of "woman writer" place her in the impossible position of attempting to disavow her own femininity while projecting it onto another so that she can then embrace it as external to herself. The intensity of L's love for M binds her to a relationship that can never satisfy her needs, threatening to destroy her if she does not free herself first—an escape that she believes can be achieved only through the death of one of the lovers. Thus, while these homoerotic relationships seem predicated on a preservation of tension between self and Other and between desire and identification, the eroticism of these bonds is simultaneously permeated by feelings of antagonism and aggression that might be described as feminine misogyny.

The undercurrent of hostility toward the Other Woman seems to result from the fact that these relationships between women are nevertheless embedded in heteronormative structures of power, resulting in narratives that reinstate familiar gendered binaries even as they appear to trouble them on other levels of analysis. While the protagonists may long for harmonious communion with the Other Woman, fundamentally these relationships are still predicated on assumptions of a binary opposition between active and passive positions, roles that are implicitly gendered as masculine and feminine, even when both parties are biologically female. Thus, while male characters remain peripheral to each of these narratives, heteronormative structures of power clearly complicate the relationship dynamics between the protagonist and the other woman.

A heightened awareness of the differences and power structures that separate women from one another, preventing real communion or solidarity among them, seems accompanied by a haunting sense of sadness as well. Each of the protagonists of these stories seems profoundly lonely in some way—Tatsuko because she is an outsider in her own family, Watashi because she is isolated and alone in a forbidding and sterile environment, and L because in striving to transcend the paradox of her status as "woman writer," she has taken up a subject position so anomalous that there now appears to be no one, male or female, with whom she can identify.

This sense of loneliness is perhaps not surprising, given that the authors of these texts, in their efforts to challenge hegemonic common sense regarding gender roles and discourses of "appropriate" femininity, seem to have been somewhat ahead of their time. Precisely because the gendered division of labor against which they struggled, in life and literature, had come to seem not only natural but necessary to Japanese society in the 1960s, founded as it was on a culture of high economic growth that produced national and individual prosperity, it was an exceptional woman indeed who dared to question the "logic" of dominant ideologies of gender. Unable to acquiesce gracefully to the models of femininity presented to them, these authors may be understood as having occupied a position in Japanese society that was as anomalous and gender indeterminate as their fictional protagonists.

Their life and works thus posed a profound challenge to the hegemonic discourses of gender that structured the high-growth period of Japan in the 1960s. It would be another decade—after the foundation of growth began to crack due to international economic events that forced Japanese to question the wisdom of a single-minded pursuit of prosperity—before Japanese society began to take this challenge seriously. As we will see in the conclusion, the "women's lib" movement of the 1970s openly debated many of the same problems of feminine subjectivity that preoccupied women writers of literature during the previous decade. These fiction writers may therefore be understood as working through the theoretical foundations of a feminist philosophy that would later emerge as an explicitly political movement.

Conclusion

Power, Violence, and Language in the Age of High Economic Growth

Gender, as envisioned by the Japanese women writers of fiction addressed in this study, is a form of power that disciplines bodies to produce certain types of behaviors and desires that are seen as advantageous to national and societal goals. In the 1960s, the goal was economic growth, and properly gendered bodies facilitated this project through total devotion either to the world of work outside the home or to roles that were supportive of such work, such as domestic labor. When bodies failed to produce the requisite behaviors and desires, "gender trouble" ensued, which threatened not only the binary model of gender that had come to seem normal, but also the national projects that were predicated on these disciplinary regimes.

The work of Michel Foucault suggests that there is no tenable position outside of power so that any resistance to disciplinary regimes must be attempted from within, through the very microchannels of power that would enforce such discipline.[1] Evidently these women writers perceived a similar dynamic in the workings of gender so that resistance to gender norms could be envisioned only from a position within the very structures that bound them to normative femininity. Literature proved to be a powerful weapon in this project of resistance, and many of these narratives reenact the process of forcible inscription of gender upon their characters so as to expose the violence and hypocrisy inherent in this process of engendering. They thus effectively parody such disciplinary mechanisms, revealing them to be void of the "natural" logic to which binary structures of gender pretend.

In this conclusion, I will highlight some of the theoretical implications of these women writers' contributions to incipient second-wave feminist discourse, comparing their work to that of prominent feminist theorists of the following decade and beyond. I hope to demonstrate that both groups were motivated to resist normative constructions of femininity imposed upon them by the gendered division of labor. In the following sections, I will outline the roles that power, violence, and language play in the theoretical architecture of these Japanese feminisms. These three categories of analysis are significant for the ways in which they constrain feminine subjectivity (and feminist expression) in some ways only to open up other possibilities for expression. Subjects are thus envisioned as engendered within networks of power, through violence that shapes their expression in language.

Power

In previous chapters we have seen the impossibility of occupying a subject position outside the structures of normative femininity, which assume a straightforward correspondence between body and gender. While all three protagonists of the stories discussed in chapter 2 may attempt to present themselves as gender-neutral, they are quickly reinscribed as feminine by the masculine gaze, a potent disciplinary mechanism that these women learn to internalize and replicate against themselves and other women. In chapter 3, although the protagonists of "Castle of Bones" and "Like a Witch" identify with their male mentors and attempt to establish themselves as provisionally "masculine," their efforts are disavowed or ridiculed by the men they strive to impress. In chapter 4, Asako of "Secret" learns that only men may transcend gender norms, just as boys in "Toddler-Hunting" represent to Akiko an ideal of freedom from the suffocating strictures of gender to which girls are subjected. On the other hand, in chapter 5, L of "Bad Summer" tries to have it both ways and possibly pays for it with her life. Although L briefly enjoys the sexual and intellectual privileges of men while keeping her feminine side close in the guise of M, this balancing act proves untenable and she is forcibly reinscribed into the heteronormative system of patriarchy in the final scene of the story. In all cases, these characters are subordinated to a disciplinary process of engendering as feminine, based solely on their occupation of female bodies. In other words, society assumes a direct correspondence between the terms female/feminine and male/masculine, regardless of whether or not these ideological concerns conform to the personal experiences and preferences of the subject in question.

Society, identified in these texts as the agent of the engendering process, is implicitly or explicitly figured as masculine, placing women in a subordinate position vis-à-vis structures of power. The term "society" therefore gestures toward the bodies of authority that administer and reinforce the disciplinary mechanisms of engendering and takes many guises in these stories. In "Broken Oath" it is represented by the legal system; in "Castle of Bones" it takes the mantle of religious authority; and in "Snake" it alternately figures as the medical establishment, the business world, the educational system, the political factions of the student movement, and even the Diet building and its representatives. In numerous stories "society" is conflated with the male-dominated intelligentsia and may even be seen as embodied in specific authority figures that hold power over the female characters—fathers, mentors, husbands, and lovers. Women are therefore understood in these stories to be embedded in asymmetrical power networks that permeate all levels of society, from the highest legislative body in Japan down to the level of the most intimate personal relationships. Precisely because these networks of power are so pervasive, cutting across all sectors of public and private life, it is difficult to resist internalizing the disciplinary mechanisms administered therein.

Japanese women faced such disciplinary mechanisms in the 1960s as they struggled with the various demands placed upon them during the era of high economic growth. Encouraged to aspire to become upwardly mobile middle-class wives and mothers, they were simultaneously exhorted to pick up the slack in the workforce as the increasing urgency of labor shortages induced both government and business interests to promote labor force participation even by married women with children. Ever greater levels of financial investment in children's education added to women's incentive to seek employment, yet they were nevertheless expected to continue to carry the full burden of domestic labor in addition to their work outside the home. In order to make outside employment compatible with their domestic responsibilities, women sought part-time positions, which were accompanied by low status and low wages. Feminist Ueno Chizuko has criticized this new model of the working wife and mother as follows:

> This "new sex-role division" is double-edged for women: it has affected the traditional power relationship between husbands and wives, but women have ended up being doubly exploited by men, both at home and at the workplace. As both part-time workers and housewives, women must be content to be "second-class citizens," while feeling guilty for being neither sufficient workers nor perfect mothers-wives. In short, "dual-

role" has not solved the "women problem." It is simply a new compromise between capitalism and patriarchy in the developed stage of capitalism.[2]

Thus, work outside the home was not experienced by Japanese women to be liberating in either a personal or economic sense, as they were effectively required to carry a double burden of labor while still remaining economically dependent on their husbands.

Within both public and private spheres, therefore, women were multiply subordinated as supportive members of highly structured organizations that placed men (whether husbands or male co-workers) in privileged positions over them. This double burden was seen as a direct result of the social and economic transformations brought on by the high-growth economy of the 1960s. As Ueno notes, challenging this structure, and the sexual division of labor upon which it was predicated, became a defining characteristic of the "second-wave" feminist movement of the following decade:

What made the second wave [of feminism] different from the first is that it questioned the sex-role division itself. Sex-roles in the modern urban nuclear family setting were seen to be the very cause that prevented women from attaining real equality despite the attainment of legal equality. This sex-role division between worker-husbands and homemaker-wives is in fact imposed on men and women by modern industrial society. To question this modern sex-role assignment is to question the modern industrial system in which we live.[3]

In this sense, then, both women writers of fiction in the 1960s and the feminist activists of the 1970s may be seen as motivated by a similar project—to challenge the ideologies of gender that form a crucial structuring mechanism of modern industrial Japanese society. Both groups understood women to be subordinated to men and highlighted the fact that this subordination was reinforced through multiple networks of power that permeated every level of society. By implication, rectifying such power imbalances would require a profound transformation of the economic structure itself. While the fiction writers focused their attention on exposing the devastating psychological impact of these gendered disciplinary mechanisms, the women's liberation activists attacked the social and economic contradictions that both facilitated and resulted from the engendering process.

Violence

The process of engendering in the stories we have discussed is fig-ured as permeated with violence—sometimes horrific in its effect on the protagonist—that is subsequently internalized and reproduced by women against themselves and other women. L's forcible reinscription as female by a gang of knife/phallus-wielding men in the final lines of "Bad Summer" is an obvious example of this kind of violence. However, as elaborated in chapter 2, the masculine gaze itself may be seen as violently penetrative, as is evident from the scenes of scopic rape in "Getting on the Wrong Train" and *Blue Journey*. Such violence is echoed in "Secret" when Asako displays herself before the gaze of her lover and his friend, keenly sensing herself as an object that must passively submit to that gaze and so hesitating to speak up regarding her own desires. She is therefore effectively deprived of language just like the protagonists of chapter 2, when they are subjected to the engendering masculine gaze.

These narratives make clear that engendering is a process rather than a single event, and its successful outcome is predicated on the extent to which it is internalized and reproduced by the subject herself. The sub-ject's complicity is evident in all the stories in chapter 2, particularly in "Getting on the Wrong Train," where the protagonist is literally inhabited by the masculine gaze in the final lines of the story. Furthermore, the protagonist in "Castle of Bones" seeks out and voluntarily submits to the torturous "training" that is imposed upon other women. Likewise, Akiko from "Toddler-Hunting" solicits violent treatment in her sexual encoun-ters with her boyfriend, willingly adopting a masochistic position vis-à-vis this embodiment of masculine authority. Asako from "Secret" seems to revel in her own quasi-crucifixion, as she stands before the two men with blood running down her breasts and is moved by the masochistic spectacle that she presents to them.

As so many of these stories indicate, women's acceptance of a position of corporeal immanence is a crucial component of this process of engen-dering. Such acceptance requires women to identify themselves with their bodies, or rather identify themselves *as* bodies vis-à-vis men, who are then able to disavow the body in order to adopt an elevated position as subjects of intellectual or spiritual transcendence. The protagonist of "Bone Meat" therefore learns to identify with the discarded possessions that her former boyfriend left behind when he abandoned her and possibly destroys herself along with the rest of the "trash" in the final lines of the story. The main character in "Castle of Bones" is forced to accept that she is "nothing but a woman" in order for the man she admires to even acknowledge her, and her reward for this assumption of a subordinate status is mortification of that body through the self-induced punishment that the "training" represents. Asako in "Secret" learns not only to identify herself with her body, but also to feel ashamed when that body fails to prove pleasing to the masculine gaze. In many stories, a loathing of the body is explicitly directed toward the female reproductive functions so that characters in *Blue Journey*, "Toddler-Hunting," "Like a Witch," and "Bad Summer" view menstruation and pregnancy as negative or empty experiences, seemingly repulsed by their own ability to reproduce.

Finally, a hatred of the feminine is directed not only internally but also externally, in the form of female characters who express chauvinism or violence toward other women. The main character of "On the Road," having adopted a masochistic position vis-à-vis her husband during their lovemaking, subsequently fantasizes about implicating her sister in this violent arrangement, which may possibly result in death. L in "Bad Summer" seems to despise other women—with the exception perhaps of the feminine side of herself, which she nevertheless disavows by projecting these characteristics onto a second self in the form of M. The protagonist of "Intercourse" has internalized the phallic principle to such an extent that she destroys the Other Woman in a metaphorically self-inflicted gesture of reinscribing the law of the father upon a fragile space of homosocial and homoerotic communion. Having struggled and failed to prove herself as provisionally masculine to her mentor and lover, in order to win his admiration and approval, the protagonist of "Like a Witch" declares that women who comply with feminine stereotypes should be "raped and killed." By highlighting the masochistic and self-destructive effects of the engendering process, the authors implicitly protest the insidious and violent consequences of normative structures of gender that induce women to denigrate themselves and other women so as to elevate men as "naturally" superior.

Women's liberation activists likewise protested the violence inherent in gendered power structures, a problem with which many of these women had personal experience during their participation in the student movement of the 1960s. Historians of the women's liberation movement in Japan have cited women's experience of chauvinism at the hands of male comrades as a primary motivating factor for women who broke away from the New Left to form their own "lib" groups in the 1970s. Setsu Shigematsu describes the nature and extent of this chauvinist behavior as follows:

Women did not break away simply because they were stuck making rice balls, or felt slighted when they were put at the rear of the marches or put in charge of first aid at the demonstrations. The sexist discrimination was also a productive part of the common sense that produced a typology of leftist women, ranging from the theoretically sophisticated "Rosa Luxembourg" types, to the beautiful Madonnas and "cute comrades," and extended to what some leftist men would refer to as those who were passed around like "public toilets."[4]

Thus, even radical student activists reproduced the engendering mechanisms of the dominant society within their own organizations, disciplining women to perform as maternal, nurturing figures or sexual objects whose primary purpose was to service male needs—even when those women proved themselves to be committed agents of social change.

Furthermore, women's lib activists were quick to point out that the pervasive sexual objectification of women within the New Left was intimately related to its dominant logic of violence, whereby male activists proved their masculinity through aggressive physical attacks on members of their own or other sects or through street battles with riot police during demonstrations. "For many New Leftists, whether or not some one [*sic*] could take up the *gebabō* [a shaft or pipe used in combat] and engage in battle became the measure of one's revolutionary intent and commitment."[5] That this employment of violence as a means of political praxis frequently took the form of misogynist treatment of women is evident in the insidious tactic of raping the women of rival sects.[6]

Such violence was then internalized and replicated by women, particularly those who remained within the New Left movement and attempted to prove themselves worthy as activists according to this masculinist logic. A striking example may be seen in the case of Nagata Hiroko, a key figure in the Japanese Red Army whose terrorist activities led to its downfall in 1972 and the arrest or death of many of its top leaders. At the height of its orgy of violence, the United Red Army lynched fourteen of its own members, including a woman who was eight months pregnant—an offense that earned Nagata a death sentence for her role in ordering the purge.[7] Shigematsu summarizes the reaction of Tanaka Mitsu, one of the most prominent theorists of the "women's lib" movement, to this event as follows:

The death of the pregnant woman in the United Red Army named Kaneko Michiyo has been remembered as the most tragic of the killings of the United Red Army. Tanaka wrote about the corpse of Kaneko Michiyo—a woman she had met before face-to-face. Her corpse—burdened with an unborn child—signified the logical outcome of the misogyny of the logic of death [that permeated the New Left]. The leaders of the United Red Army (Mori Tsuneo and Nagata Hiroko) discussed keeping the child (for its productive potential), but decided to kill the mother because of her lack of pure revolutionary intent. Within the United Red Army, the expression of traditional femininity or any sexual and erotic desire was deemed "anti-revolutionary."[8]

Given the maternalist ideology that structured conventional assumptions of femininity, it is hardly surprising that the body of Kaneko Michiyo—"burdened with an unborn child"—would be singled out by Nagata as representative of those suffocating norms. For a woman like Nagata, who was struggling to define and prove herself according to a masculine logic that denigrated femininity and all conventional expressions of feminine identity and desire, Kaneko must have seemed an embodiment of the failure to transcend woman's "inferior" status, implicitly threatening Nagata's own fragile position within this masculine hierarchy. Nagata's personal experience of rape and sexual abuse at the hands of members of her own sect may well have contributed to her conflicted mindset regarding feminine gender identity.[9] In this sense, Nagata's violent actions may be seen as consonant with the feminine misogyny—a product of the violent process of engendering—expressed by the protagonists of "Like a Witch," "Castle of Bones," and other stories analyzed in previous chapters.

Even those women who broke away from the New Left to form the women's liberation movement of the early 1970s had to deal with its legacy of violence and misogyny, as the work of Tanaka Mitsu makes evident. Violence is in fact a cornerstone of Tanaka's theory of a "disorderly women's lib," and her controversial support for Nagata Hiroko as herself a victim of the internalized misogyny of the New Left—not to mention the double standard by which she was portrayed in the media at the time—speaks powerfully to the embeddedness of "women's lib" within the very structures of power that it sought to resist. While Tanaka criticized the murder of Kaneko Michiyo as an abhorrent example of the misogynist excesses of the New Left, she simultaneously identified with Nagata, seeing her as "an ordinary woman who was symptomatic of all women who act in such a way to flatter men to gain male recognition."[10]

Thus, while a desire for solidarity among women clearly permeated lib discourse, it masked a deeper anxiety as to how this might be achieved in a society where gender difference was predicated on a misogynist logic that was frequently internalized even by women themselves.

Consistent with the lib movement's emphasis on consciousness-raising, so as to recognize the individual's role in internalizing and reproducing the gendered ideologies that confined her to hegemonic sex roles, Tanaka urged women to recognize the Nagata Hiroko within and to connect this potential for violence with the institutionalized sexism that permeated Japanese society:

> The *ribu* [lib] women decided to explicitly support the "women defendants" of the United Red Army, because they knew that the *criminalization* of women who engaged in violent action was inextricably linked to the ideological policing of women as "passive, peace-loving, and non-violent" subjects, who were rewarded for their compliant support of a masculinist social order.... They understood that Nagata was being condemned not simply because of her actions, but because she was caught acting violently *as an onna* [woman], outside of the acceptable boundaries for women to act.... *Ribu* women recognized the sexist and repressive logic that permitted men to express violent aggressive behavior, but viewed the violent actions of women as necessarily aberrant and pathological.[11]

Rejecting the master narrative of the maternal feminine that structured conventional roles for women, Nagata had attempted to establish an alternate identity for herself within a revolutionary organization that sought to transform Japanese society, only to find that this organization operated according to the same sexist power structures as the world outside. Subjected to disciplinary mechanisms that sought to reinscribe her as feminine through sexualized violence that was intended to relegate her to subordinate status, her only choice to transcend this abject state and assume a position of leadership was to redefine herself as provisionally masculine by denying those characteristics that threatened to expose her as feminine.

Within this revolutionary sphere, mastery of the language of violence was a necessary precondition for leadership. But such mastery ironically also led to Nagata's downfall, as she was subsequently convicted in the court of public opinion as a "menacing crazy-woman motivated by spite and jealousy," in contrast to her male colleague Mori Tsuneo, who was depicted merely as a "political leader whose plans went astray."[12] Even as she was sentenced to death for her assumption of the male prerogative of violence, she was reinscribed as feminine through the stereotypically "female" characteristics of spitefulness and jealousy. It is no wonder that the women's liberation activists, who had fought their own battles with a mass media that sought to trivialize their demands for social change, could identify with her plight.

The example of Nagata, and those like Tanaka who rose to her defense, poignantly underscores the double bind faced by women who struggled against "femininity" as the logical opposite of an ideology of masculine superiority. Stereotypical constructions of women as "naturally" passive, maternal, and inferior to men were clearly abhorrent, both to the participants in the women's liberation movement and to the writers discussed in this study. However, the binary logic that confined women to the negative side of this polarity made it difficult to attack ideologies of maternal femininity without appearing to also lash out at those women who complied with existing gender norms. The only position one could occupy within this structure, once one had rejected feminine inferiority, was a provisionally "masculine" subject position that carried its own chauvinist baggage. The persistence of this binary logic accounts for much of the "feminist misogyny," expressed by both writers of fiction and women's liberation activists who strove to extricate themselves from a model of femininity that rendered them mute, passive, and inferior. Just as Tanaka expressed solidarity with Nagata, seeing her as emblematic of the devastating effects of an engendering process that denigrates half of humanity, women writers of fiction likewise produced dystopic narratives of female misogyny, both self- and other-directed, that exposed this self-abnegation as a product of the misogynist logic of hegemonic gender roles.

Language

If there is any way out of this "prison-house" of gender, it seems to be through language. When the protagonists of "Broken Oath" and "Getting on the Wrong Train" finally submit to the process of engendering, the moment is signified by their loss of language, implying that they are rendered defenseless and incapable of further resistance to the disciplinary mechanisms that would contain them. On the other hand, while the protagonist of *Blue Journey* is likewise silenced during her traumatic experience of scopic rape, she is able to regain a position of empowerment by literally becoming the author of her own story. This character even explicitly articulates her intention to subvert gender norms through a perfect performance of them, effectively enunciating a posture of resistance through parody.

Subversion of gender norms is achieved on a metatextual level as well, as other narratives reenact the process of engendering so as to draw the reader's attention to the catastrophic costs of conforming to the structures that discipline and enforce such norms. The scene in "Toddler-Hunting" when the little boy is forcibly inscribed with markers of femininity may be read as a sort of hysterical parody of the disciplinary mechanisms that produce femininity in young girls. In *Blue Journey,* Kurahashi exposes the violence and cruelty of this experience of feminization by directly interpellating her audience through the second-person pronoun "you," effectively placing the reader in the position of the object of scopic rape. "Castle of Bones" reveals the hypocrisy of the double standard that discursively constructs women as inferior to men even when they demonstrate themselves capable of passing the tests that would prove their "worth" on par with men. Finally, "Snake" parodies gender norms by rendering them unnatural and incomprehensible, frustrating any attempt to align bodies with behaviors and desires that are understood to be normative. Through narratives that disturb or challenge the reader to reexamine her own preconceptions about "natural" distinctions between the sexes, these authors trouble gender norms in ways that echo the consciousness-raising tactics of the women's liberation movement of the following decade.

The purpose of consciousness-raising was to encourage women to recognize the gendered structures that confined them, toward finding practical ways of articulating new and less restrictive models of femininity in their lives. This method of praxis may be seen as similar to the project of the fiction writers we have analyzed in the sense that fiction served as a medium for exposing gendered networks of power and the violence done to women in being forced to comply with such structures. Such narratives indeed seem intended to shock women (and men) into recognizing the asymmetrical power relationships in which gender in Japanese society was embedded. But while the intent of these two groups may have been similar, their use of language to achieve this end seems to have yielded somewhat different results. Rather than parodying or disrupting existing structures of gender from within, by reenacting their effects in order to critique them, the women's lib movement sought an "authentic" feminine voice with which to articulate feminine experience as fundamentally different from that of men (yet no less valuable).

This project of articulating an "authentic" femininity, freed from the strictures of the dominant masculine paradigm, is evident in many of the publications of the women's lib movement. *Minikomi,* or "mini-communication" publications—in opposition to the *masukomi,* or mass-communication, large-circulation periodicals of mainstream society—were one important way that activists of various lib groups communicated with each other, particularly during the 1970s. As Sandra Buckley notes, these *minikomi* tended to employ characteristically feminine language as a means of creating a feminine discursive space.[13] This rhetorical strategy was then adopted by larger-circulation feminist journals such as *Onna erosu,* one of the most important periodicals to have emerged from the women's liberation movement. Buckley explains the effect of this rhetorical style as follows:

> In a review some years later one Japanese feminist who had been an avid reader of the journal recalled how important it had been to her that the language used in *Onna Erosu* was less stiff and academic than that of the U.S. feminist works translated into Japanese or the publications of the growing number of Japanese academic feminists. The frequent use of the feminine first-person pronoun (*watashi*) and the sense of familiarity created by a more colloquial or informal language was a direct carry over from the style of the *minikomi.*[14]

Academic styles of writing were indeed associated with masculine speech at this time—and to some extent today as well—and the attempt to create a language for feminism that spoke directly to the heart of women was a prime objective of the Japanese lib movement of the 1970s.

Innovative use of language was also evident in the project to translate the landmark American feminist text *Our Bodies, Ourselves* into Japanese. Feminist activists who participated in this project recall struggling to find a language that women could use to describe their bodies without shame and without the distancing effect that medical terminology brought, along with substantially chauvinist implications.[15] For example, Chinese compounds used to represent female reproductive organs frequently employ the characters for "dark/negative," "shame," and "blood," all of which traditionally connote "impurity" in Japan.[16] Feminists at this time recognized that "standard" Japanese was in fact "masculine" speech, permeated with sexist terms for anything associated with the feminine, and it would have to be rewritten before women could speak of female bodies and experiences in positive terms. In this context, "feminine" speech signified the creation of a linguistic community among women that was separate from and opposed to dominant masculine discourse.

In the realm of literature, however, women had long been confined to the separate sphere of "women's-style literature," which was seen as inherently inferior to the dominant masculine discourse. This ideological categorization of men's and women's literature was supported by a set of binary oppositions that aligned the feminine with "popular," "autobiographical," and intellectually and artistically inferior, as opposed to mainstream (that is, malestream) literature, which was purely artistic, confessional, and intellectually superior. While the fascination with confessional literature had generally fallen out of fashion by the 1960s, the qualitative distinction between "feminine" and "masculine" spheres remained.[17]

Keenly aware of these distinctions, the women writers who made their debuts during the 1960s boom in women's literature explicitly sought to inhabit this "masculine" sphere so as to disrupt it from within, challenging its privileged claim to artistic and intellectual authenticity. All of the writers analyzed in this study were considered by contemporary critics to write intellectually sophisticated stories, but Kōno's writing in particular has been described as "cerebral" and "difficult to comprehend."[18] Kurahashi goes so far as to employ that most "masculine" of discourses, mathematics, to describe her own literary style: beginning with a "hypothesis" or "axiom," she introduces several "variables" (that is, characters) and allows the plot to play out according to the logic that governs the "anti-world" that she has created.[19] Both Kurahashi and Takahashi have been described as "masculine" or "androgynous" writers for their so-called unfeminine literary styles and themes.[20] For women writers of the 1960s, the term "women's style literature" was a restrictive category ideologically imposed upon them by male conceptions of the way women "should" write, and many were therefore motivated to resist this categorization by deliberately employing language that was encoded as "masculine." In this context, then, "feminine" language signified not a liberatory expression of an authentic female self but rather a false and sexist ideology of female intellectual inferiority imposed upon women so as to characterize women's writing as second class.

There are a striking number of conceptual similarities between the literary feminism of the 1960s, and the feminist discourse of the women's lib activists of the 1970s. There are also a few differences in emphasis and articulation, most particularly having to do with generic differences between literature and political speech as modes of discourse. Literature, unbound by the requirement to "make sense" or forward a coherent political message, is in some ways freer to subvert dominant hegemonic paradigms with impunity. In the realm of fantasy, it is perhaps easier to imagine alternatives that subvert or challenge the status quo, while absolving oneself of the thorny question of how to put those ideals into practice. On the other hand, one has to first be able to envision an alternative before the status quo can be changed. Women writers of literature during the 1960s took on the difficult task of challenging gender roles that had come to seem natural and inevitable and were furthermore enforced by disciplinary mechanisms that penetrated all levels of Japanese society. The women's liberation activists of the 1970s may therefore be said to have picked up where these writers of literature left off.

The emergence of second-wave feminism in the 1970s had an extraordinary impact on the tone and content of discourse on gender and sexuality in Japanese society. In the early part of the decade, the "women's lib" movement sought to open up the field of possible expressions of feminine identity to include greater acceptance of female sexuality on its own terms and questioned conventional assumptions about the "naturalness" of gendered divisions of labor that structured public and private life. In the latter half of the 1970s, this led to the creation of "women's studies" as an academic field of study, as well as the increasing influence of female scholars and bureaucrats on government policies to promote gender equality. The explosion of political protest by women in the early 1970s could certainly be seen as one catalyst for the institutional and legal reforms of subsequent decades that opened the door to women's participation in ever broader sectors of Japanese society.[21] However, judging by the obvious feminist theoretical relevance of the authors addressed in this study, it may be time to rethink histories of feminism that privilege explicitly political speech over other methods of feminist discourse.

It is also important to stress the role of historical, economic, and social forces in shaping the forms of feminist resistance that were possible in each decade. The time frame covered by this study was designed to coincide with the end of the high economic growth period for this reason. The early 1970s saw the onset of a recession brought on by changes in the exchange rate and an international oil crisis caused by the OPEC embargo. These shocks to the economic foundation of Japanese society, in addition to increasing concerns regarding the environmental and human costs of prosperity, prompted Japan to rethink its total commitment to economic growth at the expense of other measures of quality of life.[22] In this context of soul searching and forced paradigm shifts, it became possible to credibly challenge the status quo, including the gender roles that formed the bedrock of such social structures, in ways that would have been significantly more difficult during the prosperous and freewheeling economic growth era of the 1960s. Perhaps, then, it is no wonder that feminist discourse during this period took the form of imaginative subversions of gender norms.

What a difference a decade makes.

Notes

Introduction

1. Takahashi Takako, "Onnagirai," in *Tamashii no inu* (Tokyo: Kōdansha, 1975), 231. For a complete English translation of this essay, with commentary, see chapter 2 in Julia C. Bullock, "A Single Drop of Crimson: Takahashi Takako and the Narration of Liminality" (PhD dissertation, Stanford University, 2004).

2. Kathleen S. Uno, "The Death of 'Good Wife, Wise Mother'?" in *Postwar Japan as History,* edited by Andrew Gordon (Berkeley: University of California Press, 1993).

3. By "radical feminism," I mean attempts to remake social or ideological structures that define normative gender roles, with the intent of altering Japanese society at its core. This distinguishes it from the "housewife feminism" of the same period, which advocated for certain social reforms (such as consumer protection) that would benefit women through an improvement of family life. Housewife-feminist activists tended to work within, rather than against, normative constructions of gender by emphasizing their moral authority as mothers. As this study is devoted to discursive attempts to alter gender roles and identities beyond that of the "good wife, wise mother," I am obviously more concerned with radical feminist discourse. For a thorough study of the historical development of housewife feminism in prewar Japan, see Akiko Tokuza, *The Rise of the Feminist Movement in Japan* (Tokyo: Keio University Press, 1999). For the early postwar decades, see chapter 6 of Vera Mackie's *Feminism in Modern Japan: Citizenship, Embodiment, and Sexuality* (New York: Cambridge University Press, 2003).

4. For a thorough account of the student-movement origins of "women's lib," see chapter 1 in Setsu Shigematsu, "Tanaka Mitsu and the Women's Liberation Movement in Japan: Towards a Radical Feminist Ontology" (PhD dissertation, Cornell University, 2003).

5. For example, Kurahashi Yumiko, one of the most important and critically acclaimed writers of this generation, wrote scathing critiques of the intellectual paucity of New Left political movements, even as she attempted in her own way to force readers to question reigning common sense about properly masculine and feminine gender identities.

6. For an overview of the theoretical concerns of "women's lib" activists of the 1970s, see Ichiyo Muto, "The Birth of the Women's Liberation Movement in the 1970s," in *The Other Japan: Conflict, Compromise, and Resistance since 1945,* edited by Joe Moore (Armonk, NY: East Gate/M. E. Sharpe, 1997).

7. Kurahashi debuted in 1960 with the short story "Partei" (Parutai). Kōno had been writing for some time before this but did not earn much critical attention until the publication of her short story "Toddler-Hunting" (Yōjigari) in 1961. Takahashi first began publishing in 1965 with the story "Glitter" (Kirameki). All three of these stories are available in English translation (see the works cited).

8. Michel Foucault, *The History of Sexuality: An Introduction,* vol. 1 (New York: Random House, 1990), 139–145.

9. Sheldon Garon, *Molding Japanese Minds: The State in Everyday Life* (Princeton, NJ: Princeton University Press, 1997), 5–6.

10. Judith Butler, *Gender Trouble* (New York and London: Routledge, 1999), 171–180.

Chapter 1: Party Crashers and Poison Pens

1. This historical survey has been compiled primarily from information in Elise K. Tipton, *Modern Japan: A Social and Political History* (New York: Routledge, 2002), and Andrew Gordon, *A Modern History of Japan: From Tokugawa Times to the Present* (New York and Oxford: Oxford University Press, 2003).

2. The United States had begun pressuring Japan to remilitarize even before the Occupation ended, resulting in the creation of a National Police Reserve that evolved into what is currently known as the Self-Defense Forces (SDF) in 1954. This U.S. pressure for remilitarization was highly ironic in light of the fact that the new (American-authored) Japanese constitution prominently featured a renunciation of all forms of aggressive military force (Article 9).

3. Socialist Party members who tried to obstruct the vote were physically removed from the Diet building on the orders of Prime Minister Kishi Nobusuke, and when the rest of the socialists boycotted the session, the LDP passed the bill anyway over strenuous protests not just from the opposition parties, but also from a large portion of the Japanese citizenry. Large-scale riots ensued, and Kishi was forced to step down as the news media criticized him for precipitating this "crisis for parliamentary democracy." Takafusa Nakamura, *A History of Shōwa Japan, 1926–1989,* trans. Edwin Whenmouth (Tokyo: University of Tokyo Press, 1998), 347.

4. Early postwar victories by organized labor had been undermined first by the Occupation's "reverse course" and then by increasingly cozy relations between the Japanese government and business interests throughout the 1950s. As Japan transitioned from coal to oil as its primary source of fuel for industry, there was a rash of mine closures and cutbacks. At Miike these included the involuntary "retirement" of selected workers. When it became evident that a disproportionate

number of union leaders had been targeted for retirement, a strike was called, leading to a lockout of unionized workers.

5. Tipton, 166.

6. Gordon, *A Modern History of Japan*, 279. Ikeda's plan cannot be solely credited for these changes, as the trend toward high economic growth actually began in 1950, with the onset of the Korean War. Japan's strategic location, not to mention its role as subordinate nation under the Occupation by the United States (and later as ally under the U.S.-Japan Security Treaty), made it the logical choice as a supply base for U.S. troops during that conflict. Japan's growth should also be seen against a backdrop of global economic growth facilitated by booming international trade. See ibid., 246.

7. Tipton, 169, 177.

8. Ibid., 170, 182.

9. Ibid., 167–168.

10. *Shōwa niman'nichi no zenkiroku: Anpo to kōdo seichō*, vol. 12 (Tokyo: Kōdansha, 1990), 206–207.

11. Kumiko Fujimura-Fanselow, "College Women Today: Options and Dilemmas," in *Japanese Women: New Feminist Perspectives on the Past, Present and Future*, edited by Kumiko Fujimura-Fanselow and Atsuko Kameda (New York: Feminist Press, 1995), 126–132.

12. For more on this ideology of femininity, see Uno.

13. For a thorough explanation of this term, see Foucault, *The History of Sexuality*, 139–145.

14. Gordon, *A Modern History of Japan*, 214–215.

15. Andrew Gordon, "Managing the Japanese Household: The New Life Movement in Postwar Japan," in *Gendering Modern Japanese History*, edited by Barbara Molony and Kathleen Uno (Cambridge, MA: Harvard University Press, 2005), 428.

16. Tiana Norgren, *Abortion before Birth Control: The Politics of Reproduction in Postwar Japan* (Princeton, NJ: Princeton University Press, 2001), 56.

17. Ibid., 5–6.

18. See ibid., chapter 5, for an overview of these movements.

19. Ibid., 56, 96. On "purity education," see chapter 3 in Sonia Ryang, *Love in Modern Japan: Its Estrangement from Self, Sex, and Society* (London and New York: Routledge, 2006).

20. See Norgren, chapter 7, on the politics surrounding legalization of the pill.

21. The cooperation of the male partner is obviously true of condoms because of the nature of the method. Additionally, a male partner's consent was legally required before an abortion could be performed.

22. Barbara Sato, *The New Japanese Woman: Modernity, Media, and Women in Interwar Japan* (Durham, NC: Duke University Press, 2003), 159.

23. Ryang, 69.

24. Ibid., 88.

25. Donald Roden, "From 'Old Miss' to New Professional: A Portrait of Women Educators under the American Occupation of Japan, 1945–52," *History of Education Quarterly* 23, no. 4 (1983): 471.

26. Ibid., 471.

27. Ibid., 476.

28. See, for example, her reminiscences of this time in *Takahashi Kazumi no omoide,* discussed below under "Texts and Contexts."

29. For example, Atsuko Kameda finds that as late as 1975, Japanese school textbooks in various subjects were riddled with portrayals of boys and girls in stereotypically gender-coded behavior, informally indoctrinating students into their future roles as appropriately gendered men and women. See Atsuko Kameda, "Sexism and Gender Stereotyping in Schools," in Fujimura-Fanselow and Kameda, *Japanese Women,* 112–113.

30. Ibid., 111. As Sally Hastings notes, girls growing up in the United States at this time would have experienced a similarly sex-segregated vocational curriculum (personal communication).

31. Kameda, 112.

32. Hiroko Hirakawa, "Maiden Martyr for 'New Japan': The 1960 Ampo and the Rhetoric of the Other Michiko," *U.S.-Japan Women's Journal,* no. 23 (2002): 95.

33. Yoko Kawashima, "Female Workers: An Overview of Past and Current Trends," in Fujimura-Fanselow and Kameda, *Japanese Women,* 276.

34. Ibid., 281.

35. Eiko Shinotsuka, "Women Workers in Japan: Past, Present, Future," in *Women of Japan and Korea: Continuity and Change,* edited by Joyce Gelb and Marian Lief Palley (Philadelphia: Temple University Press, 1994), 115.

36. Ibid., 102.

37. Gordon, "Managing the Japanese Household," 425.

38. Ibid., 447.

39. Jan Bardsley, "Discourse on Women in Postwar Japan: The Housewife Debate of 1955," *U.S.-Japan Women's Journal,* no. 16 (1999): 8–9.

40. Ibid., 11–12.

41. For a history of the *bundan* prior to the end of World War II, see Irena Powell, *Writers and Society in Modern Japan* (Tokyo: Kodansha International, 1983). For a variety of perspectives on the genre of *shishōsetsu,* see Edward Fowler, *The Rhetoric of Confession: Shishōsetsu in Early Twentieth Century Japanese Fiction* (Berkeley: University of California Press, 1988); James Fujii, *Complicit Fictions: The Subject in the Modern Japanese Prose Narrative* (Berkeley: University of California Press, 1993); and Tomi Suzuki, *Narrating the Self: Fictions of Japanese Modernity* (Stanford, CA: Stanford University Press, 1996).

42. "Ichiyō had to rewrite her submissions until they struck [mentor Nakarai] Tōsui as appropriately feminine." Rebecca Copeland, *Lost Leaves: Women Writers of Meiji Japan* (Honolulu: University of Hawai'i Press, 2000), 44.

43. Joan Ericson, "The Origins of the Concept of 'Women's Literature,'" in *The Woman's Hand: Gender and Theory in Japanese Women's Writing*, edited by Paul Gordon Schalow and Janet A. Walker (Stanford, CA: Stanford University Press, 1996), 101.

44. The characterization of Sono's writing is taken from Sachiko Schierbeck, *Japanese Women Novelists in the 20th Century* (Copenhagen: University of Copenhagen, Museum Tusculanum, 1994), 133.

45. Chieko M. Ariga, "Text Versus Commentary: Struggles over the Cultural Meanings of 'Woman,'" in Schalow and Walker, *The Woman's Hand*. Ariga demonstrates that *kaisetsu*, or explanatory essays appended to the paperback editions that were responsible for bringing women's work to a mass audience, frequently served to neutralize feminist literary challenges to the status quo. She specifically addresses *kaisetsu* that accompanied the publication of the work of Takahashi and Kōno.

46. Chieko M. Ariga, "Who's Afraid of Amino Kiku? Gender Conflict and the Literary Canon," in Fujimura-Fanselow and Kameda, *Japanese Women*. Ariga demonstrates how such gendered expectations of women's literary production worked to exclude one popular prewar writer from the canon. According to Ariga, Amino Kiku (1900–1978), a writer of "semi-autobiographical fiction" and a contemporary of more well-known writers like Miyamoto Yuriko, was apparently quite popular with mainstream audiences and was rewarded with literary prizes and critical acclaim. Yet today she is largely unknown because she was almost uniformly excluded from all the major volumes of collected works that have secured the lasting reputations of many of her contemporaries. Ariga attributes this neglect to Amino's consistent portrayal of female protagonists who are completely independent of relationships with men, as well as her depiction of female bodily experiences in frank, unsentimental, and sometimes grotesque ways that alienated male critics.

47. The term *zenshū* refers to any collection of works by a single author or group of authors, but here I am referring to large anthologies such as *Nihon kindai bungaku taikei*. These collections present themselves as a selection of the best literature published during a period of time (anywhere from specific eras such as "Shōwa literature" to all-inclusive periods like "modern Japan"). As such, they purport to determine for posterity which works of literature survive as "timeless" and which ones are quickly forgotten.

48. Margaret Hillenbrand, "Doppelgängers, Misogyny, and the San Francisco System: The Occupation Narratives of Ōe Kenzaburō," *Journal of Japanese Studies* 33, no. 2 (2007): 399.

49. Michael S. Molasky, *The American Occupation of Japan and Okinawa: Literature and Memory* (London and New York: Routledge, 1999), 132.

50. Douglas N. Slaymaker, *The Body in Postwar Japanese Fiction* (London and New York: RoutledgeCurzon, 2004), 35–36.

51. Susan J. Napier, *Escape from the Wasteland: Romanticism and Realism in the Fiction of Mishima Yukio and Oe Kenzaburo* (Cambridge, MA: Harvard University Press, 1991).

52. Ibid., 92–93.

53. *To the End of the Heavens* is one obvious example of this type of story.

54. Atsuko Sakaki, "Kurahashi Yumiko's Negotiations with the Fathers," in *The Father-Daughter Plot: Japanese Literary Women and the Law of the Father,* edited by Rebecca L. Copeland and Esperanza Ramirez-Christensen (Honolulu: University of Hawai'i Press, 2001).

55. Biographical information on Kōno has been compiled from Kōno Taeko, "Kōno Taeko nenpu," in *Shōwa bungaku zenshū,* edited by Yasushi Inoue (Tokyo: Shōgakukan, 1987).

56. Davinder L. Bhowmik, "Kōno Taeko," in *Modern Japanese Writers,* edited by Jay Rubin (New York: Charles Scribner's Sons, 2001), 171. Enemy cultural products were banned during the height of the Pacific War conflict. The work of the Brontë sisters, in particular, would profoundly influence her later development as a writer.

57. The decision to draft young unmarried women was also consistent with government policy to preserve the integrity of the family unit by keeping married women with children at home. See Sandra Buckley, "Altered States: The Body Politics of 'Being-Woman,'" in *Postwar Japan as History,* edited by Andrew Gordon (Berkeley: University of California Press, 1993), 365.

58. For a brief account of such disciplinary regimes, see "Japan in Wartime," chapter 12 of Gordon, *A Modern History of Japan.*

59. For readers who cannot read Japanese, see "Full Tide" (Michishio, 1964), translated by Lucy North, in *Toddler-Hunting and Other Stories* (New York: New Directions, 1996). Other stories that treat this topic are "Inside the Fence" (Hei no naka, 1962) and "Distant Summer" (Tōi natsu, 1964). Both are included in volume one of Kōno's untranslated collected works, *Kōno Taeko zenshū* (Tokyo: Shinchōsha, 1994).

60. Indeed, most families saw college attendance for young women as a means of improving their marriage prospects rather than preparing them for any sort of career, and in this sense Kōno's family may be seen as typical of the mainstream opinion regarding gender-appropriate life choices. See Chizuko Uema, "Resisting Sadomasochism in Kōno Taeko" (PhD dissertation, University of Oregon, 1998), 9–10.

61. In English, see "Crabs" (Kani, 1963), "Toddler-Hunting" (Yōjigari, 1961), and "Ants Swarm" (Ari takaru, 1966) in North. "On the Examining Room Table" (Utena ni noru, 1965) and "The Next Day" (Akuru hi, 1965), in volume two of Kōno's collected works, also deal with these themes.

62. Uema, 3.

63. Kōno, *Kōno Taeko zenshū,* vol. 2, 143.

64. Several scholars have noted a progression in Kōno's literature from protagonists who play the masochist role in her early works to those who take up the role of sadist in later stories. Some interpret these themes as a metaphor for women's subordinate role in Japanese society and see her heroines' eventual

assumption of roles of power (as opposed to submission) in later works as a kind of literary closure of this theme, illustrating women's liberation from the bounds of patriarchal oppression. One example of this type of interpretation is Uema.

65. Other prestigious prizes included the Tanizaki Jun'ichirō Award (for *Ichinen no bokka*, 1980) and the Noma Literary Award (for *Miiratori ryōkitan*, 1991). Kōno's work has appeared in anthologies such as the *Nihon bungaku zenshū* (Collection of Japanese Literature, Kawade shobō shinsha, 1971); *Gendai bungaku taikei* (Compendium of Contemporary Literature, Chikuma shobō, 1968, 1977); and *Shōwa bungaku zenshū* (Shōwa Era Literature Collection, Shōgakukan, 1987).

66. Yonaha Keiko, *Gendai joryū sakkaron* (Tokyo: Shinbisha, 1986), 7.

67. Bhowmik, 170.

68. As recalled in Takahashi's 1975 essay, "Coeducation" (Danjo kyōgaku), in *Kioku no kurasa* (Kyoto: Jinbun shoin, 1977). This is echoed in other essays in this volume and in Takahashi Takako, *Tamashii no inu* (Tokyo: Kōdansha, 1975).

69. Takahashi, *Takahashi Kazumi no omoide*, 92. Unless otherwise indicated, all translations in the book are mine.

70. This information is compiled from anecdotal evidence in *Takahashi Kazumi no omoide* (ibid.), a memoir recounting their married life together until Kazumi's premature death from cancer in 1971, and from Takahashi's self-authored personal chronology at the end of her selected works: Takahashi Takako, "Jihitsu nenpu," in *Takahashi Takako jisen shōsetsu shū* (Tokyo: Kōdansha, 1994).

71. See, for example, "Doll Love" (Ningyōai, 1976), "Secret Rituals" (Higi, 1978), and *The House of Rebirth* (*Yomigaeri no ie*, 1980). While the stories that depict Takahashi's fascination with this particular theme fall temporally outside the parameters of this study, Maryellen Mori has published extensively on this topic; see "The Quest for Jouissance in Takahashi Takako's Texts," in Schalow and Walker, *The Woman's Hand*, and "The Liminal Male as Liberatory Figure in Japanese Women's Fiction," *Harvard Journal of Asiatic Studies* 60, no. 2 (2000).

72. Having completed a graduation thesis on Baudelaire in 1954, which stimulated her interest in philosophical problems of good and evil, Takahashi immersed herself in a study of the works of François Mauriac, which led her to complete a master's thesis on this author in 1958. Some of her first publications were in fact not works of literature but literary criticism of authors like Mauriac and Endō Shūsaku, who grappled with such questions from a Catholic perspective. She later devoted herself to translation of Mauriac's story *Thérèse Desqueyroux* (published in 1963), a tale of a woman who tries to poison her husband and comes face to face with the evil impulses that lurk beneath the surface of her everyday life.

73. Yonaha, 35.

74. Mark Williams, "Double Vision: Divided Narrative Focus in Takahashi Takako's *Yosōi Seyo, Waga Tamashii Yo*," in *Ōe and Beyond: Fiction in Contemporary Japan*, edited by Stephen Snyder and Philip Gabriel (Honolulu: University of Hawai'i Press, 1999), 111.

75. Biographical information on Kurahashi is taken primarily from *Chikuma gendai bungaku taikei* 82 (Tokyo: Chikuma shobō, 1977). See also Faye Yuan Kleeman, "Kurahashi Yumiko," in *Japanese Fiction Writers since World War II*, edited by Van C. Gessel (Detroit: Gale Research, 1997), 93–101.

76. NHK, the Japanese national television network, is functionally equivalent to the BBC in the United Kingdom.

77. Sakaki, "Kurahashi Yumiko's Negotiations with the Fathers," 311.

78. See, for example, "Like a Witch" (Yōjo no yō ni, 1964), in which "femininity" is explicitly defined as thoroughly subsuming oneself in love for a man. The protagonist's writing career begins, she says, when she loses the ability to love men and therefore "stops being a woman"; her ability to write originates from the "third eye," which develops at the site where her "female parts" shrivel away (*Kurahashi Yumiko zensakuhin*, vol. 4, 247–248).

79. A remarkable exception to this trend is "Virginia," an unusually (for Kurahashi) realistic story loosely based on her stay in the United States, written just after her return to Japan. In this story the author seems to be working through some of her own anxieties regarding her conflicting identities of wife/mother and published author. For more on this work, see Julia C. Bullock, "We'll Always Have Iowa: Gender and National Identity in Kurahashi Yumiko's 'Virginia,'" *Proceedings of the Association for Japanese Literary Studies (PAJLS)* 7 (2007).

80. Kurahashi Yumiko, "Symbiosis" (Kyōsei), in *Kurahashi Yumiko zensakuhin*, vol. 6 (Tokyo: Shinchōsha, 1976), 109.

81. Ibid., 93.

82. For a thorough account of the vituperative debates surrounding *Blue Journey* and subsequent works, see Sakaki, "Kurahashi Yumiko's Negotiations with the Fathers."

83. Takeo Okuno, "Is Fiction Inherently the Realm of Women?" in *Woman Critiqued: Translated Essays on Japanese Women's Writing*, edited by Rebecca L. Copeland (Honolulu: University of Hawai'i Press, 2006). For a list of the women writers honored by both the Akutagawa and Naoki prize committees, see Chieko Ariga, "Onna ga teigi suru 'onna': Akutagawa shō, Naoki shō sakuhin ni miru," *Nichibei josei jānaru* 18 (1995). Ariga notes a marked increase in female winners of both prizes beginning in the 1960s and then accelerating dramatically from 1980 to the time of writing.

84. For more on Kurahashi's popularity in the 1960s and her relationship to the countercultural milieu, see Suzuki Naoko, "Ribu zen'ya no Kurahashi Yumiko—Josei shintai o meguru seiji," in *Karuchuaru poritikusu 1960/70* (Tokyo: Serika shobo, 2005). For an account in English of Kurahashi's unfortunate experiences with the *bundan*, see Atsuko Sakaki, "(Re)Canonizing Kurahashi Yumiko: Toward Alternative Perspectives for 'Modern' 'Japanese' 'Literature,'" in Snyder and Gabriel, *Ōe and Beyond*.

85. See Shimizu Yoshinori, "Arano no soko kara todoku koe," in *Doko ka aru ie: Takahashi Takako jisen essei shū* (Tokyo: Kōdansha, 2006).

Chapter 2: The Masculine Gaze as Disciplinary Mechanism

Epigraph. Laura Mulvey, "Visual Pleasure and Narrative Cinema," in *Feminism and Film Theory,* edited by Constance Penley (New York: Routledge, 1988), 64.

1. Michel Foucault, *Discipline and Punish: The Birth of the Prison,* trans. Alan Sheridan, 2nd ed. (New York: Vintage Books, 1995), 200–201.

2. Ibid., 228.

3. Laura Mulvey, "Afterthoughts on 'Visual Pleasure and Narrative Cinema' Inspired by 'Duel in the Sun.'" In Penley, *Feminism and Film Theory,* 69–79.

4. See, for example, Lois McNay, *Foucault and Feminism: Power, Gender, and the Self* (Boston: Northeastern University Press, 1992), and Caroline Ramazanoğlu, ed., *Up against Foucault: Explorations of Some Tensions between Foucault and Feminism* (London and New York: Routledge, 1993).

5. Gordon, *A Modern History of Japan,* 221.

6. For example, Garon notes the role of home inspections by grassroots New Life Association activists in campaigns to inculcate frugality and resource conservation as late as the 1980s (175). Likewise, in "Managing the Japanese Household," Gordon notes that such home visits were also integral in the movement's promotion of birth control (444–445), as well as intervention into family disputes (435–436), demonstrating the degree to which outside surveillance penetrated to the most intimate corners of women's lives.

7. Kōno Taeko, "Broken Oath" (Haisei), in *Kōno Taeko zenshū,* vol. 2 (Tokyo: Shinchōsha, 1995), 289. Subsequent page citations will appear parenthetically in the discussion of the text. All translations are mine unless otherwise indicated.

8. Foucault, *Discipline and Punish,* 200.

9. Kasumigaseki is a neighborhood in Tokyo where the headquarters of Japanese government bureaucracies are located, and the name of the area itself is used metonymically to refer to this seat of administrative power, just as "Wall Street" is used to refer to the center of financial power in the United States.

10. Takahashi Takako, "Getting on the Wrong Train" (Jōsha sakugo), in *Hone no shiro* (Kyoto: Jinbun shoin, 1972), 221–222. Subsequent page citations will appear parenthetically.

11. Kurahashi Yumiko, *Blue Journey (Kurai tabi),* in *Kurahashi Yumiko zensakuhin* (Tokyo: Shinchōsha, 1975), 98–99. Ellipsis in original. Subsequent page citations will appear parenthetically.

12. Chapter 1 in Atsuko Sakaki, "The Intertextual Novel and the Interrelational Self: Kurahashi Yumiko, a Japanese Postmodernist" (PhD dissertation, University of British Columbia, 1992).

13. This is not to suggest that only women are subordinated to disciplinary mechanisms that produce them as gendered subjects. While a definitive conclusion regarding the production of masculine gender identity is clearly unwarranted

given the parameters of this study, I hypothesize that men are likewise subjected to a different type of societally inflicted gaze that polices their behavior and crafts them into appropriately "masculine" subjects. Take, for example, the scene in Mishima Yukio's *Confessions of a Mask,* in which the young male protagonist dresses in his mother's clothes and performs in drag for an audience of friends and family, only to be made to understand, via the horrified looks in the eyes of his loved ones, that his behavior and desires are "abnormal."

Chapter 3: Feminist Misogyny? or How I Learned to Hate My Body

Epigraph. Susan Gubar, "Feminist Misogyny: Mary Wollstonecraft and the Paradox of 'It Takes One to Know One,'" *Feminist Studies* 20, no. 3 (1994): 462.

1. See chapter 1, "Approaching Abjection," of Julia Kristeva, *Powers of Horror* (New York: Columbia University Press, 1982), 1–4.

2. Kōno Taeko, "Bone Meat," in North, *Toddler-Hunting,* 259. As "Bone Meat" is one of two stories analyzed in this book that exist in English translation and since the translated version of this story is widely used and cited in English-language scholarship, I have opted to quote from this version rather than provide my own translations of the original. Subsequent page citations will appear parenthetically and are from the translation by Lucy Lower so that English readers can easily locate the quoted passages.

3. Kurahashi Yumiko, "Like a Witch" (Yōjo no yō ni), in *Kurahashi Yumiko zensakuhin,* vol. 4 (Tokyo: Shinchōsha, 1976), 217. All translations are mine. Subsequent page citations will appear parenthetically.

4. This notion of being impregnated by his gaze is eerily reminiscent of the denouement of Takahashi's "Getting on the Wrong Train," where the eyes of the young boy likewise "take up residence" inside the protagonist in the final lines of the story.

5. While the inclusion of "female Diet members" in this list of abhorrent types may sound far from the Western idea of a feminine stereotype, in the Japanese context, "housewife feminism" gave certain women license to participate in politics on the condition that they did so on the basis of their moral authority as wives and mothers. Many female Diet members in the first few postwar decades ran on such platforms. One example of this "feminine" approach to politics is Ichikawa Fusae; though Ichikawa herself ironically did not marry or have children, she rose to power on a platform that embraced "housewife-feminist" issues as central to social reform. The symbol of her campaign for inclusion in this predominantly male-dominated structure of authority was the rice ladle, evocative of home and hearth, and a mother's "natural" instinct to nurture. Another example would be Oku Mumeo, who is said to have lobbied male Diet members with a baby on her back even before women were legally granted the right to vote. For more on "housewife feminism," see Tokuza.

6. Takahashi Takako, "Castle of Bones" (Hone no shiro), in *Hone no shiro* (Kyoto: Jinbun shoin, 1972), 19. Subsequent page citations will appear parenthetically.

7. For example, Watashi seems to sense the purpose of the man's "training" without being told (8), and the old man expresses the reason for Watashi's wandering city streets in exactly the same language she uses to narrate it, even though there is no evidence that she has explained her motivation to *him* (12).

Chapter 4: Odd Bodies

Epigraph. Luce Irigaray, *This Sex Which Is Not One,* trans. Catherine Porter with Carolyn Burke (Ithaca, NY: Cornell University Press, 1985), 78.

1. Ibid., 72.

2. Kōno Taeko, "Toddler-Hunting," 45–46. Because this text is available in English, I have chosen to cite from the translation by Lucy North so that English readers can readily locate the passages in question. All page numbers are from the translated version and will henceforth appear parenthetically.

3. Gretchen Jones, "Deviant Strategies: The Masochistic Aesthetic of Tanizaki Jun'ichirō and Kōno Taeko" (PhD dissertation, University of California, 1999), 115–116.

4. This is not to say that boys are not in fact also coercively inscribed with signifiers of masculinity as they develop into young men. I have no doubt that this is true, but it is not recognized by the text, devoted as it is to detailing the restrictive practices of feminine discipline.

5. Takahashi Takako, "Hi," *Shinchō,* no. 822 (1973): 66. Subsequent page citations will appear parenthetically.

6. White and red are fairly conventional signifiers for masculine and feminine respectively in Japanese society.

7. The renewal of ANPO, the U.S.-Japan Security Treaty, in 1960, the year this story was written, caused the largest mass demonstration in Japanese history as citizens from all sectors of society, led by student activists and left-wing political parties, rioted outside the Diet building while the conservative ruling party forced passage of the ratification of the treaty. (See chapter 1.)

8. "Anti-world" is Kurahashi's own term for the narrative universe depicted by her literature. Atsuko Sakaki describes it in the following terms: "The relationship between the 'Anti-world' and the 'real' world is [such that]...the former is not a representation of the latter, and yet it is a deformed version of the latter, and thus subject to it." Sakaki, "The Intertextual Novel and the Interrelational Self," 9. See below for more on this term as it applies to Kurahashi's critique of binary models of gender.

9. Kurahashi Yumiko, "Hebi," in *Kurahashi Yumiko zensakuhin* (Tokyo: Shinchōsha, 1975), 86. Subsequent page citations will appear parenthetically.

10. Irigaray, 72.

11. Kurahashi quoted in Sakaki, "The Intertextual Novel and the Interrelational Self," 10; italics in original.

Chapter 5: The Body of the Other Woman

1. Here, the term "Other Woman" is meant to signify that the character in question is "not-self"—that is, a character different from the female protagonist in some fundamental way that prevents complete understanding or intimacy between the two characters, in spite of the fact that they are both women and assumed to be fundamentally similar. The concept of the "Other Woman" thus serves as an ironic critique of theories of gender difference that present Woman as a monolithic category that is sexually Other (and implicitly inferior) to Man.

2. Gregory M. Pflugfelder, "'S' Is for Sister: Schoolgirl Intimacy and 'Same-Sex Love' in Early Twentieth-Century Japan," in Molony and Uno, *Gendering Modern Japanese History*. Pflugfelder notes that usage of the term "S," used to denote such passionate female friendships, persisted well into the 1960s in Japan (174–175). This would suggest that the phenomenon it described continued roughly up to the time that lesbian activists who emerged from the "women's lib" movement began to organize in more visible and explicitly politicized ways (see below).

3. Mark McLelland, *Queer Japan: From the Pacific War to the Internet Age* (Lanham, MD: Rowman and Littlefield, 2005).

4. Ibid., 93. In making this statement, I do not mean to suggest that lesbians did not exist in Japan before the 1970s. However, it is clear from the difficulties recounted by Japanese lesbians seeking partners in the decades prior to the "women's lib" movement that outside of the perverse press described by McLelland, lesbians were virtually invisible to mainstream Japanese society. It appears that it was only with the creation of Wakakusa no Kai, considered to be the first lesbian organization in Japan, in 1971, and subsequent efforts by lesbian women's lib activists later in the decade to produce publications aimed explicitly at the emerging lesbian community, that information about lesbianism as a distinct form of sexuality and lifestyle choice became more readily available, even to women seeking to build networks of like-minded women. See Sharon Chalmers, *Emerging Lesbian Voices from Japan* (London and New York: RoutledgeCurzon, 2002), and Mark McLelland, Katsuhiko Suganuma, and James Welker, eds., *Queer Voices from Japan: First-Person Narratives from Japan's Sexual Minorities* (Lanham, MD: Rowman and Littlefield, 2007).

5. I have written about such triangular relationships in Takahashi's literature at length elsewhere; see Julia C. Bullock, "Fantasizing What Happens 'When the Goods Get Together': Female Homoeroticism as Literary Trope," *Positions* 14, no. 3 (2006).

6. Kōno Taeko, "On the Road" (Rojō), in *Kōno Taeko zenshū*, vol. 2 (Tokyo: Shinchōsha, 1995), 19. Subsequent page citations will appear parenthetically.

7. "Christmas cake" is a rather callous expression for an unmarried woman past the age of twenty-five. Like the sweet for which they are named, such women tended not to "sell" (on the marriage market) after the twenty-fifth. This expression has rapidly fallen out of use in recent years as Japanese women have prolonged the average age of first marriage well into the thirties.

8. For other stories dealing with this theme, see also "Final Moments" (Saigo no toki, 1966) and "Snow" (Yuki, 1962), translated by North in *Toddler-Hunting*.

9. Takahashi Takako, "Intercourse" (Majiwari), in *Hone no shiro* (Kyoto: Jinbun shoin, 1972), 150. Subsequent page citations will appear parenthetically.

10. Ibid., 155. The character for "woman," used along with *kanojo* (she) as the only appellations given to the female other in this story, is written accompanied by a phonetic equivalent instructing the reader to pronounce it as *hito*, which likewise seems to imply an erotic relationship between the women. (Phrases like *ano hito*, or "that person," are commonly used as euphemisms for a lover or significant other. *Kanojo*, of course, can also be used to refer to one's girlfriend.)

11. This is in marked contrast to the penetrative gesture of Watashi's carving her initial into the woman's body at the conclusion of the story. While the diffuse eroticism of these homoerotic encounters acts as a positive expression of intimacy between the women, the phallic act of inscribing her identity upon the other woman—perhaps a parody of the way women's identities are reassigned upon marriage to a man?—brings the relationship to an untimely end. This is evocative of Luce Irigaray's argument in *This Sex Which Is Not One* that women, who possess erogenous zones everywhere and may climax repeatedly, have a fundamentally different sort of sexuality to that of men. It therefore seems possible to read this scene as a conflict between two opposing models of sexuality that concludes with the heteronormative imperative reasserting its authority.

12. In fact, in a number of Takahashi stories, homoerotic relationships between women obtain according to a triangular structure that is mediated by a male, who serves as both an object of rivalry and a medium for intimacy between the women. See Bullock, "Fantasizing What Happens."

13. The text hints that this may be cancer, but the nature of the illness is never clearly stated.

14. Kurahashi Yumiko, "Bad Summer" (Warui natsu), in *Kurahashi Yumiko zensakuhin* (Tokyo: Shinchōsha, 1975), 144. Subsequent page citations will appear parenthetically.

15. Interpreting fictional literature as a more or less transparently realistic portrayal of the life of the author, a genre known in Japan as the "I-novel" (*shishōsetsu*), had become the dominant mode of reading by the 1960s, when experimental writing by Kurahashi and other writers influenced by the European anti-novel arose to challenge this paradigm. Kurahashi's anti-"I-novel" stance is evident within this text, when L scorns the inclination of critics to offer biographical readings of her literature (136). Kurahashi's propensity for frustrating autobiographical readings

of her texts by simultaneously suggesting and denying their relationship to events in her own life is part of the "postmodern" aesthetic that Atsuko Sakaki details in her study of Kurahashi, "The Intertextual Novel and the Interrelational Self." For more on the "I-novel" genre, see Tomi Suzuki.

16. This is unclear because nouns in Japanese are typically not designated as to singular or plural, as is the case in this passage, so the "place" from which the blood emanates may in fact be one or many.

Conclusion

1. Foucault, *Discipline and Punish*. See especially the chapter entitled "Docile Bodies."

2. Chizuko Ueno, "The Japanese Women's Movement: The Counter-Values to Industrialism," in *The Japanese Trajectory: Modernization and Beyond*, edited by Gavan McCormack and Yoshio Sugimoto (Cambridge and New York: Cambridge University Press, 1988), 177–178.

3. Ibid., 170.

4. Shigematsu, 64.

5. Ibid., 75.

6. Ibid., 64, fl16.

7. Ibid., 225–242. See also Patricia Steinhoff, "Three Women Who Loved the Left: Radical Woman Leaders in the Japanese Red Army Movement," in *Re-Imaging Japanese Women*, edited by Anne E. Imamura (Berkeley: University of California Press, 1996).

8. Shigematsu, 87.

9. Steinhoff, 309.

10. Shigematsu, 239.

11. Ibid., 229–230.

12. Steinhoff, 311.

13. Japanese speech exhibits a relatively high degree of gender marking, extending even to its morphology (sentence-final particles, use of polite language and verb endings, etc.). For a brief study of "characteristically feminine speech" as employed selectively by middle-class, middle-aged Tokyo women, see Yoshiko Matsumoto, "Gender Identity and the Presentation of Self in Japanese," in *Gendered Practices in Language*, edited by Sarah Benor et al. (Stanford, CA: CSLI Publications, 2002), 339–354. For other articles on the gendered aspects of the Japanese language, see also Okamoto (91–113), Yuasa (193–209), and Miyazaki (355–374) in the same volume. For a comprehensive study of the historical development and transformation of Japanese "women's language," see Miyako Inoue, *Vicarious Language: Gender and Linguistic Modernity in Japan* (Berkeley: University of California Press, 2006).

14. Sandra Buckley, "A Short History of the Feminist Movement in Japan," in Gelb and Palley, *Women of Japan and Korea*, 173.

15. Sandra Buckley, *Broken Silence: Voices of Japanese Feminism* (Berkeley: University of California Press, 1997). See Buckley's interview with Nakanishi Toyoko, 185–198.

16. Ibid., 193; see also Buckley's translation of the preface to the Japanese version of *Our Bodies, Ourselves,* 202–203.

17. Joan Ericson, *Be a Woman: Hayashi Fumiko and Modern Japanese Women's Literature* (Honolulu: University of Hawai'i Press, 1997), 27–29.

18. Jones, 102.

19. Sakaki, "(Re)Canonizing Kurahashi Yumiko," 159.

20. Ericson, *Be a Woman,* 31–32.

21. Scholars are not in agreement on the degree of connection between the radical *ūman ribu* (women's lib) movement and the more "institutionalized" academic and bureaucratic trend that characterized Japanese feminism following the formation of the International Women's Year Group in 1975. It seems clear that while there were many differences in emphasis and rhetoric (and some antagonism) between the two camps, there were also common goals, and in some cases women affiliated themselves with both. For varying accounts of this transition, see Shigematsu (epilogue), Mackie (chapters 7 and 8), and Kazuko Tanaka, "The New Feminist Movement in Japan, 1970–1990," in Fujimura-Fanselow and Kameda, *Japanese Women,* 343–352. At any rate, it seems difficult to see these two as entirely unconnected either to one another or to the radical literary feminism of the previous decade given their common origin in the social and economic pressures of the gendered division of labor that underwrote the era of high economic growth.

22. Beginning in the late 1960s, Japan was hit with a succession of scandals revealing the harmful effects of industrial pollution on the health and welfare of ordinary Japanese citizens—for example, incidents of mercury poisoning that came to be known as the infamous "Minamata disease." See chapter 11 in Tipton.

Works Cited

Ariga, Chieko. "Onna ga teigi suru 'onna': Akutagawa shō, Naoki shō sakuhin ni miru." *Nichibei josei jānaru* 18 (1995): 27–46.

Ariga, Chieko M. "Text versus Commentary: Struggles over the Cultural Meanings of 'Woman.'" In Schalow and Walker, *The Woman's Hand*, 352–381.

———. "Who's Afraid of Amino Kiku? Gender Conflict and the Literary Canon." In Fujimura-Fanselow and Kameda, *Japanese Women*, 43–60.

Bardsley, Jan. "Discourse on Women in Postwar Japan: The Housewife Debate of 1955." *U.S.-Japan Women's Journal*, no. 16 (1999): 3–47.

Benor, Sarah, Mary Rose, Devyani Sharma et al. *Gendered Practices in Language.* Stanford, CA: CSLI Publications, 2002.

Bhowmik, Davinder L. "Kōno Taeko." In *Modern Japanese Writers*, edited by Jay Rubin. New York: Charles Scribner's Sons, 2001.

Buckley, Sandra. "Altered States: The Body Politics of 'Being-Woman.'" In Gordon, *Postwar Japan*, 347–372.

———. *Broken Silence: Voices of Japanese Feminism.* Berkeley: University of California Press, 1997.

———. "A Short History of the Feminist Movement in Japan." In Gelb and Palley, *Women of Japan and Korea*, 150–186.

Bullock, Julia C. "Fantasizing What Happens 'When the Goods Get Together': Female Homoeroticism as Literary Trope." *Positions* 14, no. 3 (2006).

———. "A Single Drop of Crimson: Takahashi Takako and the Narration of Liminality." PhD dissertation, Stanford University, 2004.

———. "We'll Always Have Iowa: Gender and National Identity in Kurahashi Yumiko's 'Virginia.'" *Proceedings of the Association for Japanese Literary Studies (PAJLS)* 7 (2007).

Butler, Judith. *Gender Trouble.* New York and London: Routledge, 1999.

Chalmers, Sharon. *Emerging Lesbian Voices from Japan.* London and New York: RoutledgeCurzon, 2002.

Chikuma gendai bungaku taikei 82. Tokyo: Chikuma shobō, 1977.

Copeland, Rebecca L. *Lost Leaves: Women Writers of Meiji Japan.* Honolulu: University of Hawai'i Press, 2000.

Ericson, Joan. *Be a Woman: Hayashi Fumiko and Modern Japanese Women's Literature*. Honolulu: University of Hawai'i Press, 1997.

———. "The Origins of the Concept of 'Women's Literature.'" In Schalow and Walker, *The Woman's Hand*, 74–115.

Foucault, Michel. *Discipline and Punish: The Birth of the Prison*, 2nd ed. Translated by Alan Sheridan. New York: Vintage Books, 1995.

———. *The History of Sexuality: An Introduction*. Vol. 1. New York: Random House, 1990.

Fowler, Edward. *The Rhetoric of Confession: Shishōsetsu in Early Twentieth Century Japanese Fiction*. Berkeley: University of California Press, 1988.

Fujii, James. *Complicit Fictions: The Subject in the Modern Japanese Prose Narrative*. Berkeley: University of California Press, 1993.

Fujimura-Fanselow, Kumiko. "College Women Today: Options and Dilemmas." In Fujimura-Fanselow and Kameda, *Japanese Women*, 125–154.

Fujimura-Fanselow, Kumiko, and Atsuko Kameda, eds. *Japanese Women: New Feminist Perspectives on the Past, Present, and Future*. New York: Feminist Press, 1995.

Garon, Sheldon. *Molding Japanese Minds: The State in Everyday Life*. Princeton, NJ: Princeton University Press, 1997.

Gelb, Joyce, and Marian Lief Palley, eds. *Women of Japan and Korea: Continuity and Change*. Philadelphia: Temple University Press, 1994.

Gordon, Andrew. "Managing the Japanese Household: The New Life Movement in Postwar Japan." In Molony and Uno, *Gendering Modern Japanese History*, 423–460.

———. *A Modern History of Japan: From Tokugawa Times to the Present*. New York and Oxford: Oxford University Press, 2003.

———, ed. *Postwar Japan as History*. Berkeley: University of California Press, 1993.

Gubar, Susan. "Feminist Misogyny: Mary Wollstonecraft and the Paradox of 'It Takes One to Know One.'" *Feminist Studies* 20, no. 3 (1994): 453–473.

Hillenbrand, Margaret. "Doppelgängers, Misogyny, and the San Francisco System: The Occupation Narratives of Ōe Kenzaburō." *Journal of Japanese Studies* 33, no. 2 (2007): 383–414.

Hirakawa, Hiroko. "Maiden Martyr for 'New Japan': The 1960 Ampo and the Rhetoric of the Other Michiko." *U.S.-Japan Women's Journal*, no. 23 (2002): 92–109.

Inoue, Miyako. *Vicarious Language: Gender and Linguistic Modernity in Japan*. Berkeley: University of California Press, 2006.

Irigaray, Luce. *This Sex Which Is Not One*. Translated by Catherine Porter with Carolyn Burke. Ithaca, NY: Cornell University Press, 1985.

Jones, Gretchen. "Deviant Strategies: The Masochistic Aesthetic of Tanizaki Jun'ichirō and Kōno Taeko." PhD dissertation, University of California, 1999.

Kameda, Atsuko. "Sexism and Gender Stereotyping in Schools." In Fujimura-Fanselow and Kameda, *Japanese Women*, 107–124.

Kawashima, Yoko. "Female Workers: An Overview of Past and Current Trends." In Fujimura-Fanselow and Kameda, *Japanese Women*, 271–293.

Kelly, William. "Finding a Place in Metropolitan Japan: Ideologies, Institutions, and Everyday Life." In Gordon, *Postwar Japan*, 189–216.

Kleeman, Faye Yuan. "Kurahashi Yumiko." In *Japanese Fiction Writers since World War II*, edited by Van C. Gessel. Detroit: Gale Research, 1997.

Kōno Taeko. "Akuru hi" (The Next Day). In *Kōno Taeko zenshū*, vol. 2, 131–150.

———. "Ants Swarm." In North, *Toddler-Hunting*, 166–184.

———. "Ari takaru" (Ants Swarm). In *Kōno Taeko zenshū*, vol. 2, 37–50.

———. "Bone Meat." In North, *Toddler-Hunting*, 250–266.

———. "Crabs." In North, *Toddler-Hunting*, 135–165.

———. "Final Moments." In North, *Toddler-Hunting*, 185–213.

———. *Fui no koe* (A Sudden Voice). In *Kōno Taeko zenshū*, vol. 5, 111–200.

———. "Full Tide." In North, *Toddler-Hunting*, 27–44.

———. "Haisei" (Broken Oath). In *Kōno Taeko zenshū*, vol. 2, 271–296.

———. "Hei no naka" (Inside the Fence). In *Kōno Taeko zenshū*, vol. 1, 51–88.

———. "Hone no niku" (Bone Meat). In *Kōno Taeko zenshū*, vol. 3, 103–115.

———. *Ichinen no bokka* (A Year's Pastoral). In *Kōno Taeko zenshū*, vol. 8, 7–135.

———. "Kani" (Crabs). In *Kōno Taeko zenshū*, vol. 1, 171–193.

———. "Kōno Taeko nenpu." In *Shōwa bungaku zenshū*, edited by Yasushi Inoue, 1026–1030. Tokyo: Shōgakukan, 1987.

———. *Kōno Taeko zenshū*. Vol. 1. Tokyo: Shinchōsha, 1994.

———. *Kōno Taeko zenshū*. Vol. 2. Tokyo: Shinchōsha, 1995.

———. "Michishio" (Full Tide). In *Kōno Taeko zenshū*, vol. 2, 51–62.

———. *Miiratori ryōkitan* (The Strange Tale of a Mummy Hunter). In *Kōno Taeko zenshū*, vol. 8, 137–348.

———. "Rojō" (On the Road). In *Kōno Taeko zenshū*, vol. 2, 7–24.

———. "Saigo no toki" (Final Moments). In *Kōno Taeko zenshū*, vol. 2, 189–210.

———. "Sōkyū" (Twin Arches). In *Kōno Taeko zenshū*, vol. 2, 231–270.

———. "Toddler-Hunting." In North, *Toddler-Hunting*, 45–68.

———. "Tōi natsu" (Distant Summer). In *Kōno Taeko zenshū*, vol. 1, 267–294.

———. "Utena ni noru" (On the Examining Room Table). In *Kōno Taeko zenshū*, vol. 2, 101–129.

———. "Yōjigari" (Toddler-Hunting). In *Kōno Taeko zenshū*, vol. 1, 7–23.

———. "Yume no shiro" (Dream Castle). In *Kōno Taeko zenshū*, vol. 1, 141–169.

Kristeva, Julia. *Powers of Horror.* New York: Columbia University Press, 1982.

Kurahashi Yumiko. "Hebi" (Snake). In *Kurahashi Yumiko zensakuhin*, vol. 1, 79–121.

———. "Kekkon" (Marriage). In *Kurahashi Yumiko zensakuhin*, vol. 5, 5–70.

————. "Kon'yaku" (Engagement). In *Kurahashi Yumiko zensakuhin,* vol. 1, 123–181.

————. *Kurahashi Yumiko zensakuhin.* Tokyo: Shinchōsha, 1975–1976.

————. *Kurai tabi (Blue Journey).* In *Kurahashi Yumiko zensakuhin,* vol. 3, 27–171.

————. "Kyōsei" (Symbiosis). In *Kurahashi Yumiko zensakuhin,* vol. 6, 65–129.

————. "Partei." In *This Kind of Woman: Ten Stories by Japanese Women Writers, 1960–1976,* edited by Yukiko Tanaka and Elizabeth Hanson. Stanford, CA: Stanford University Press, 1982.

————. "Parutai" (Partei). In *Kurahashi Yumiko zensakuhin,* vol. 1, 19–36.

————. "Virginia." In *Kurahashi Yumiko zensakuhin,* vol. 6, 185–234.

————. "Warui natsu" (Bad Summer). In *Kurahashi Yumiko zensakuhin,* 131–183.

————. *The Woman with the Flying Head and Other Stories.* Trans. Atsuko Sakaki. Armonk, NY: M. E. Sharpe, 1998.

————. "Yōjo no yō ni" (Like a Witch). In *Kurahashi Yumiko zensakuhin,* vol. 4, 209–249.

Mackie, Vera. *Feminism in Modern Japan: Citizenship, Embodiment, and Sexuality.* Cambridge: Cambridge University Press, 2003.

Matsumoto, Yoshiko. "Gender Identity and the Presentation of Self in Japanese." In Benor et al., *Gendered Practices in Language,* 339–354.

McLelland, Mark. *Queer Japan: From the Pacific War to the Internet Age.* Lanham, MD: Rowman and Littlefield, 2005.

McLelland, Mark, Katsuhiko Suganuma, and James Welker, eds. *Queer Voices from Japan: First-Person Narratives from Japan's Sexual Minorities* (Lanham, MD: Rowman and Littlefield, 2007).

McNay, Lois. *Foucault and Feminism: Power, Gender, and the Self.* Boston: Northeastern University Press, 1992.

Miyazaki, Ayumi. "Relational Shift: Japanese Girls' Nontraditional First Person Pronouns." In Benor et al., *Gendered Practices in Language,* 355–374.

Molasky, Michael S. *The American Occupation of Japan and Okinawa: Literature and Memory.* London and New York: Routledge, 1999.

Molony, Barbara, and Kathleen Uno, eds. *Gendering Modern Japanese History.* Cambridge, MA: Harvard University Press, 2005.

Mori, Maryellen. "The Liminal Male as Liberatory Figure in Japanese Women's Fiction." *Harvard Journal of Asiatic Studies* 60, no. 2 (2000): 537–594.

————. "The Quest for Jouissance in Takahashi Takako's Texts." In Schalow and Walker, *The Woman's Hand,* 205–235.

Mulvey, Laura. "Afterthoughts on 'Visual Pleasure and Narrative Cinema' Inspired by 'Duel in the Sun.'" In Penley, *Feminism and Film Theory,* 69–79.

————. "Visual Pleasure and Narrative Cinema." In Penley, *Feminism and Film Theory,* 57–68.

Murase, Miriam. *Cooperation over Conflict: The Women's Movement and the State in Postwar Japan.* New York: Routledge, 2006.

Muto, Ichiyo. "The Birth of the Women's Liberation Movement in the 1970s." In *The Other Japan: Conflict, Compromise, and Resistance since 1945*, edited by Joe Moore, 147–171. Armonk, NY: East Gate/M. E. Sharpe, 1997.

Nakamura, Takafusa. *A History of Shōwa Japan, 1926–1989*. Trans. Edwin Whenmouth. Tokyo: University of Tokyo Press, 1998.

Napier, Susan J. *Escape from the Wasteland: Romanticism and Realism in the Fiction of Mishima Yukio and Oe Kenzaburo*. Cambridge, MA: Harvard University Press, 1991.

Norgren, Tiana. *Abortion before Birth Control: The Politics of Reproduction in Postwar Japan*. Princeton, NJ: Princeton University Press, 2001.

North, Lucy, ed. and trans. *Toddler-Hunting and Other Stories*. New York: New Directions, 1996.

Okamoto, Shigeko. "Ideology and Social Meanings: Rethinking the Relationship between Language, Politeness and Gender." In Benor et al., *Gendered Practices in Language*, 91–113.

Okuno, Takeo. "Is Fiction Inherently the Realm of Women?" In *Woman Critiqued: Translated Essays on Japanese Women's Writing*, edited by Rebecca L. Copeland, 66–72. Honolulu: University of Hawai'i Press, 2006.

Penley, Constance, ed. *Feminism and Film Theory*. New York: Routledge, 1988.

Pflugfelder, Gregory M. "'S' Is for Sister: Schoolgirl Intimacy and 'Same-Sex Love' in Early Twentieth-Century Japan." In Molony and Uno, *Gendering Modern Japanese History*, 133–190.

Powell, Irena. *Writers and Society in Modern Japan*. Tokyo: Kodansha International, 1983.

Ramazanoğlu, Caroline, ed. *Up against Foucault: Explorations of Some Tensions between Foucault and Feminism*. London and New York: Routledge, 1993.

Roden, Donald. "From 'Old Miss' to New Professional: A Portrait of Women Educators under the American Occupation of Japan, 1945–52." *History of Education Quarterly* 23, no. 4 (1983): 469–489.

Ryang, Sonia. *Love in Modern Japan: Its Estrangement from Self, Sex, and Society*. London and New York: Routledge, 2006.

Sakaki, Atsuko. "The Intertextual Novel and the Interrelational Self: Kurahashi Yumiko, a Japanese Postmodernist." PhD dissertation, University of British Columbia, 1992.

———. "Kurahashi Yumiko's Negotiations with the Fathers." In *The Father-Daughter Plot: Japanese Literary Women and the Law of the Father*, edited by Rebecca L. Copeland and Esperanza Ramirez-Christensen, 292–326. Honolulu: University of Hawai'i Press, 2001.

———. "(Re)Canonizing Kurahashi Yumiko: Toward Alternative Perspectives for 'Modern' 'Japanese' 'Literature.'" In Snyder and Gabriel, *Ōe and Beyond*, 153–176. Honolulu: University of Hawai'i Press, 1999.

Sato, Barbara. *The New Japanese Woman: Modernity, Media, and Women in Interwar Japan*. Durham, NC: Duke University Press, 2003.

Schalow, Paul Gordon, and Janet A. Walker, eds. *The Woman's Hand: Gender and Theory in Japanese Women's Writing*. Stanford, CA: Stanford University Press, 1996.

Schierbeck, Sachiko. *Japanese Women Novelists in the 20th Century*. Copenhagen: University of Copenhagen, Museum Tusculanum, 1994.

Shigematsu, Setsu. "Tanaka Mitsu and the Women's Liberation Movement in Japan: Toward a Radical Feminist Ontology." PhD dissertation, Cornell University, 2003.

Shimizu Yoshinori. "Arano no soko kara todoku koe." In *Doko ka aru ie: Takahashi Takako jisen essei shū*, 300–311. Tokyo: Kōdansha, 2006.

Shinotsuka, Eiko. "Women Workers in Japan: Past, Present, Future." In Gelb and Palley, *Women of Japan and Korea*, 95–119.

Shōwa niman'nichi no zenkiroku: Anpo to kōdo seichō. Vol. 12. Tokyo: Kōdansha, 1990.

Slaymaker, Douglas N. *The Body in Postwar Japanese Fiction*. London and New York: RoutledgeCurzon, 2004.

Snyder, Stephen, and Philip Gabriel. *Ōe and Beyond: Fiction in Contemporary Japan*. Honolulu: University of Hawai'i Press, 1999.

Sono Ayako, Kurahashi Yumiko, Kōno Taeko shū. Vol. 50, *Gendai Nihon no bungaku*. Tokyo: Gakushū kenkyūsha, 1971.

Steinhoff, Patricia. "Three Women Who Loved the Left: Radical Woman Leaders in the Japanese Red Army Movement." In *Re-Imaging Japanese Women*, edited by Anne E. Imamura. Berkeley: University of California Press, 1996.

Suzuki Naoko. "Ribu zen'ya no Kurahashi Yumiko—Josei shintai o meguru seiji." In *Karuchuaru poritikusu 1960/70*, 29–48. Tokyo: Serika shobo, 2005.

Suzuki, Tomi. *Narrating the Self: Fictions of Japanese Modernity*. Stanford, CA: Stanford University Press, 1996.

Takahashi Takako. "Byōbō" (Endless Expanse). In Takahashi, *Kanata no mizuoto*, 113–164.

———. "Congruent Figures." Trans. Noriko Mizuta Lippit. In *Stories by Contemporary Japanese Women Writers*, edited by Noriko Mizuta Lippit and Kyoko Iriye Selden, 153–181. Armonk, NY: M. E. Sharpe, 1982.

———. "Danjo kyōgaku" (Coeducation). In *Kioku no kurasa*, 158–160.

———. "Glitter." *U.S.-Japan Women's Journal*, no. 26 (2004).

———. "Hi" (Secret). *Shinchō*, no. 822 (1973): 63–81.

———. *Hone no shiro* (Castle of Bones). Kyoto: Jinbun shoin, 1972.

———. "Hone no shiro." In *Hone no shiro*, 6–31.

———. "Jihitsu nenpu." In *Takahashi Takako jisen shōsetsu shū*, 553–578. Tokyo: Kōdansha, 1994.

———. "Jōsha sakugo" (Getting on the Wrong Train). In *Hone no shiro*, 213–238.

———. *Kanata no mizuoto*. Tokyo: Kōdansha, 1971.

———. "Keshin" (Transformation). In *Hone no shiro*, 34–55.

———. *Kioku no kurasa*. Kyoto: Jinbun shoin, 1977.

———. "Kodomosama" (Honorable Child). In *Kanata no mizuoto*, 167–199.

———. *Lonely Woman*. Trans. Maryellen Toman Mori. New York: Columbia University Press, 2004.

———. "Majiwari" (Intercourse). In *Hone no shiro*, 148–164.

———. "Natsu no fuchi" (Summer Abyss). In *Ushinawareta e*, 183–232.

———. "Onnagirai" (Woman-Hating). In *Tamashii no inu*, 229–232.

———. "Sōjikei" (Congruent Figures). In *Kanata no mizuoto*, 7–53.

———. *Sora no hate made* (To the End of the Heavens). Tokyo: Shinchōsha, 1973.

———. *Takahashi Kazumi no omoide*. Tokyo: Kōsōsha, 1977.

———. *Tamashii no inu*. Tokyo: Kōdansha, 1975.

———. "Unmei no wakareme" (Fateful Departure). In *Tamashii no inu*, 212–214.

———. *Ushinawareta e*. Tokyo: Kawade shobō shinsha, 1981.

Tanaka, Kazuko. "The New Feminist Movement in Japan, 1970–1990." In Fujimura-Fanselow and Kameda, *Japanese Women*, 343–352.

Tipton, Elise K. *Modern Japan: A Social and Political History*. New York: Routledge, 2002.

Tokuza, Akiko. *The Rise of the Feminist Movement in Japan*. Tokyo: Keio University Press, 1999.

Uema, Chizuko. "Resisting Sadomasochism in Kōno Taeko." PhD dissertation, University of Oregon, 1998.

Ueno, Chizuko. "The Japanese Women's Movement: The Counter-Values to Industrialism." In *The Japanese Trajectory: Modernization and Beyond*, edited by Gavan McCormack and Yoshio Sugimoto, 167–185. Cambridge and New York: Cambridge University Press, 1988.

Uno, Kathleen S. "The Death of 'Good Wife, Wise Mother'?" In Gordon, *Postwar Japan*, 293–322.

Williams, Mark. "Double Vision: Divided Narrative Focus in Takahashi Takako's *Yosōi Seyo, Waga Tamashii Yo*." In Snyder and Gabriel, *Ōe and Beyond*, 104–129.

Yonaha Keiko. *Gendai joryū sakkaron*. Tokyo: Shinbisha, 1986.

Yuasa, Ikuko Patricia. "Empiricism and Emotion: Representing and Interpreting Pitch Ranges." In Benor et al., *Gendered Practices in Language*, 193–209.

Index

abjection, 10–11, 76, 78, 83, 99
abortion, 13, 18, 19–21, 22, 115, 171n21
activism: feminist, 4, 6, 12, 156, 158, 159, 162, 164, 165–166, 169n3, 170n6, 180n4; student, 15, 48, 115, 117, 159, 179n7 (*see also* student movement)
Akutagawa prize, 43, 49, 51, 176n83
Amino Kiku, 173n46
androgyny, 98, 108, 110–114, 143, 145, 148–149, 165
ANPO (U.S.-Japan Security Treaty), 4, 15, 26, 48, 115, 171n6, 179n7
anti-novel, 181n15
anti-world, 115, 118, 120, 122–123, 125, 165, 179n8
"Ants Swarm" (Ari takaru). *See* Kōno Taeko
Anzen Hoshō Jōyaku. *See* ANPO
Ariga, Chieko M., 32, 173nn45–46, 176n83
Article 9 (of the Japanese Constitution), 170n2
autoeroticism, 140, 145
avant-garde, 51, 141

"Bad Summer" (Warui natsu). *See* Kurahashi Yumiko

Bardsley, Jan, 29
Baudelaire, Charles, 175n72
beauty (as disciplinary regimen), 88, 89–96 passim, 98, 105–114 passim, 125
Bhowmik, Davinder, 44, 174n56
biopower, 6, 7, 14, 18, 41, 52. *See also* Michel Foucault
birth control, 18, 19–21, 177n6
Blue Journey (Kurai tabi). *See* Kurahashi Yumiko
Bluestocking (Seitō), 3, 9
"Bone Meat" (Hone no niku). *See* Kōno Taeko
Breton, André, 38
"Broken Oath" (Haisei). *See* Kōno Taeko
Buckley, Sandra, 164, 174n57, 183nn15–16
bundan (Japanese literary world), 4, 8, 9, 30–33, 34, 36, 51, 52, 172n41, 176n84
Butler, Judith, 8. *See also* gender: performativity of

Camus, Albert, 39, 49
"Castle of Bones" (Hone no shiro). *See* Takahashi Takako
Chalmers, Sharon, 180n4
chauvinism, 1, 3, 4, 24, 29, 34, 45, 77, 94, 95, 158, 162, 164

"Christmas cake," 131, 181n7
"coeds ruining the nation" debate,
    25–26
"Coeducation" (Danjo kyōgaku).
    See Takahashi Takako
Cold War, 15
"Congruent Figures" (Sōjikei). See
    Takahashi Takako
Copeland, Rebecca, 172n42
corporeality, 10, 11, 34, 36, 52,
    67, 71, 74, 76, 77, 86, 87, 89,
    91–94, 96, 97, 104, 105, 107,
    113, 114, 125, 142, 144, 145,
    157
"Crabs" (Kani). See Kōno Taeko

deformity, 98, 105–114 passim
"Distant Summer" (Tōi natsu). See
    Kōno Taeko
"Doll Love" (Ningyōai). See Taka-
    hashi Takako
doppelganger, 11, 129, 133, 138,
    140, 143, 149–150
"Dream Castle" (Yume no shiro).
    See Kōno Taeko

"economic miracle," 16. See also
    high economic growth
education: coeducation, 9, 22,
    38–39, 44–46; higher educa-
    tion, 16–17, 23–26; Ministry of,
    22, 24–25; sex education, 20,
    22, 171n19; and women's roles,
    20, 21–27, 155; and women
    writers, 9, 31, 38, 44–46, 84,
    127, 140, 146, 155
employment, 16, 27–30, 155
Enchi Fumiko, 9, 32
"Endless Expanse" (Byōbō). See
    Takahashi Takako
Endō Shūsaku, 175n72
"Engagement" (Kon'yaku). See
    Kurahashi Yumiko

Ericson, Joan, 31
Etō Jun, 51

Fifteen Year War. See Pacific War
"Final Moments" (Saigo no toki).
    See Kōno Taeko
Foucault, Michel, 6–8, 14, 18,
    52, 53–56, 59, 64, 74, 153,
    171n13
Fowler, Edward, 172n41
Fujii, James, 172n41
"Full Tide" (Michishio). See Kōno
    Taeko

Garon, Sheldon, 7, 55, 177n6
gender: binary models of, 2–3, 5, 6,
    10–11, 26–27, 28, 68–70, 74,
    76, 93–96, 97–99, 102, 114,
    118–125, 127, 149, 151, 153,
    162, 165, 179n8; disciplinary
    mechanisms of, 6–8, 10, 18–19,
    23, 28, 30, 32–33, 52, 53–56,
    60–65, 74–76, 77, 89, 96, 101,
    104, 106, 113, 125, 153–156,
    161–163, 166, 177n13, 179n4;
    and division of labor, 2, 8, 14,
    17, 18–21, 26, 27–30, 50, 102,
    125, 151, 154, 156, 183n21;
    performativity of, 8, 75, 95. See
    also androgyny; Butler, Judith;
    "good wife and wise mother";
    masculinity
gender-neutral, 56, 67, 74, 154. See
    also androgyny
"Getting on the Wrong Train"
    (Jōsha sakugo). See Takahashi
    Takako
"Glitter" (Kirameki). See Takahashi
    Takako
"good wife and wise mother," 2, 18,
    28, 67, 169n3
Gordon, Andrew, 28–29, 55,
    170n1, 171n6, 174n58, 177n6

Green, Julien, 38
gross national product (GNP), 15–16
Gubar, Susan, 77

Haniya Yutaka, 51
Hastings, Sally, 172n30
high economic growth, 2, 6, 8, 14, 16, 27, 67, 151, 155, 166, 171n6, 183n21
Higuchi Ichiyō, 172n42
Hirakawa, Hiroko, 25
Hirano Ken, 39
homoeroticism, 109–110, 128–129
"Honorable Child" (Kodomosama). See Takahashi Takako
House of Rebirth, The (Yomigaeri no ie). See Takahashi Takako
"housewife debates," 29–30
"housewife feminism," 3, 169n3, 178n5

Ichikawa Fusae, 178n5
ie (household) system, 21
Ikeda Hayato, 16, 171n6
immanence, 76, 78, 82, 87, 94–95, 97, 145, 157
imperialism, 7, 34, 55
infanticide, 13, 47
infertility, 86, 99, 102, 104
Inoue, Miyako, 182n13
"I-novel," 31, 34, 51, 172n41, 181n15
"Inside the Fence" (Hei no naka). See Kōno Taeko
"Intercourse" (Majiwari). See Takahashi Takako
International Women's Year Group, 183n21
Irigaray, Luce, 97–98, 114, 121–122, 125, 181n11
Ishigaki Ayako, 29–30
Izumi Kyōka, 39

"Japan, Inc.," 15, 125
Jones, Gretchen, 103
joryū bungaku. See women's (style) literature

Kafka, Franz, 39, 49
kaisetsu, 173n45
Kameda, Atsuko, 25, 172n29
Kaneko Michiyo, 159–160
Kasumigaseki, 59, 177n9
Kishi Nobusuke, 170n3
Kleeman, Faye Yuan, 176n75
Kōno Taeko
—biography, 5, 13, 37–44, 46, 51–52
—works of: "Ants Swarm" (Ari takaru), 42, 174n61; "Bone Meat" (Hone no niku), 78–83, 94, 157; "Broken Oath" (Haisei), 56, 57–65, 73–75, 155, 162; "Crabs" (Kani), 43, 174n61; "Distant Summer" (Tōi natsu), 174n59; "Dream Castle" (Yume no shiro), 42; "Final Moments" (Saigo no toki), 43, 181n8; "Full Tide" (Michishio), 174n59; "Inside the Fence" (Hei no naka), 174n59; "The Next Day" (Akuru hi), 41, 174n61; "On the Examining Room Table" (Utena ni noru), 174n61; "On the Road" (Rojō), 129, 130–134, 150, 158; "Snow" (Yuki), 181n8; The Strange Tale of a Mummy Hunter (Miiratori ryōkitan), 175n65; A Sudden Voice (Fui no koe), 43; "Toddler-Hunting" (Yōjigari), 13, 41, 43, 98, 99–105, 113, 154, 157, 158, 163, 170n7, 174n61; "Twin Arches" (Sōkyū), 42; A Year's

Pastoral (Ichinen no bokka), 175n65
Korean War, 15, 171n6
Kristeva, Julia, 78
Kumaya Tomihiro, 49
Kurahashi Yumiko
—biography, 5, 6, 13, 37–39, 47–52
—works of: "Bad Summer" (Warui natsu), 130, 141–149, 150, 154, 157, 158; *Blue Journey (Kurai tabi)*, 49, 56, 70–73, 74, 75, 100, 157, 158, 162, 163, 176n82; "Engagement" (Kon'yaku), 50; "Like a Witch" (Yōjo no yō ni), 78, 83–89, 94–96, 154, 158, 176n78; "Marriage" (Kekkon), 50; "Partei" (Parutai), 13, 49, 170n7; "Snake" (Hebi), 49, 98, 115–125, 155, 163; "Symbiosis" (Kyōsei), 50

language, 11–12, 56, 59, 64, 73, 154, 157, 161, 162–165, 182n13
lesbianism. *See under* sexuality
Liberal Democratic Party (LDP), 15, 170n3
"Like a Witch" (Yōjo no yō ni). *See* Kurahashi Yumiko
"literature of the flesh." *See nikutai bungaku*

Mackie, Vera, 3, 169n3, 183n21
marriage, 2, 17, 19, 20, 21–27, 29, 32, 51, 56, 155, 174n57, 181n7; and Kōno Taeko, 40, 42–43, 57, 64, 78, 130–134, 174n60; and Kurahashi Yumiko, 49–51, 70, 84–85, 117, 124; and Takahashi Takako, 5, 38, 46–47, 105, 113, 175n70, 181n11

"Marriage" (Kekkon). *See* Kurahashi Yumiko
masculine gaze, 10, 52, 53–56, 57, 63, 67, 69, 70, 72, 73–76, 77, 92–93, 97, 106–107, 154, 157, 158
masculinity, 2–3, 11, 28, 30, 34–36, 50, 51, 70, 77–78, 85, 87, 91, 93, 95, 96, 97–99, 102, 104, 113–114, 115, 118–119, 121–125, 127, 146, 147, 149, 151, 154–165 passim, 179n4
masturbation, 13, 22. *See also* auto-eroticism
masukomi, 164
Matsumoto, Yoshiko, 182n13
Mauriac, François, 38, 175n72
McLelland, Mark, 129, 180n4
McNay, Lois, 177n4
menstruation, 56, 71–73, 86–87, 100–101, 103–104, 114, 158
Miike coal mine strike, 15–16, 170n4
Minamata disease, 183n22
minikomi ("mini-communication" publications), 164
Ministry of Education. *See under* education
Mishima Yukio, 36–37, 177n13
misogyny, 3, 34–37, 42, 69, 76, 77–78, 85, 88–89, 94–96, 143, 151, 159–162
Miyamoto Yuriko, 173n46
Molasky, Michael, 35
Mori, Maryellen, 175n71
motherhood, 2, 5, 20, 23, 26–27, 40, 46–47, 49–50, 64, 99
Mulvey, Laura, 53–56, 59
Muto, Ichiyo, 170n6

Nagata Hiroko, 159–162
Nakamura Mitsuo, 51
Nakamura, Takafusa, 170n3

Naoki Prize, 176n83
Napier, Susan, 36
New Left, 4, 51, 158–160, 169n5
New Life Movements, 28–29
"Next Day, The" (Akuru hi). *See*
    Kōno Taeko
Nihon Hōsō Kyōkai (NHK), 49,
    176n76
nikutai bungaku (literature of the
    flesh), 34–36
Norgren, Tiana, 171n20

Occupation, Allied, 2, 9, 14–15, 24,
    34–35, 37–38, 44–45, 78, 146,
    170n2, 170n4, 171n6
Ōe Kenzaburō, 36–37
Oku Mumeo, 178n5
Onna erosu, 164
"On the Examining Room Table"
    (Utena ni noru). *See* Kōno
    Taeko
"On the Road" (Rojō). *See* Kōno
    Taeko
Other Woman, 11, 126, 128–129,
    133, 138–140, 148–151,
    180n1, 181n11

Pacific War, 39, 55, 174n56. *See also*
    World War II
"Partei" (Parutai). *See* Kurahashi
    Yumiko
pedophilia, 13
Pflugfelder, Gregory M., 180n2
Popular Rights Movement, 9
Powell, Irena, 172n41
power: "hard" vs. "soft," 10–11,
    32–33
pregnancy, 56, 67, 69, 87, 104, 114,
    118, 142, 158
prostitution, 22
purity education, 22, 171n19. *See
    also under* education: sex
    education

queer (theory): and "odd bodies,"
    11, 96, 124

radical feminism, 4, 169n3
Ramazanoğlu, Caroline, 177n4
Red Army, 4, 159–162
Roden, Donald, 24
romantic love (ideology), 21, 23, 70
Ryang, Sonia, 22, 171n19
ryōsai kenbo. See "good wife and wise
    mother"

sadomasochism, 13, 42–43, 83, 95,
    102–103, 132–133
Sakaki, Atsuko, 49, 51, 73, 122,
    176n82, 176n84, 177n12,
    179n8, 180n11, 182n15
salaryman, 8, 14, 18, 27–28, 68, 98
Sartre, Jean-Paul, 39, 48, 49
Sato, Barbara, 21
Schierbeck, Sachiko, 173n44
scopic rape, 10, 66, 68, 70–71, 75,
    157, 162–163
second-wave feminism, 3, 23, 124,
    153, 156, 166
"Secret" (Hi). *See* Takahashi Takako
"Secret Rituals" (Higi). *See* Taka-
    hashi Takako
Security Treaty (U.S.-Japan). *See*
    ANPO
Seitō (Bluestocking) group, 3, 9
Self-Defense Forces (SDF), 170n2
sexual indifference, 97–98, 105,
    114, 121–122, 124–125, 127.
    See also Irigaray, Luce
sexuality, 4–5, 34, 37, 51, 129, 166,
    180n4; feminine, 5, 19–23, 26,
    56, 63, 88, 166; heterosexual-
    ity, 23, 35, 43, 47, 57, 128,
    142–149; lesbianism, 128–129,
    180n2, 180n4
Shigematsu, Setsu, 158–159, 169n1,
    183n21

Shimizu Yoshinori, 176n85
shishōsetsu. *See* "I-novel"
Shōwa One-Digit Generation, 13,
    17, 21, 45
Slaymaker, Douglas, 35
"Snake" (Hebi). *See* Kurahashi
    Yumiko
"Snow" (Yuki). *See* Kōno Taeko
Socialist Party, 170n3
Sono Ayako, 32, 173n44
Steinhoff, Patricia, 182n7
*Strange Tale of a Mummy-hunter, A
    (Miiratori ryōkitan)*. *See* Kōno
    Taeko
student movement, 4, 13, 15, 48,
    120, 155, 158, 169n4
subjectivity, 33, 101, 145; feminine,
    3, 4, 10, 11–12, 19, 41, 44, 56,
    63, 69, 71, 73, 78, 96, 99, 105,
    111, 113–114, 134, 149–152,
    154; masculine, 11, 30, 34–37,
    77, 96, 102, 121, 125
Sudden Voice, A (Fui no koe). *See*
    Kōno Taeko
Suganuma, Katsuhiko, 180n4
"Summer Abyss" (Natsu no fuchi).
    See Takahashi Takako
Suzuki Naoko, 176n84
Suzuki, Tomi, 172n41, 182n15
"Symbiosis" (Kyōsei). *See* Kurahashi
    Yumiko

Takahashi Kazumi, 46, 175n70
Takahashi Takako
—biography, 2, 5, 13, 24, 37–39,
    44–47, 51–52
—works of, "Castle of Bones"
    (Hone no shiro), 78, 89–94,
    95, 154, 155, 157, 163; "Co-
    education" (Danjo kyōgaku),
    175n68; "Congruent Figures"
    (Sōjikei), 46; "Doll Love"
    (Ningyōai), 175n71; "Endless

Expanse" (Byōbō), 47; "Getting
    on the Wrong Train" (Jōsha
    sakugo), 56, 65–70, 73–75,
    157, 162; "Glitter" (Kirameki),
    170n7; "Honorable Child"
    (Kodomosama), 47; *The House
    of Rebirth* (Yomigaeri no ie),
    175n71; "Intercourse" (Maji-
    wari), 130, 134–140, 150, 158;
    "Secret" (Hi), 98, 105–114,
    154, 157, 158; "Secret Ritu-
    als" (Higi), 175n71; "Summer
    Abyss" (Natsu no fuchi), 47,
    174n53; *To the End of the Heav-
    ens (Sora no hate made)*, 47;
    "Transformation" (Keshin), 47;
    "Woman-hating" (Onnagirai),
    1–2, 169n1
Tanaka, Kazuko, 183n21
Tanaka Mitsu, 159–162
Tanizaki Jun'ichirō, 39
Teruoka Yasutaka, 25–26, 29
Tipton, Elise K., 170n1
"Toddler-Hunting" (Yōjigari). *See*
    Kōno Taeko
Tokuza, Akiko, 169n3
*To the End of the Heavens (Sora
    no hate made)*. *See* Takahashi
    Takako
transcendence (of the body), 34–36,
    89, 92–96, 101, 110–114, 157
"Transformation" (Keshin). *See*
    Takahashi Takako
"Twin Arches" (Sōkyū). *See* Kōno
    Taeko

Uema Chizuko, 41, 174n60,
    175n64
Ueno Chizuko, 155–156
ūman ribu (women's lib), 3, 4, 5,
    9, 11, 12, 183n21. *See also*
    women's liberation movement
United Red Army. *See* Red Army

Uno, Kathleen, 171n12
U.S.-Japan Security Treaty. *See*
    ANPO

violence, 4, 11, 12, 15, 37, 40, 43,
    75, 114, 127, 148, 153, 154,
    157–162, 163
"Virginia." *See* Kurahashi Yumiko

Wakakusa no kai, 180n4
Welker, James, 180n4
Williams, Mark, 47
"Woman-hating" (Onnagirai). *See*
    Takahashi Takako

women's liberation movement, 3, 4,
    5, 11, 23, 129, 152, 153–167
    passim
women's (style) literature, 11,
    31–32, 165
World War II, 2, 7, 9, 15, 18, 19,
    34, 40, 128, 172n41

Year's Pastoral, A (Ichinen no bokka).
    See Kōno Taeko
Yonaha Keiko, 43, 47

zenshū (collected works), 32,
    173n47

About the Author

Julia C. Bullock is assistant professor of Japanese at Emory University in Atlanta, Georgia. Her research interests are in the areas of modern Japanese literature, film, popular culture, and gender theory. She has published articles on feminine subjectivity, gender and national identity, female homoeroticism, misogyny, and Japanese feminism. She is currently working on projects that explore the reception of Simone de Beauvoir's feminist theory in postwar Japan, as well as the gendered discourses that underwrote debates regarding the role of intellectual women in Japanese society during the 1960s.

Production Notes for Bullock | *The Other Women's Lib*

Cover design by Julie Matsuo-Chun

Text design by University of Hawai'i Press production staff
with display type in Arctic and text type in Galliard

Composition by Terri Miyasato

Printing and binding by Sheridan Books, Inc.